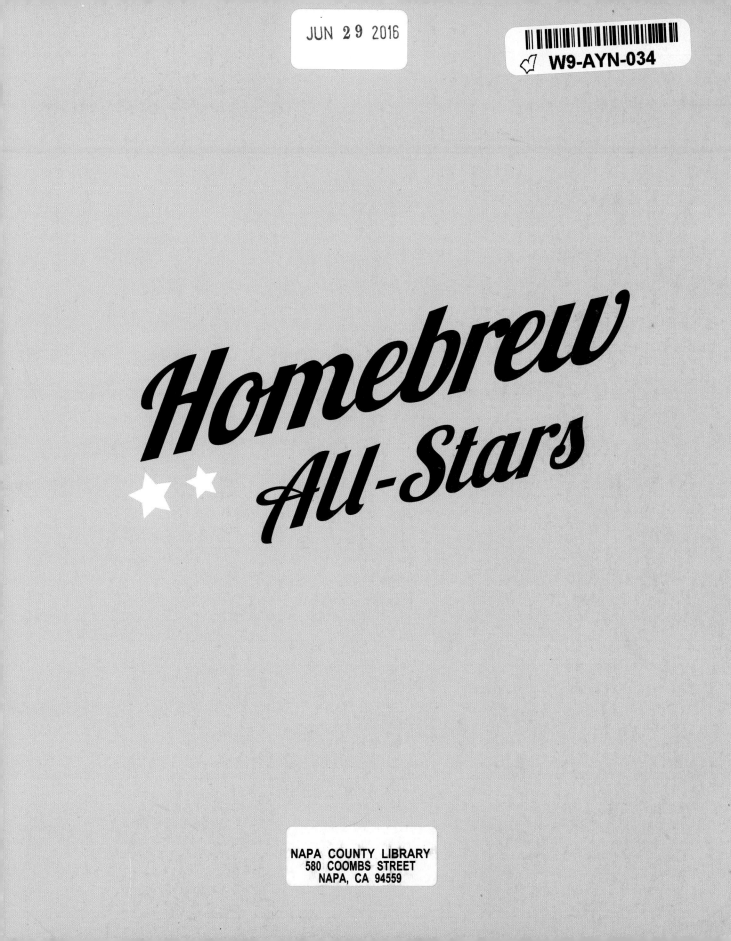

Homebrew
All-Stars

Quarto is the authority on a wide range of topics.

Quarto educates, entertains and enriches the lives of our readers—enthusiasts and lovers of hands-on living.

www.quartoknows.com

First published in 2016 by Voyageur Press, an imprint of Quarto Publishing Group USA Inc., 400 First Avenue North, Suite 400, Minneapolis, MN 55401 USA. Telephone: (612) 344-8100 Fax: (612) 344-8692

quartoknows.com
Visit our blogs at quartoknows.com

Voyageur Press titles are also available at discounts in bulk quantity for industrial or sales-promotional use. For details contact the Special Sales Manager at Quarto Publishing Group USA Inc., 400 First Avenue North, Suite 400, Minneapolis, MN 55401 USA.

10 9 8 7 6 5 4 3 2 1

ISBN: 978-0-7603-4961-8

Library of Congress Cataloging-in-Publication Data
Names: Beechum, Drew, author. | Conn, Denny.
Title: Homebrew all-stars : top homebrewers share their best techniques and recipes / Drew Beechum amd Denny Conn.
Description: Minneapolis : Voyageur Press, 2016.
Identifiers: LCCN 2015040521 | ISBN 9780760349618 (paperback)
Subjects: LCSH: Brewing--Amateurs' manuals. | BISAC: COOKING / Beverages /Beer.
Classification: LCC TP570 .B435 2016 | DDC 663/.42--dc23
LC record available at http://lccn.loc.gov/2015040521

Photo Credits
Laura Schott: 6, 8–9, 12, 14, 20, 22–28, 30, 43–44, 51, 56, 61–62, 67, 69, 78, 87, 89, 96–97, 102–103, 105, 107, 125, 133, 136, 138, 140, 144, 151, 155, 170, 174, 189, 194, 201, 208, 212, 216
Eric Gaddy: 41, 47, 53, 59, 65, 71, 77, 90, 93, 99, 111, 116, 121, 129, 135, 147, 153, 157, 159, 165, 166, 176, 185, 191, 197, 203, 204, 211
Shutterstock: Front cover, glass (gstockstudio), 33 (anandoart), 82 (Gyuszko-Photo)
Library of Congress: Front cover, baseball player (ggb2005022615)

Acquiring Editor: Thom O'Hearn
Project Manager: Caitlin Fultz
Art Director: James Kegley
Cover Designer: Amelia LeBarron
Layout: Amelia LeBarron

Printed in China

Homebrew

★ ★ ## All-Stars

TOP HOMEBREWERS SHARE THEIR BEST
Techniques and Recipes

DREW BEECHUM AND DENNY CONN

Voyageur
Press

CONTENTS

CHAPTER 1

Welcome to the Big Leagues

*I*t's inevitable. Put a group of folks together in a room with a bunch of beers and sooner or later the conversation is going to turn to some variant of, "So and so was the greatest to ever play the game!" The names change from generation to generation and sport to sport, but the conversation remains the same. Heck, it doesn't even have to be a sport; it could be philosophers, bands, artists, and more. Beatles versus Stones, Yankees versus Red Sox, Harlem Globetrotters versus the Washington Generals, Adam Smith versus Karl Marx . . . the list goes on!

DENNY: For the record, it's the Beatles, Drew would kill me if I answered the baseball question, and it's Groucho, not Karl.

Even when it comes to beer, where there's certainly no stopwatch or ruler to determine objective winners and losers, you'll see comparisons flying out of the woodwork. Just look at the endless "Top 100 Best Beer Lists." Homebrew is no different. We've both spent horrifyingly large parts of our lives devoted to the art of judging beer, with hours and hours spent studying and tasting to learn to detect minute differences in technique, process, and approach. We've cultivated bad posture as we sat scrunched over cups and score sheets armed with mechanical pencils and wishing for a computer to type on (at least the entrants getting score sheets from Drew wish he was typing on a computer for legibility's sake). All that work is devoted to answering the question, "So does this beer suck or is it awesome?"

Every weekend around the globe, people are judging beers and submitting beers to be judged. But are ribbons and medals the key to being an all star? While we admit medals are awesome and tough to win, we're going to argue that there's much more to being an All-Star brewer. Read on!

Our Book's Manifesto

We are both big believers in the idea that brewing is a skill best learned by doing. It may seem ironic that a couple of crusty old bearded fellows who've written a few books about beer are now telling you to put down the book and go hang out with other brewers. However, it actually makes perfect sense: what we've tried to present in our books is a distilled essence of all the lessons we've learned in our solo and partnered brewing adventures.

DREW: When I bought my first kettle in 1999, the biggest thing that helped me learn the fine art of homebrewing was going around and brewing with others. Every few batches, a special trip was made to the house of a different member of my homebrew club. Lots of lessons were learned; some were even directly related to brewing! Sure, not every member was a classic "All-Star," but they all had experience to share. By learning from all of them, I was able to forge my own brewing style and a willingness to play around with different techniques.

DENNY: I went through a similar homebrewing evolution, although mine was based on the Internet. I was not a member of a club at that time, so I discovered the UseNet discussion group rec.crafts.brewing, and the people in that group became my mentors. I quickly figured out how to tell who had the bright ideas and who just thought they did. However, I eventually learned lessons big and small by brewing with friends. For example, in the days when I bottled I had always done so kneeling, with the bottles on the floor. Why? Because the most popular homebrewing book at the time showed pictures of people doing it that way. So, for at least a couple of years, that's the way I did

You'll never be a better brewer if you don't fire up the kettle.

it, on the kitchen floor! Then one day I was bottling a split batch with a friend who brought out two chairs and set them next to the counter with the bottling bucket. He sat in one chair and put the bottles he was filling on the seat of the other. Revelation! Now, maybe this is one of those things that everybody else had already thought of. But for me it was the first lesson about what you can learn from others!

In short, there are millions of folks out there who have homebrewing experience. Quite a number of them are obsessive, with deeply held brewing views. Most of us can't meet them all and learn their lessons. So we thought, "Wouldn't it be great to gather up the wisdom of the best and brightest and bring it to everyone?"

Who Is the Average Homebrewer?

Before we get into the subject of who's an All-Star homebrewer, we should take a moment to figure out who the average homebrewer is. We'll also want to take a look at the makeup of the advanced homebrewing crowd.

There are two pools of data we're drawing from here. One is from our good friends at the American Homebrewers Association (AHA) who put together a massive nationwide survey in an attempt to better understand their constituency. The survey went out to both members and non-members of the AHA. They received over 18,000 responses which, when combined with their other market research, gives a pretty complete picture of active American homebrewers.

Note: Both of us have close ties with the AHA including writing, speaking, and serving on the governing committee. We believe the organization is valuable in defending homebrewing rights and spreading knowledge, plus it provides a kickass annual party where you can let your beer obsession fly without fear of rolled eyes or exasperated sighs. We're grateful they shared the results of their survey with us.

By current estimates, there are approximately 1.2 million homebrewers in the United States,

Is this a "typical" group of homebrewers? According to the data, they are probably pretty close.

about 0.4 percent of the US population. That means you may not be one in a million, but you are one in 250! You're either really elated or disappointed, depending on how much importance you put on being "unique." If you look only at the population who drinks beer and wine, then we're approximately 1 percent!

Our hobby has a bit of reputation too: many think it's made up of nothing but slightly pudgy white dudes who have college degrees in a technical field. Supposedly we all have an affinity for novelty T-shirts, beer glassware, and beards. While we'd like to disabuse you of that notion, the fact remains that roughly 60 percent of respondents were 40 years old, 69 percent had college degrees, 88 percent self-identified as

If you're interested in drilling down further into the AHA survey results, here are a few of the most interesting findings:

BREWING METHODOLOGY IN THE PAST 12 MONTHS:

72%	all grain (7.6 batches average)
50%	extract with grains (4 batches average)
24%	partial mash (3.1 batches average)
18%	extract only (2.6 batches average)

PRIMARY MASHING PROCESS IN THE PAST 12 MONTHS:

31%	all grain, batch sparge
29%	all grain, traditional fly sparge
22%	single pot/extract
9%	partial mash
6%	brew in a bag
1%	no sparge

One of the most surprising results of the AHA's survey was where it asked how many people were making other fermentation products (mead, wine, cider, etc.). The answers broke down like so:

57%	beer only
12%	beer and cider
7%	beer and mead
7%	beer and wine
6%	beer, cider, and mead
4%	everything
3%	beer, wine, and cider
3%	beer, wine, and mead
1%	wine only

All we can say is this indicates a number of folks aren't taking advantage of the wider world of fermentation. If you're in that majority, making beer and beer alone, we'd suggest giving a new fermentation project a try. Many are shockingly easy!

Caucasian, and 94 percent were male. However, 30 percent said they brew with their spouse, which dilutes the exceedingly testosterone-laden environment a bit.

Note: A fact not looked at by the AHA is that given the number of homebrewers in the U.S. and the number of new craft breweries opening up daily, we calculate (the rate of change times success rate, carry the one . . .) that all of America's homebrewers, except us, will have opened up a craft brewery in the next ten years. Make sure to send us samples!

How much beer does the average homebrewer make in a year? Roughly 64 gallons. The good news is that means people are staying well below the legal threshold of 200 gallons per two-adult household! But it also means y'all got some work to do, so get busy brewing!

OUR SURVEY FOR ADVANCED HOMEBREWERS

Armed with a good sense of who the average homebrewer is (thanks to the AHA), we wanted to

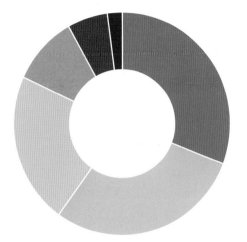

- ■ Batch Sparge   31%
- ▦ Fly Sparge   29%
- ▥ Extract   22%
- ▧ Partial Mash   9%
- ■ Brew in a Bag   6%
- ■ No Sparge   1%

tackle the picture of the more advanced brewer. So we crafted a forty-question survey intended to probe at the heart of the matter. In a few weeks of active survey gathering, we received over five hundred responses.

Since the AHA's survey was largely focused on gathering a better understanding of the homebrewer market, we decided to focus on how and why homebrewers do their magic.

We asked participants a simple self-identifying question of what type of brewer they were (more on this later), followed by a series of questions meant to help us understand how a particular type of brewer thinks and operates.

Our questions ranged from the simple, such as, "What styles of beer do you brew?" all the way to philosophical questions like, "Why do you brew?" Trust us when we say *a lot* of people have asked us that very same question over the years except it sounds more like: "Why are you so obsessive . . . *about beer?!*"

The data we gathered was broken down between two target segments: active homebrewers in general and our selected All-

Stars. In each chapter devoted to brewers, we'll present breakdowns of how each group answered our survey and dig out the really interesting tidbits.

Note: It should be said that all of the survey respondents for both the AHA's massive national survey and our survey were volunteers who had the wherewithal and desire to sit down for twenty to thirty minutes answering our questions. We can expect that skews the results a bit. The truly average homebrewer is a rapidly changing group of people interested in the hobby for a slew of reasons.

What Makes Someone an All-Star Homebrewer?

The very first question you must answer when sitting down to talk about all-stars, no matter the occupation or sport, is, "What makes someone an all-star?" Remember, this is the stuff of legendary bar discussions that never end. You will never reach agreement with someone you're related to, never mind with us, but we think that's part of the fun!

All-Star homebrewers do more than enter competitions. They're committed to the hobby in a variety of ways, such as teaching and supporting other homebrewers.

Since we knew we'd be starting arguments, here's what we came up with to pinpoint an All-Star. The All-Star homebrewer is someone who does much of the following:

COMPETES

We have a big note on this one (see page 13), so don't get uptight yet. But as we talked about earlier, it's definitely something easy you can point to. If Person A won 80 medals and Person B only won 5, Person A may well be a better brewer.

It's a central part of human nature to compete and quantify quality in a measurable fashion. It's inevitable. But is it a complete measure of an All-Star? Not at all.

TEACHES

We cannot understate the importance of teaching and sharing knowledge. Without teaching, the fine art of homebrewing would wither on the vine. It's not just about teaching the mechanics of brewing either. It's also about demonstrating the other aspects of the hobby: tasting, culture, judging, history, and so on. It's about offering guidance and doing so in a way that is uplifting, not denigrating.

We hope that everyone has a little bit of "teacher" in them, but the All-Star takes it to the next level. Maybe they host lessons at home or always reach out to help the new folks. And since we're a little biased, we think writing totally counts. Having said that, we don't think writing a book is the important piece. Look online and you'll find many passionate homebrewers toiling away at their blogs, writing up their experiments, and freely sharing information. That's an All-Star move right there.

DREW: Why do we want to go beyond the definition of "all-star" that's defined by millennia of competition-enthused civilizations? I can't speak for Denny's experience, but in mine, competing has been about the most boring, tedious affair I can imagine. I hate bottling. I hate packing stuff for shipment. I hate going to the shipping store. I really hate paying shipping and entry fees. And so on.

All in all, even though I'm an egotistical sort, I just don't care enough to go through all the work to get an opinion or a medal anymore. I have other avenues for beer evaluation and endless options for people to tell me how badly I've screwed up.

So, since competing isn't my bag, does that mean I can't qualify as an All-Star? I'd hope not! I do a ton of research, brewing, writing, and a lot of work with my club. And I'm not alone. There are plenty of other folks who are messing around out there making their beers, teaching, and so on.

Remember, I work closely with the AHA, organizers of the largest homebrew competition in the world. I'm not anti-competition or anti-winning. I just feel that a 100-percent emphasis on that is limiting and only part of a more complete picture.

DENNY: I admit to sharing most of Drew's "hates." I went through competing quite a bit early in my brewing. I did it for the feedback from people who (supposedly) know what they're talking about, but I also admit to being a ribbon whore. There's something about having qualified beer judges acknowledge that your beer is better than someone else's that gave me quite a thrill.

But those days are pretty much behind me now. Laziness was a factor. I keg my beer and the process of bottling some, along with packing them up and shipping them, were things that I just didn't want to do any more. Another part of it comes from being a national level Beer Judge Certification Program (BJCP) judge with quite a bit of beer-judging experience behind me. At this point, I'm pretty good at giving myself the feedback I was looking for from judges. And because I'm so into experimenting, I know how to assemble a tasting panel to give me objective feedback on my beer that I can't provide to myself.

Again, like Drew, I'm not anti-competition, and I applaud those who enter and win. However, simply winning ribbons doesn't make someone an All-Star, in my opinion. You can't ignore the folks who discover innovative ways to make great beer and have a great time doing it and then share those methods and enthusiasm with others.

INNOVATES

One of the greatest things about the homebrewing community is the innovation we see from its members. If there's a better, cheaper, more logical way of doing things, one of us will discover it. There may be fights about it, wars over whether of not it's a legitimate way of brewing, but innovation will happen.

Think of the guys down in Australia who made all-grain homebrewing more accessible with the whole brew-in-a-bag setup. Or even coauthor Denny, who promulgated the "Cheap 'n' Easy" batch sparge setup that's so common these days. Or take Drew, who taught people how to put clams into beer. Okay, maybe that last one isn't the best example. But you get the idea: an All-Star is someone who's out there beating new pathways.

DENNY: This doesn't mean you have to be discovering new techniques or new ingredients or new uses for things, but you need to be willing to update your own brew process and not remain hidebound by "this is the way I've always done it!"

The next time you get together and brew with your friends, take the quiz on page 17 and figure out your brewer archetypes!

SUPPORTS OTHERS

Since we both have done a lot of work with the AHA, it's clear we consider supporting the homebrew community incredibly important. We've already covered the aspect of supporting your fellow brewers one-on-one with the teaching characteristic. This is more about supporting the larger community.

Plenty of people still hold the opinion that homebrewers are just creative alcoholics—drunks looking to legitimize their drinking hobby. We've both encountered that attitude often. There's a telling smirk in their eye when you talk about the hobby.

DREW: My landlord used to hound me repeatedly about the legality of my activities despite my repeated assurance that it's legal and the fact that I could show her the laws.

So, an All-Star can also be the person who puts a good face on the homebrewing community. Look at the Carolina Brewmasters who've raised gobs and gobs of money for charity. Look at the folks who've done the ground work to *finally* make homebrewing legal in all fifty states of the United States. Look at all of the folks who've made an effort to show folks that homebrewers are good, outstanding members of the whole community.

BREWS

If you don't brew, how can you be a homebrew All-Star? Maybe you can be the wise old guru, sitting loftily on the mountain of your previous brewing exploits, but there's stagnation there. So, if this is you, hopefully you find this to be your clarion call to stand back behind the kettles and get to making magic once more.

We've noticed that the majority of our All-Star candidates have rocked their brew systems impressively when it comes to the number of batches brewed. Is it the obsessive nature that drives you to brew multiple times per month that makes a person an All-Star, or is it the repetitious

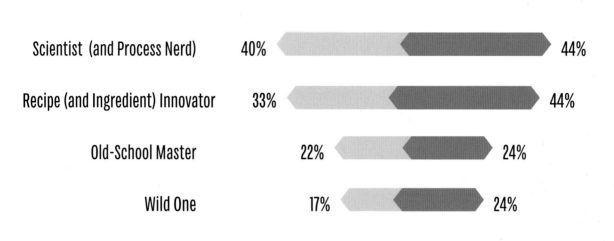

ARCHETYPE TEST RESULTS

◆ AVERAGE HOMEBREWERS   ◆ ALL-STAR HOMEBREWERS

Scientist (and Process Nerd)   40% ▰▰▰ 44%

Recipe (and Ingredient) Innovator 33% ▰▰▰ 44%

Old-School Master   22% ▰▰ 24%

Wild One   17% ▰▰ 24%

building of muscle memory that creates the "second nature" instinct that we see so often?

The Brewer Archetypes

If you look at the homebrewing world and talk to homebrewers for about thirty seconds, you quickly realize that, like other endeavors, people develop approaches and fascinations. More interestingly, patterns to individuals' approaches develop. With enough data, it's possible to develop distinct classifications and group brewers by their common traits. We do this all the time without thinking about it: "Oh, he's a real gadget freak. She's a sour nut . . . " From a psychological point of view, we can say that the base personality types are homebrewing archetypes. People naturally slot into these groups (and usually into multiple groups).

Let's start with thirty-second psychology lesson. The modern science of psychology and psychoanalysis is largely credited to Sigmund

Freud in the 1880s. Freud is the source of the couch-laying form of "talking therapy" often depicted in popular culture. His movement to understand the weird, wooly pathways of the human mind soon attracted followers—most notably, Carl Gustav Jung.

After nearly a decade of collaboration, Jung and Freud broke apart, never to speak again, due to a developing disagreement over the nature of the unconscious mind. Where Freud saw the human psyche driven largely by sexual compulsion, Jung saw a deeper collective unconscious driven by fundamental shared human experiences that innately shaped our minds. To help communicate this concept, Jung developed a notion of archetypes and images. These images represent deeply important cultural touchstones that shape the human psyche—the mother, the trickster, the god, and so on. In a modern sense, we can think of Jung's archetypes as software that comes preloaded in our brains.

The popular culture upshot of this deeply shallow summation of fifty years of psychological theory development is this: Freud is remembered for being a sexual pervert with a funny quip about a cigar whereas Jung is best remembered for inspiring the whole world of psychological personality tests like the Myers-Briggs Type Indicator or the endless online quizzes for "Which School of Magic Do You Belong To?"

We'll get to the quiz in a moment, but first let's discuss the archetypes we've discovered in the course of writing. There are four main types we'll discuss in this book and a boatload of ancillary types found on pages 32, 80, 138, and 168, and at www.HomebrewAllStars.com.

HOMEBREW ALL-STARS ARCHETYPES

Where did these four final types come from? We've joked for years about brewers having types. (Most of the jokes centered on the types of the "Non All-Star," because let's face it, they're funny and totally true.) But for this book we began asking around in earnest and plotting out the behaviors we've seen in our collective forty years of brewing.

Together, we forged an initial list of types and people who fit them and then reviewed and winnowed them into the four primary All-Star types. Once we began collecting brewers to be profiled in the book, we asked them to identify the archetypes they felt applied to them. Please note that we're certain there are more, but this is what worked for our All-Stars.

THE OLD-SCHOOL MASTERS
There can be no deeper respect than what these brewers hold for brewing tradition. Many worship at the feet of the *Reinheitsgebhot*, and any newfangled technique is considered suspect. They refuse to even consider the possibility that step mashes and decoctions may not end up making a noticeably better beer. They may not be producing a wacky Maple Bacon Smoked Belgian Porter, but they can knock your socks off with a clean and classic rendition of a Bohemian pilsner.

THE SCIENTISTS (AND PROCESS NERDS)
These brewers are all about the process and understanding how brewing on their system works. Experimentation and repeatability is the name of their game. They'll be able to tell you exactly what temperature their mash tun settles at, exact volumes that their system will produce, and how their fermentations respond.

THE WILD ONES
These are the folks who've never met a fermentation they didn't love. They are on a first name basis with Brett(anoymces). Mead is normal. Bring on the kombucha, kefir, and anything weird and wild. If it makes a winemaker cringe in fear or a brewer confused, then it's perfect for this type of brewer.

THE RECIPE (AND INGREDIENT) INNOVATORS
No ingredient is too obscure, no recipe idea is too outré to tackle. These brewers take their pleasure and inspiration from the flavors around the world. This type also includes the subtle innovators, those great recipe designers who nudge existing styles little by little into something new and wonderful—from British IPA to American IPA, or say from IPA to Double IPA and Session IPA. They're all innovations!

Quiz:
What Brewer Type Are You?

We'd bet good money that right now you're glancing through these lists and categorizing not only yourself, but your friends and fellow brewers! Now's the time to take the almighty quiz! We hope you studied, because this test will determine your brewing fate for the next 200 or so pages.

Grab a pen and paper and write down your answers. Rank the responses in terms of fit. Make sure to rank each answer (1 being the best match, 4 being the worst—don't repeat ranks).

Not sure about an answer? Go with your gut! Despite our earlier assertion, the fate of the world is not riding on your test-taking abilities. When you're finished, see page 19 for the key.

1) It's 2 a.m. on a sleepless night. To lull yourself to sleep, you begin to think about your next brew day.
   A. "That blot of mustard on my shirt from earlier tonight reminds me: a mustard beer would be interesting to try."
   B. "Hm, which malt and hop should I use in my next SMaSH beer?"
   C. "I should brew an English barleywine so I'm ready for Christmas."
   D. "When do the fruit orchards begin to bloom this year?"

2) For dinner, which would you prefer?
   A. Thai Tom Yum Guy soup with coconut milk
   B. Sous vide steak, seared
   C. A Sunday roast
   D. Sausage and limburger served on sourdough rye toast

3) Where are you when inspiration strikes you for your next batch of beer?
   A. At your local micro flour mill discovering they have Tibetan Purple Barley (or reading online about Neo-Mexicanus hops or wanting to now that you've heard the name)
   B. Flipping through the pages of Cynmar or AS&S's latest catalog
   C. Your local English pub
   D. Watching a documentary on the bee men of Africa

4) In order of importance, rank these elements in terms of your brewing priorities (1 being the highest priority and 4 being the lowest):
   A. Developing a beer that makes people go "wha?"
   B. Dialing in on your process
   C. Using traditional techniques to make perfect beer
   D. Coaxing complex characters from multiple microorganisms

5) You're at a bar or beer store and see a new beer that contains chocolate, red wine, and coffee. What is your first thought?
   A. "What if I swapped the coffee for tea?"
   B. "What kind of mash schedule and yeast did they use?"
   C. "Good God, are they trying to kill me?"
   D. "Wonder if it's sour . . ."

6) When you design a new recipe, what generally drives the development?
   A. An ingredient
   B. A question
   C. A tradition
   D. A bug

7) Where is the ideal place to have a beer?
  A. Someplace you've never been before
  B. Someplace not distracting, preferably familiar
  C. In the old part of the city where the beer is brewed
  D. Out in the woods or in a very small, dark café

8) When you sit down with a glass of beer, what are you looking for on the first sip?
  A. A flavor that makes you think, "How did they do this?"
  B. A beer that tastes just like the last one you had from this brewery
  C. A reassuring blend of familiar flavors
  D. Something so sour you make a scrunchy face

9) Imagine yourself in the plumbing department of a large home improvement store. As you peruse the aisles, what are you thinking?
  A. I don't know what that thing is, but I need it!
  B. How would that affect my mash runoff?
  C. That's just like the valve I saw in a picture of a German brewery.
  D. I could use that to make a separate fermenter for my wild beers.

10) What books are you reading?
  A. *Experimental Homebrewing* by two well-regarded gentlemen, *Radical Brewing* by Randy Mosher, *Extreme Brewing* by Sam Calagione
  B. *How to Brew* by John Palmer, *Principles of Brewing Science* by George Fix, *Brewing* by Dr. Michael Lewis
  C. *The Brewer's Publications Style Series*
  D. *American Sour Beers* by Michael Tonsmeire, *Wild Brews* by Jeff Sparrow

Now turn to page 19 to tabulate your results!

BUT, BUT . . . I'M NOT ONE THING!

Before you object too strenuously to the category you fit into, we know that any attempt to quantify an individual with a simple test and a pithy paragraph is folly. To paraphrase Walt Whitman, "We are large, we contain multitudes."

Even the people with PhDs in this topic—you know, the ones who actually know what they're doing—will tell you that no simple categorization system will capture the various intricacies of an individual. We're not quite that hive minded. But a system like this can help you focus on information that is pertinent to your natural leanings or point you in directions that you need to explore.

DREW: As an example, I'm classified as an Innovator. I make a "classic" recipe once, and then new ingredients or goofy ideas distract me. I think it may be time to focus a bit more on the traditional elements I embraced when I first started brewing. Did you know, for instance, that I've won medals for milds, barleywines, and bocks that contained nothing but "normal" ingredients? Nope, you probably didn't. Instead I'm the Guacamole Clam Chowder Saison guy. Hopefully, our Old-School Masters can lend me some wisdom and help me work on that aspect of myself—or I'll have forgotten that I wrote this and when the book is published, I'll be announcing my creation of a Nitrogenated Salt Cod Quadruple IPA. Place your bets!

DENNY: I'm basically the Scientist kind of guy. I like to figure out why things do or don't work and how to make them work better. I take great joy in brewing a recipe multiple times and having it come out the same way every time. I love to analyze why something happens, then try to find a way to have the same result with an easier process. But that creeps over the boundaries to being a recipe geek too. While I almost always prefer "beer-flavored beer" and generally eschew a lot of the ingredients Drew thrives on, I also like to think through new flavors using traditional ingredients and figure out how to make those flavors end up in my glass, or to figure out how to make the perfect German pilsner or Belgian dark strong.

Let's see how you did. To learn your brewing archetype, simply add up the ranks you gave to each of the A/B/C/D responses. Your strongest affinity is for the letter with the lowest total score.
Here's how the archetypes fit into the responses.

A   The Recipe (and Ingredient) Innovator
B   The Scientist (and Process Nerd)
C   The Old-School Master
D   The Wild One

In other words, let's say Drew took this quiz—his scores would look something like this:

Answer	Q1	Q2	Q3	Q4	Q5	Q6	Q7	Q8	Q9	Q10
A	1	1	1	1	2	1	1	1	1	1
B	3	2	4	3	3	2	4	4	2	4
C	4	4	3	4	4	3	3	3	4	3
D	2	3	2	2	1	4	2	2	3	2

A: 11
B: 31
C: 35
D: 23

With a low score of 11, this indicates Drew's clear preference for The Innovator archetype with the least affinity for The Old-School Master since that score is so much higher.

So which type did you end up being? Want to go visit your fellow archetypes?

The Old-School Master (Traditionalist) (starts on page 30)
The Scientist (and Process Nerd) (starts on page 78)
The Wild One (starts on page 136)
The Recipe (and Ingredient) Innovator (starts on page 166)

CHAPTER 2

Getting Started

★ ★ ★

*T*he 1978 omnibus transportation bill that legalized homebrewing at the federal level (which naturally happened through a secret backroom–negotiated amendment) says that any and all books pertaining to the subject of homebrewing must contain a description of the homebrewing process. So to be compliant with the law and avoid federal raids on our homes, we present an extremely simplified tour of the homebrewing process.

Okay, it's not really law. But for the few that may have picked up this book needing a refresher, we've got you covered. We're also including some All-Star tips and our recipe standards toward the end of the chapter. So even if you know everything about brewing, you might want to flip to page 21 and at least read a few pages before moving on to the next chapter. On the other hand, if you need a more in-depth review of basic homebrewing procedures, you can refer to Drew's *The Everything Homebrewing Book*. Or, for a more "medium" depth review of basic homebrewing combined with a disturbing amount of more advanced techniques, pick up a copy of our *Experimental Homebrewing*.

STEP 1

STEP 2

The Homebrewing Process in a Nutshell

Brewing is easy to do, but a brew day also includes plenty of hard work. (One of our brewing pals describes brewing as two hours of hard work crammed into eight hours of time—that sounds about right!) Okay, before we get into any specifics, let's take a real quick look at the brewing process from the outer space level. DANGER! DANGER! GROSS OVERSIMPLIFICATIONS AHEAD! *We have to post that warning lest we're inundated with eleventy billion emails saying "How could you forget this?" or "That's not how I do it, and I make fantastic beer!"*

STEP 1: DISSOLVE

First things first: We have to create a sugary liquid for our yeasts to snack on. Most of the world's alcoholic beverages start with simple sugars (fruit juice, honey, and so on). With beer, we start with malted barley, extract the starches in it, and break them down with a long hot steep. Either that or we start with malt extracts created by manufacturers who performed that task for us.

STEP 2: BOIL

Once the sugars have been dissolved into our "soon-to-be-beer" water (a.k.a. wort), we have to boil it. The boil kills any native creepy crawlies (like *Lactobacillus* harbored on the barley husk) and extracts the aromatic and bittering compounds of beer's constant companion, hops.

STEP 3: CHILL

Freshly boiled wort is a clean playground for yeast to get their feast on, but the same heat that killed the other microorganisms would do a number on the good guys. So we need to chill the beer down to the optimum temperature range for our yeast. In most cases, that's going to be in the 60 to 70°F range. Ideally, you should strive

STEP 3

STEP 4

to do this as fast as possible with the resources on hand for better clarity and less chance of a creeper taking root.

STEP 4: FERMENT

Now we reach the magic stage where you and I step back. As the old brewing slogan goes, "Brewers make wort. Yeast makes beer." After you pitch the yeast, they get busy reproducing until they have enough buddies to tackle the smorgasbord laid out in front of them. Once they start eating, they break sugar into alcohol, carbon dioxide, and other flavorful compounds. This goes on for a few days to a few weeks until the food is gone, the energy is all spent, and the yeast need a good long nap.

DENNY: Keep in mind that the stages of fermentation actually aren't this distinct. Technically, all that reproduction is going on at the same time that alcohol is being produced. Sounds kinda like a yeast party, huh?

STEP 5: PACKAGE

Before we can call the beer done, it has to be packaged. In modern contexts, since we like carbonated beer, that means getting it into a sealed bottle or keg. This allows us to capture or inject carbon dioxide, which will dissolve into the beer. Later, when the beer is served, the carbon dioxide will come rushing back out in the form of bubbles and foam. Both serve to promote the aromatic nature of the beer.

STEP 6: CONSUME

This is far and away the most fun step: grab a clean, unfrosted glass and pour your beer down the side. Keep the yeast in the bottle. Sniff, sip, and enjoy!

That's it! Everything else about brewing is details and noise and exceptions to the "rules." This goes for extract versus all-grain, ales versus lagers, and yeast versus wild critters. Once you internalize those six steps, fermentation is your orchestra to guide.

STEP 1

Extract with Grains 101

This is also known as the way everyone gets started (we hope). In short, steps 2 through 5 here contain so much new information for folks new to brewing that it makes perfect sense to let the professional maltsters handle the work of extracting starch from grain and converting it to sugar. Once you've got a handle on these steps, then you should feel free to explore the intricacies of mashing to extract starch and create sugar.

DREW: Does this mean everyone needs to be brewing all-grain eventually? Nope, not even close. Later, we'll meet a veteran homebrewer who brews with extract and can kick your beer to the curb. We'll also dispel the myth that extract always means poor quality beer. Usually the problem with extract brews is the brewer's inexperience, not the ingredients.

THE INGREDIENTS

Liquid or dry malt extract, flavoring/character grains (crystals, roasts, and so on), hops, yeast, water, and plenty of other fixings if you don't believe in the *Reinheitsgebot*!

DENNY: Gesundheit!

THE GEAR

A pair of pots in which to heat up water, a plastic bucket with an airlock or glass carboy with a stopper and an airlock, and sanitizer (preferably a no-rinse like StarSan or Iodophor).

THE PROCESS

STEP 1: DISSOLVE

Add your character grains in a fine mesh bag to approximately 3 quarts of 170°F filtered water in a 20-quart or larger pot. Steep for 30 to 45 minutes. Heat another 3 quarts of water to 170°F. Chill an additional 4 to 5 gallons of filtered water in the fridge until cold.

After steeping, pull the bag of grains out and place in a colander over the pot and drain. Take your additional hot water and pour it over the grain to rinse. Congratulations, you've made wort—beer's sugary larval stage!

STEP 2: BOIL

Bring the wort to a boil and remove from the heat. Add one-third of the liquid or dry malt extract. Stir well to fully incorporate the extract. Bring back to a boil and add your first hops, which starts a 60-minute countdown. Add your other hops as directed by your recipe. With 15 minutes left, again pull the pot from the heat, add the remaining extract, and return to the boil.

STEP 3: CHILL

Turn off the heat and cover the wort. If you can, place the pot in a sink full of ice-cold water and stir occasionally with a sanitized spoon until the wort reaches 95°F. Add 1 gallon of chilled water to your sanitized fermenter. Carefully pour the warm wort into the fermenter. Add enough chilled water to come up to 5 gallons and measure the temperature.

STEP 4: FERMENT

Once the temperature is below 75°F (ideally lower, closer to 65°F), add the yeast and stand back. Stash your ferment somewhere that's dark and nice and cool—for ales about 65°F, for lagers about 50°F. A refrigerator or other cooling rig with temperature control works like a charm. Leave the fermenter alone for 2 to 4 weeks. Check the gravity to determine if the ferment is finished.

STEP 5: PACKAGE

If bottling, transfer your beer to a bottling bucket on top of ¾ cup of corn sugar that's been dissolved and boiled in ¾ cup of water. Fill the sanitized bottles, leaving two fingers of space and cap securely. Wait 2 weeks.

If kegging, transfer the beer to the sanitized keg. Cool overnight to the low 30s (°F) and then inject carbon dioxide at 12 psi while rocking for 10 minutes. Wait 1 hour and serve.

STEP 3

All-Grain 101

THE INGREDIENTS

Base grain (a.k.a. 2-row pale malt, pilsner malt, and the lighter Munich malts—basically any grain that has enough enzyme power to convert itself). Character grains and all the other stars—hops, water, sugars, flavorings, and yeast.

THE GEAR

All the same gear as your extract batch, but now with larger pots. You need to be able to comfortably boil 6 or more gallons of wort. You'll also need a cooler or pot with a straining mechanism to separate the sugary liquid away from the grain. We both use steel hose braids, but there are endless variations on that idea.

STEP 1

THE PROCESS

STEP 1: MASH

Heat 1.5 quarts of water per pound of well-crushed malt to about 164°F. Mix the grain and the heated water together in a pot or cooler that has a filtering mechanism installed to a spigot. The temperature of the mash should be between 148°F and 158°F. The filtering mechanism will let you separate the soaking liquid from your barley. Denny and Drew both use stainless braids, others use metal sheets with many small holes, and still others use copper pipes with hacksaw cuts. (Go really old school and use a woven conical basket that you shove into the mashed grains.)

Slowly run the wort out of the mash vessel. Add the first few quarts of output back to the mash tun until the wort clears. Then run all the wort into your boiling pot.

Calculate the amount of liquid in your kettle. Subtract the kettle volume from your batch size plus 1 gallon. Add that amount of 170–180°F water to the grains and recirculate. Once the wort is clear, run it into the boil kettle, combining it with your initial runoff for your full pre-boil volume.

Note: We're both all grain batch-sparging fools, but we highly recommend that you find what works for you. In fact, this whole book is about trying to expose you to different top-notch examples of brewers doing the things that make them great brewers. You should feel encouraged that none of us do this the exact same way—even the two of us who use the same general procedure differ in a great many ways.

DREW: Seriously, Denny, John Palmer, and I brewed together at my house while we were writing this book. I think my brewing process, which from a high level looks the same as Denny's, drove him nuts!

DENNY: Not nuts exactly, but I did wonder how anybody could brew the way Drew does! Seriously though, it's more about minor differences.

STEP 2: BOIL

Boil and then add your hops. This step is the same as when using extract except you don't have to worry about the malt extract.

STEP 3: CHILL

Using an immersion or counter-flow chiller, chill your wort to 65°F or the appropriate temperature for your yeast.

STEP 4: FERMENT AND STEP 5: PACKAGE

There's nothing different here from the brewing with extract process.

VARIATION: FLY SPARGE

For Step 1, follow the process for all-grain batch sparge. However, instead of running all the wort out at once and adding fresh water, slowly add water to the mash as you're running into the boil kettle. Stop adding water when you only need to collect approximately 1 more gallon.

VARIATION: BREW IN A BAG

For Step 1, add your grain to a fine mesh bag. Place the bag in a brew kettle filled with 162°F water equal to the total volume of your batch (say 5 gallons), plus 0.1 gallons of water per pound of grain (10 pounds of grain equals 1 extra gallon). Stir the grains around to ensure proper wetting. Make sure the bag gives the grain room to expand! After 60 minutes, pull the bag out of the boil kettle and suspend it over the brew pot to drain. No sparging necessary.

All-Star Homebrewing Tips

These are the tips that any good homebrewer worth their salt is going to tell you. Why? Because these encompass the common wisdom of the ages passed down from our predecessors. Some may eventually fade with exposure to the harsh light of science and experimentation, while others will remain with the fervent force of the right and true. So, yes, this list is ever evolving.

- Don't be surprised if you see some of our All-Stars advocate conflicting advice. As we've discovered in life, universal truths aren't so universal. Or, as Denny likes to say, "There are many roads to the same destination." (Yeah, he really talks like that.) Just be aware, that when you see someone promulgating the heretical, you are either in the presence of madness or revolution. (See the rise of brew-in-a-bag or small-batch brewing for examples.)

Temperature control is important for yeast health before and during fermentation.

A clean, well-organized brewery is more important than fancy equipment—though who doesn't love fancy equipment?

- Clean as you go. It'll make life a lot easier at the end of a long brew day.

- Treat yeast right—starters are key.

- Sanitize, sanitize, sanitize! Don't waste your brew day effort by lazing out. Get your post-boil gear squeaky clean and (relatively) microbe free.

- Some variety of temperature control, at least for the first seventy-two hours, will really step up your brew quality. It's not that hard to build a temperature-controlled brew chamber either. Plenty of plans exist online to build something sturdy and cheap.

- All the fancy equipment in the world isn't going to make your beer better, but it might be fun to have.

- Take good notes. If you make an incredible beer, you'll want to remember what you did so you can do it again. If, on the other hand, you end up with 5 gallons of drain cleaner, you'll want to remember what you did so you'll *never* do that again!

- Have fun and don't stress out! This is a hobby, and malted barley wants to become beer! If you're not having fun, you're doing something wrong.

Here's one last recommendation from us: you need to play around. Embrace your fear of failing because that's how you progress. Seriously, beer-making is one of those things where you can find a way that works and stick to it. But if you do that and that alone, you lose out on the chance of discovering better ways to do something, more interesting beers, or heck, even just a better tale to tell your drinking companions.

Recipe Standards for This Book

- Recipes are written for all-grain brewing. If you want to brew with extract, we recommend substituting dry or liquid malt extract (DME/LME) for the base malt. Use an online calculator for adjustments based on what you're using and the recipe, but a safe rule of thumb is 0.60 pounds of DME or 0.75 pounds of LME for each pound of "base" grain (a.k.a., 2-row, pilsner, etc.).

- The recipes in this book clearly state batch size and assume 75 percent efficiency. If your batch size or efficiency are different, be sure to adjust accordingly.

- Unless the recipe states otherwise, it assumes you'll be mashing with a ratio of 1.25 quarts of water per pound of grain, batch sparging, and performing a full boil for sixty minutes.

- Even though we sometimes specify whole or pellet hops, feel free to use whichever you have that is of good quality.

- Recipes assume the IBU contributed from first wort hopping is counted as a twenty-minute hop addition.

- For the best utilization of hops, wait until the hot break subsides, then add bittering hops and start your timing.

- All hop IBU calculations in this book are done using the Tinseth formula. (Don't use Tinseth? Don't sweat it—remember all IBU calculations are rough estimations. Pick a formula, train yourself in what 20 IBUs, etc., means in that formula, and run with it.)

- If the alpha acid of the hops you have is different from what we listed, use the alpha acid units (AAU) method to substitute: multiply the alpha acid (AA) of the hops by the amount used. For example: 1 ounce of 5 percent AA hops gives you 5 AAU (1 × 5 = 5). If the hops you have are 4 percent, then you need 1.25 ounces (1.25 × 4 = 5). Use this substitution for any hops that will contribute to bitterness (up to the fifteen-minute addition). After fifteen minutes, you can simply substitute ounce for ounce for flavor and aroma contributions.

- Yeasts are listed by company, strain number, and strain name. White Labs (WLP) and Wyeast (WY) are the main companies you'll see, but you'll also find East Coast Yeast (ECY), Safale, and a couple other manufacturers. Check online if you want to track down a specific yeast from a small manufacturer.

- Unless otherwise noted, we insist on good yeast health. That means you should make a starter, rehydrate dry yeast, or use a yeast slurry from a previous batch. Use an online yeast calculator such as Brewers Friend or Mr. Malty to determine the correct amount of yeast to pitch. (Or use Drew's rough rule of thumb of 1 to 2 quarts of starter for every 5 gallons of wort below 1.065.) Treat your yeast right to get great beer. The ABV listed for each recipe is an estimate only. Your true ABV may be slightly above or below what's listed for the recipe.

- CHAPTER 3 -

The Old-School Masters

*W*here else should we start our exploration of brewers' archetypes but with the folks who hold tradition in the highest regard? You've seen them at beer festivals and classes holding forth on the righteousness of old brewing techniques and tradition. You will know them by their beers (and sometimes by their lederhosen, fancy appropriate glassware, and mash paddles).

What makes someone an Old-School Master? Usually it's a fascination with a singular locale or tradition. You know the brewer in your club who can't stop raving about the old serving methods of the British? Or maybe *Reinheitsgebot* is their holy word and they see no reason to break from hundreds of years of rules regarding what makes a beer a true beer. Yet Old-School Masters exist for every aspect of brewing. It's not just a devotion to the brewing traditions of Europe (particularly Germany, Belgium, and Britain/Ireland); it's an abiding love of beer, history, and stories that propels them forward.

The Positives

Aside from Wild Ones (see page 136), the Old-School Masters (OSM) tend to be the most passionate of brewers. We have never met an OSM who didn't have a deep and abiding love of all things good and beery. It's just that their definition of *good* may be different from yours, or ours. But no matter your opinion, these are the guys and gals who first got people to pay attention to beer as a thing suited to more than something to sip while watching the game.

One of their main strengths is their incredible depth of knowledge. Sometimes it's only about a single subject. But get them started on their primary obsession, then try to stop them. If humanity ever figured out how to generate electricity from nerdish obsession, the world's breweries would never run out of power.

Yet here's what we consider the most important part of the traditionalists: they persevere. As the brewing world pursues the next "hot" beer, perhaps Purple Sticky Icky IPA or a Pickled Habanero Helles, the Old-School Masters hold firm. Whether it's a matter of pride, visions of their brewing forefathers, or a fervent belief that things done the "old-fashioned way" are better, they drop a firm anchor and hold their vast store of knowledge safe. Thanks to them, other brewers can keep a thread to the past in place while they traipse off in search of new beer discoveries. Look at our profile of Lars M. Garshol (page 36), who

★ OLD-SCHOOL MASTER SUB-ARCHETYPES ★

- **The Strict Semanticist:** This is the person who is very persnickety about getting all of his or her facts right. Correctness matters more than anything else. The mild form of this disorder results in a beer being called something like "Bavarian-style hefeweizen" since it wasn't brewed in Bavaria. See also those who work for the Alcohol and Tobacco Tax and Trade Bureau (TTB) and insist that consumers will be confused by the term "Russian imperial stout."

- **The Romantic Historian:** One of Drew's favorite movies is *The Man Who Shot Liberty Valence*, which contains the classic line, "When the legend becomes fact, print the legend." The beer world is filled with a number of colorful tales of varying truthfulness. Some traditionalists love the romantic story and find it far more important to believe fanciful facts than the truth.

- **The Hardcore Historian:** These folks are mortally opposed to the Romantic Historians and their half-truths. (Okay, as mortally opposed as you can get in the beer world.) These are Herzog's accountants, and they're the ones who spoil the beautiful legends. Do they do it because it's fun or because the truth is that important?

- **The Pilsner Perfectionist:** To many, this is the apex traditionalist. This kind of brewer will brew over and over with minute tweaks, trying to finally nail that image of the perfect classic style. It may take them a decade, but they'll keep at it until they succeed!

- **The Merchant and Ivory Costume Dramatist:** More than the others, this version of the traditionalist is a completist about all the trappings of their target culture. These are the guys who only want to drink their perfect Bavarian beers from the appropriate *Maßkrug* while wearing lederhosen and eating wurst. But here's the funny part: they're so obsessed with these parts of the package that they often seem to skip over the same detail in the beer. In other words, they pay lip service to tradition while still doing things like substituting US domestic 2-row for German pilsner in their helles recipe.

is wandering Northern Europe investigating and documenting traditional farmhouse ales like a latter day beery Alan Lomax. That's the kind of magic that's needed in the world.

DENNY: To me, Lars is a fascinating example and his dedication to learning about and recreating ancient beers almost leaves me breathless. This guy is one of the most exciting All-Stars (see page 36)!

The Negatives

We can sum up OSMs in two words: myopia and rigidity. We've all encountered singularly hard-headed brewers who can't break their tunnel vision. That same laser-like focus that gives them incredible knowledge of the changes made by Guinness's third brewmaster to the souring protocol used on the beloved stout blinds them to the ongoing efforts of others. It's no surprise; we all know the human brain is capable of only holding so much before losing patience with acquiring more information.

Think of the old *Saturday Night Live* skit "All Things Scottish" with the store motto "If it's no' Scottish, it's crap!" That summarizes some of the Old-School Master conversations that we've had. "Seriously,

Oktoberfest celebrations near and far are possible thanks to brewers like the Old-School Masters.

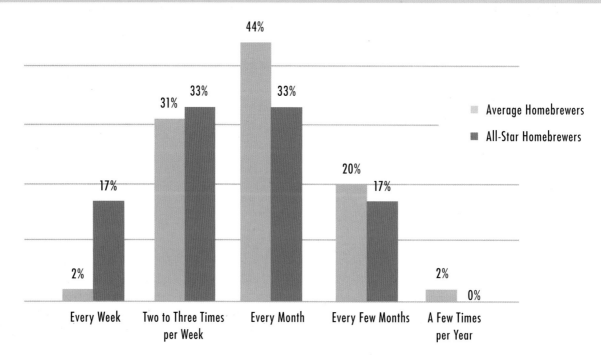

you should try this IPA, it's mind-blowing." "No thanks, I only like Belgians." It's this same mentality that can lead to beery monocultures.

DREW: This sort of attitude isn't just about old-school styles either. I've had a great many fun arguments with folks about the historical truthiness of saison as "farmhouse ale" and how the story we know about beers brewed for farmhands on a farm is probably a romantic load of codswallop. Some people really, really want to brew the story, and all I can say is, "Go forth, have fun, etc., etc."

The lack of flexibility also comes at a cost when looking at the commercial beer world. Look at the flattening sales of mass-market lager here in the United States. Look at declining beer consumption in, of all places, Germany, land of beery beer. You know the one segment of the market that's growing everywhere though? That's right: craft beers with more flavor!

Old-School Masters by the Numbers

Based on our data collection, they're surprisingly young: the average age is just thirty! Still, that doesn't mean they don't have the experience; the average OSM has been brewing for nearly eleven years. On the All-Star side, the years balloon to an average of 17.5.

What's more interesting to us, though, is that the average experience of all the regular respondents together was 6.8 years. This means our Old-School Masters, on average, have nearly four more years of brewing experience compared to the average homebrewers. I think it's safe to say that's the passion at play, and it keeps them brewing for a long time. Speaking of which, OSMs brew more frequently than the average homebrewer as well—at least monthly. Perhaps there's truth to the aphorism, "practice makes perfect!"

When we look more closely at the brewing practices of the Old-School Masters, you'll see it varies widely depending upon their particular focus. Those with a penchant for process and repetition favor more tightly controlled, automated systems along with decoction (for the masochists). Almost all OSMs have a greater focus on preparing for a brew day than the other personality types, including pre-grinding, precise start schedules, and so on.

Choice Quotes from Old-School Masters

We asked all of our survey respondents to provide us with some thoughts about homebrewing. Collected below are some of the best responses we received from the regular brewers. For the All-Stars, read on for their profiles. (Yes, we know some of the quotes throughout the book are contradictory, but that's what you get when it comes to homebrewers.)

- "Batch sparging: I don't trust it!"

- "There's no need for hop additions other than sixty minutes, whirlpool, and dry hopping. It seems like a lot of people are very concerned with exact mash temperatures, but I've found that being somewhere in the (fairly large) sweet spot gets the job done without significant variability."

- "Fermentation temperature control for ales is crucial, but it's even more crucial for certain strains, particularly some Belgian strains. With some Belgian yeasts in particular, a too-low ferment temp creates the risk of under-attenuation. But go too high and you risk fusel alcohol formation."

- "Simple beers are unsung heroes."

DREW: Of course, we have to include anything negative about batch sparging just to tweak Denny!

- "Brewing isn't rocket science; it's as much art as science. Relaxation and patience are the keys."

- "The more I learn, the more I realize I know nothing but this: there is no right way to brew, but there is a wrong way. I don't think it can be qualified, but if your beer tastes/smells/looks bad, it's probably been brewed the wrong way."

- "Taste everything. Be open to every style and learn what good examples taste like."

- "Some bits of common knowledge are backed by experience and science. Others are nothing more than a guess or superstition. It is very hard for new brewers to know which are which."

★ OUR OLD-SCHOOL MASTER SIDES ★

DREW: I express my traditionalist side with my love of saisons and milds. Of course, I immediately go and muck them up with other stuff, like my Clam Chowdah Saison (page 178).

DENNY: I recognize a lot of myself in the Pilsner Perfectionist but without quite the rigid adherence to style and process. I do like to start with very traditional styles and techniques but often put my own spin on things.

Lars Marius Garshol

Lars is dedicated to learning and recreating traditional techniques and recipes from his native Norway. He meticulously researches recipes, ingredients, and equipment in his quest to brew and taste these historic beers. He's even started working with White Labs in Europe to preserve a number of these traditional strains before they disappear. (Unfortunately for American homebrewers, Lars's yeasts aren't available as of this writing.) He posts his research and results at www. garshol.priv.no/blog/beer.

BREWING SINCE: This is a bit tricky. Lars doesn't consider himself a homebrewer and in fact claims to have never brewed a batch of beer by himself. (But he has made batches at home to test yeasts.) The first time he brewed with someone else was in 2005.

BREWING MOTTO: *Wir müssen wissen. Wir werden wissen.* (We must know. We will know.)

FAVORITE BREW STYLES: Traditional farmhouse ales in many styles.

FAVORITE BREWING COUNTRY: Lithuania

BREWING METHODOLOGY: Because Lars considers himself more of a researcher than a homebrewer, he brews with friends in a traditional brewery or with homebrewers in their houses, using their equipment. His interest lies in the process and results. "When I brew I typically try to reproduce some traditional beer to understand the process and how it works. So the process is always different, since the traditional brewing processes vary dramatically."

But who says tradition is boring? When brewing with a traditional homebrewer in Voss, Norway, Lars co-created a beer with a yeast strain inherited from the brewer's uncle and a huge 300-liter copper kettle from the eighteenth century. Now, he's trying to crack the code on a Hornindal-style recipe for "raw ale" (a.k.a. unboiled beer).

HOW HE GOT STARTED: He wanted to fully understand traditional beers, and there was no better way to do it.

FANCIEST PIECE OF EQUIPMENT: Erlenmeyer flask, because something has to keep the yeast going!

FAVORITE INGREDIENTS: Juniper branches, myrica gale

FAVORITE YEASTS: Local yeasts with a long history. He mentions Hornindal kveik, a blend of eight different *Saccharomyces* strains and a few fun bacteria. "That delicate aroma is just unbelievable."

Lars on Maltøl: Norwegian Farmhouse Beer

As with Lithuanian *kaimiškas*, and probably also Finnish *sahti*, *maltøl* is an umbrella term for several very different styles of beer. However, it seems that this was the term used for a loose style of farmhouse beers produced across almost the entire country of Norway.

The basic ingredients seem to be the same everywhere: there is juniper in the recipes in addition to the traditional water, barley malts, hops, and yeast. In fact, hops are often used very sparingly, mainly to prevent infection or as a light bittering agent together with the juniper. There's no filtering. The beer is carbonated by racking before fermentation is entirely complete.

Yet alcohol strengths vary widely and color can range from pale yellow to dark. The pale yellow color is actually traditional, as in many places people would dry their malts in the sun. On the process side of things, there are also huge differences from region to region, but one thing seems constant: the use of big, wood-fired copper or iron kettles. An open question is to what degree these affect the flavor. From my own experiments, I know that the heat from the wood fire definitely does affect the color.

Although some people describe the tradition as unchanged for thousands of years, that's obviously untrue, even if the tradition almost certainly is *unbroken* for thousands of years. There have been many changes over the centuries. The biggest was perhaps the transition to an all-malt beer. Other changes were the introduction of copper kettles, the boiling of the wort (probably), the reuse of yeast (probably), the introduction of hops, and a few more.

Some of these brewers don't use modern lab yeast because they still have the yeast cultures that their ancestors used, which are referred to as *kveik*. These have been used for generations beyond count, and some of them produce aromas unlike any commercial yeast. There are many kveik cultures, and they are very different from one another. Some brewers keep the yeast in a glass jar in the fridge, while others dry it and keep it in the freezer. Before pitching, the yeast is always tasted to make sure it's good. If it's bad, the brewer will find a different jar or go to another brewer in the region who has good yeast. Pitch temperatures range from 86 to 109°F (30 to 43°C).

STYLES

Identifying separate styles of beer out of the tangled mess of data is by no means easy, and for a long time it wasn't even clear that it was a good idea. By now, however, a few clusters are beginning to emerge. All of the styles listed below share the commonalities listed above. I'm restricting myself to the styles that are still alive today.

VOSSAØL/HARDANGERØL

These are quite strong beers (7 to 8 percent), made from pale, unsmoked malts, with a long mash of at least three hours and a boil of three to four hours. The result is amber or reddish. A key factor in the character of these beers is the use of kveik. The main flavors are an orangey aroma from the kveik, as well as a juniper taste, and key to brewing a good one seems to be blending the kveik flavor harmoniously in with the juniper, while balancing the hop/juniper bitterness with the malty sweetness.

Making the juniper infusion at Kaupanger. *Photo courtesy of Lars Marius Garshol*

I helped brew one beer like this in Voss and tasted two others that were quite similar. Afterward, Voss Bryggeri brewed a commercial version following much the same recipe, producing a beer rather like the first three. I later brewed two more with modern equipment, and again they came out much like the originals. So it's clear that the different *vossaøl* are all very close in flavor and consistent enough to be considered a single style. The flavor is totally unlike anything else I've ever had, so I have no hesitation naming this a separate style.

Discussions with two homebrewers from Hardanger (which is not far from Voss) indicate that the process is the same there. Interestingly, the local history society in Hardanger published a recipe from 1898 which seems to follow the same outline: mashing three to four hours, boiling "preferably for several hours." The process from 1898 seems to be to split the wort and boil the first part with the hops, then boil the last part for several hours. Frustratingly, the recipe is a bit ambiguous there.

Anyway, it's likely the maltøl from these two areas are similar enough to form a single type. Whether it's one style or two hinges on the flavor of kveik from Hardanger, and that flavor is still totally unknown to me. It may be that it the combined style should be named *hardangerøl*, since that was a recognized beer style in Norway a century ago.

RÅØL

The *råøl* (raw ale) is characterized by the wort not being boiled. Typically, a small part of the wort is taken off and boiled with hops, and the result is then added to the unboiled wort and fermented directly. It seems that some people lightly smoke the malt. Some use kveik and others use bread yeast if the kveik is gone.

Geographically, these beers are somewhat spread out. We found one in Oppland, but it's also found in Sunnmøre. It used to be brewed in Stranda (and might still be), and it's still brewed in Hornindal just across the province border to Sogn og Fjordane. It probably lives in more places I just don't know about yet.

The raw ale must, as far as I can tell, vary quite a lot, so perhaps this is in reality more than a single beer style, but since it stands out so clearly in terms of both flavor and process from other maltøl, it seems to deserve a category of its own. Raw ale made with kveik stands out quite clearly from the ones made with bread yeast.

STJØRDALSØL

These beers are from the region around Stjørdal near Trondheim, and this is a style that's already established among Norwegian beer enthusiasts. Everyone there knows about *stjørdalsøl*. Within the style there is considerable variety, and some brewers like to use more specific terms, like *Hegra maltøl*, but it really does seem like a single style. The defining characteristic is that the brewers make their own malts: they're usually lightly roasted and between somewhat smoked to heavily smoked.

The beers are generally 5.0 to 7.5 percent alcohol, dark amber to dark brown, and defined by the malt flavor. The locals like to say, "If you have good malts, you can hardly fail to make good beer," showing what emphasis they place on the malts. As far as I know, all of these beers have a smoke flavor, but it varies from light and delicate to intense and overpowering. The baking yeast they use gives a rough, fruity flavor to the beer that goes well with the smoky malts.

OTHERS

There are lots of maltøl that don't fall within one of these three styles, including the one I helped brew in Sogndal, for example, as well as the one from Holo Gardstun, and a whole range of others. At the moment I am not sure how to classify these, so for now I think they are best described simply as generic maltøl.

REGIONS

Geographically, the brewing that survives is fairly spread out, as you can see from the range of cities that follows.

VOSS

This stands out as one of the two key farmhouse areas in Norway (the other is Stjørdal—more on that area at right). There are lots of farmhouse brewers here, and the original style is amazingly well preserved. They've preserved the ancestral Norwegian yeast strains (kveik), as well as Norwegian hop varieties. As recently as two decades ago, people were even making their own malts! Even more important, the beer is really, really good. The process of making these traditional beers more widely available has begun as well, which is good for all of us.

HARDANGER

I have made little progress on this region, but it seems to still have a good number of active brewers and to be very similar to Voss. The kveik lives on, but how well preserved it is and whether it's like the one from Voss is unknown.

SOGN

This region has many brewers that brew in different ways. The tradition seems less well preserved here, but the style and process are still mostly traditional. Malts and hops are now all imported, and most people use lab yeast.

SUNNMØRE

Again, there are many brewers, and they are quite spread out geographically, but they are actually fairly well organized. How well preserved the original styles are is not clear based on my travels, but there are still people who know how to brew in the traditional way and make their own malts. Their kveik lives on and is quite different from the kveik in Voss.

OPPDAL

There is a fairly small cluster of brewers here, but some of them have preserved their tradition amazingly well. The kveik has not survived, and local hops seem to be gone, but they do make their own malts.

Mashing in Voss. *Photo courtesy of Lars Marius Garshol*

STJØRDAL

This is the other key area of Norwegian farmhouse brewing with hundreds of brewers, nearly all of them making their own malts. There's no kveik or hops, but the original style and processes are preserved. They have even begun the process of commercializing the farmhouse ales, which is very promising.

TELEMARK

Brewing nearly died in the 1970s in this region, then was revived. They import all the ingredients. They make boiled beer and actually mash in the kettle. They used to boil the mash in the kettle, but brewing has been slightly modernized, so that they now step-mash instead. Step-mashing is not unknown in Norwegian farmhouse brewing, so it could still be considered traditional.

SETESDAL

This is the dark north-south furrow southwest of the two dots in Telemark, across into the next province. The brewing appears to be the same as in Hardanger.

Lars's Recipe

★

NORWEGIAN FARMHOUSE ALE

This brew is inspired by Lars's research notes and is our best attempt at "standardizing" one of his brews from that trip. This recipe requires some extra work and kettle manipulation on your part as you must infuse your mash and sparge water with juniper and build a juniper bed in your lauter tun. Mmmm . . . juniper water.

FOR 5.5 GALLONS AT 1.115 OG, 19 SRM, 18 IBUs, 12% ABV

GRAIN BILL
15.00 lb.   Munich malt
6.00 lb.   2-row pale malt
1.75 lb.   Weyermann CaraRed malt
2.00 oz.   Weyermann Carafa II malt

MASH
Rest   161°F   60 minutes

HOPS
1.00 oz.   Hallertauer   4.8% AA   60 minutes
0.25 oz.   Hallertauer   4.8% AA   15 minutes

YEAST
Fermentis Safale US-05

ADDITIONS
Common juniper branches, largely free of berries, enough to fill your hot liquor tank (HLT) and layer in your mash tun. (Make sure you're using an edible variety of juniper. Add a North American twist by using *Juniperus virginiana*, also known as Eastern Red Cedar.)

NOTES
Fill your HLT with juniper and water. Heat to 176°F while prepping the mash.

Mash in a large pot with juniper water and grain. Add enough water to stabilize around 161°F. Lars says you will know the ratio is right when your mash paddle is just barely able to stay upright.

Refill your HLT with water and reheat to 176°F.

Fill your mash/lauter tun with a few inches of juniper branches. After 1 hour of mashing, move the mash into the lauter tun and sparge with your fresh juniper water.

Boil, add hops, chill, and pitch as normal.

Fred Bonjour

Fred was the assistant education director for the BJCP and taught numerous classes for others studying for BJCP certification. His own beers have won many awards, but what sets Fred apart is his obsession: BIG beers. Since he began brewing, at least one-third of his beers have been 1.100 OG or higher. Not many brewers spend three hours boiling and then rouse their yeast three times a day, but Fred does. Fred's website is www.beerbonjour.com.

BREWING SINCE: 2001

BREWING MOTTO: Everything under 1.100 is a session beer.

BREWING PHILOSOPHY: Enjoy!

FAVORITE BREW STYLES: Barleywine, Russian imperial stout, wee heavy, porter, and dark mild (which Fred calls a yeast starter!). Fred's beers almost always have an OG of 1.091 or above. "I really prefer to brew the big beers, and mostly the English barleywine and Scottish wee heavy. When I was getting started, I would judge how good an IPA was by how much I hated it."

FAVORITE BREWING COUNTRY: England

BREWING METHODOLOGY: All-grain fly sparge

BREWING LOCATION: Back patio

BREWING SYSTEM: Fred uses a pretty basic system. He mashes in a round 10-gallon Igloo cooler with a false bottom. He fly sparges his big beers, but smaller beers are usually batch sparged. He fly sparges into two kettles on two burners. Small beers are boiled for sixty to ninety minutes, and his big beers can be boiled all day. He uses a simple copper coil immersion chiller, which he moves up and down in the wort to provide aeration. Sometimes the beers go into his fermentation fridge to cool overnight. His fermentation is done in either a refrigerator or swamp cooler setup. His goal is to maintain fermentation temperatures in the low 60s (°F).

HOW HE GOT STARTED: Fred received a Mr. Beer kit as a Christmas gift and says he never looked back. The first beer he brewed was a Mr. Beer Octoberfest kicked up with DME.

FANCIEST PIECE OF EQUIPMENT: Fred says that his fanciest piece of equipment is the jockey box he uses for serving his beer.

FAVORITE INGREDIENTS: Fred's favorite malt is Maris Otter. He says it brings complexity to a beer and is his "go-to" malt. The only exception is when he brews a very light beer and uses pilsner malt.

FAVORITE YEASTS: Fred's favorite yeast strain is Danstar Nottingham Ale since he mainly brews ales.

MOST UNUSUAL INGREDIENTS AND RECIPES: "Brewers Licorice for a Bell's Kalamazoo Stout Clone. I'm fairly tame."

Fred on How to Brew a Really Big Beer

If you're talking about just 1.070 or 1.080, you have to be kidding; I'm talking about brewing a *really* big beer! The information that follows is for beers in the 1.100 and up range. Why? Well, I can buy a lot of beers, but very few of them are truly big. Life begins at 100 . . . 1.100 that is. Let's hear it for "century" beers!

Like every beer, you need to decide what your original gravity will be. There's no magic here; just formulate your grain bill in your normal manner. Here's where things get different: choose a target final gravity. Yes, I said final gravity.

Part of the art of brewing a truly big beer is to hit your FG. The achieved FG provides a lot of character to your beer, mostly in mouthfeel and residual sweetness. How dry or sweet do you want your beer? The residual sweetness left behind determines a lot of this character in the beer.

For really big beers, the FG is actually difficult to predict since none of the brewing software packages are built to predict it (they assume an average attenuation for the yeast used), and none of the current literature addresses this. So we each have to deal with this based on our own experience and the principles of what we can do to impact FG.

Let's take one of my favorites, an English barleywine, as an example. The style guidelines (BJCP style guidelines at www.BJCP.org) say:

OG 1.080 to 1.120+
FG 1.018 to 1.030+
IBUs 35 to 70
SRM 8 to 22
ABV 8 to 12+%

For a 1.080 barleywine that finishes at 1.020, this is an attenuation of 75 percent, which is easily attainable with most grain bills and most yeasts. At the upper end of the

Expect a very full mash tun when you brew big beers!

Rousing yeast regularly is a key to success with big beers.

spectrum, we have a 1.120 barleywine that finishes at 1.030. This again is an attenuation of 75 percent, but it's a harder-to-achieve 75 percent. I would actually expect it to finish with an FG of 1.035 to 1.040. Let's look at one more—a true monster—a 1.150 barleywine with that same 75 percent attenuation, which is now very difficult and provides an FG of 1.038. In practice, brewed with no special techniques, it will likely finish higher at 1.045 to 1.050, which in my opinion is a bit too high and into the cloyingly sweet range.

The bottom line when brewing big beers is that we need to get our attenuation up to achieve a FG lower than we would normally achieve. These attenuation issues can be addressed with several variables, which we'll now explore.

SELECT THE RIGHT YEAST

Since you are dealing with attenuation, you need to select a very attenuative yeast whenever possible. In some styles, all you are looking for is a neutral yeast, while in others you need the character of the yeast to come through. For those styles, you may consider a yeast blend, a neutral high attenuative yeast, and your character yeast. My last barleywine used a WY1007 German Ale yeast cake and a WY1318 London Ale III starter for a bit of English character.

ADJUST THE GRAIN BILL

In a nutshell, you want to squeeze as much attenuation as you can out of your brew. First let's limit our use of malts, which yield higher FGs, which are the crystals- and carapils-type malts. Additionally, we can add some sugar, up to 10 percent. Remember, this is not some light beer we are trying to brew—there is more than enough malt backbone here to carry the sugar. Almost any kind of sugar will do, but I like to add a "character" sugar: think maple sugar or syrup, molasses, light or dark brown sugar, honey, or candi sugar. All of these sugars are more fermentable than wort and will effectively lower your FG given the same OG because they are all nearly completely fermentable.

If you are using extracts, do not use the lower fermentable extracts (such as Laaglanders, which is great in a Scottish 80/-). You will have plenty of nonfermentables from the size of your grain bill.

MAKE A STARTER

A pitchable tube or an activator pack is *not* enough yeast for any of these beers. A large starter—at least a cup of thick slurry or yeast sediment—or pitching on top of a yeast cake is what you need instead. With big beers, you really can't have too much yeast.

CRAFT A MASH SCHEDULE

Attenuation is influenced by mash temps, and for different mash temps you can expect a different range. With a single infusion mash at 149°F, you can generally achieve 75 to 80 percent attenuation. For a big Belgian, which by style has a dry finish, you will need to mash for even higher fermentability, more in the 80- to 87-percent attenuation range.

However, if you are brewing a big thick beer such as a Thomas Hardy clone or a wee heavy, you want a higher than normal FG. For a normal-strength beer, up to about 1.080, you would perform a single-step infusion mash of around 155 to 158°F to achieve this. Yet if you were to attempt this with a 1.120+ beer, you could probably sell the result as molasses! What is needed is a counterintuitive, highly fermentable mash schedule. I would suggest a 146 to 149°F to 154 to 156°F step mash with about forty to forty-five minutes at the initial step and an hour at the higher step. Do not be afraid to extend your mash times. While conversion occurs quickly (ten to fifteen minutes), longer mashes guarantee maximum efficiency. I also recommend a thin mash, greater than or equal to 2 quarts per pound of malt, to promote greater fermentability.

AERATE THE WORT

Your wort needs to be well oxygenated or aerated to provide a good environment for your growing yeast. Vigorous agitation, which is what I do, is sufficient, though direct oxygenation with an O_2 gas injection would be even better.

ROUSE THE YEAST

As the yeast is completing its task, it is flocculating or falling out of solution. It does not matter if the yeast flocculates at a high or a low rate; with a big beer it will flocculate out before fermentation is finished. To compensate, we must rouse the yeast at frequent intervals to keep it in suspension and able to ferment the remaining fermentable sugars. I recommend rousing the yeast two to three times per day (before you go to work, when you get home, and just before you go to bed). Note that this does not need to start until fermentation is slowing down.

CONTROL FERMENTATION TEMPERATURE

Fermentation temperature is the largest single success factor in brewing a big beer. High ester and fusel alcohol production is a function of the yeast working at higher temperatures. Ideal fermentations for me with WY1007 German Ale or 1728 Scottish Ale are at 55°F (yes, this is an ale). I would also consider WY2112 California Lager. For those in the ice belt, your basement during December and January should be fine.

Fred's Recipe

★

KILT LIFTER: A SCOTTISH WEDDING BEER

This beer showcases Fred's love of brewing and drinking big beers. How much bigger does it get than his take on a wee heavy? We imagine that the guests at this wedding had to be carried out! Be sure to follow all of Fred's advice about brewing big beer.

FOR 5.5 GALLONS AT 1.133 OG, 1.043 FG, 20 SRM, 14.5 IBUs, 12% ABV

GRAIN BILL

16 lb.	Maris Otter malt
6 lb.	Weyermann Munich I malt
1 lb.	caramel/crystal 20°L malt
1 lb.	caramel/crystal 80°L malt
1 lb.	Weyermann Caramunich I malt
1 lb.	Caravienne malt
4 oz.	Weyermann Rauch malt

MASH

Rest	146°F	40 minutes Infuse with 26 quarts of water
Decoct	156°F	40 minutes Boil 5.25 quarts of mash and add back to main mash
Sparge	168°F	4 gallons water

HOPS

2 oz.	East Kent Goldings (pellets)	4.1% AA	60 minutes

YEAST

WY1728 Scottish Ale

NOTES

Age for 28 days.

Agitate fermenter frequently to encourage fermentation and keep the yeast in suspension.

MALTED BLISS

Another sipping beer from Fred! This one involves a decoction mash. While we don't know if a decoction really adds a lot of flavor to the beer, other brewers disagree with us, so go for it! You'll have a full brew day to reflect on it as you drink this beer. Seriously, Fred's brought this one to AHA Governing Committee meetings and passed it around. It tends to derail the proceedings!

FOR 5.5 GALLONS AT 1.137 OG, 14.7 SRM, 43 IBUs, 12% ABV

GRAIN BILL

18.00 lb.	Maris Otter malt
2.50 lb.	crystal 20°L malt
2.25 lb.	cara-pils (dextrine) malt
2.00 lb.	Weyermann Munich I malt
1.00 lb.	white wheat malt
2.00 oz.	chocolate malt

MASH

Rest	146°F	40 minutes Infuse with 30 quarts of 165°F water
Decoct	158°F	40 minutes Boil 5.25 quarts of mash and add back to main mash
Sparge	168°F	5.25 gallons water

HOPS

4 oz.	East Kent Goldings	4.1% AA	60 minutes
2 oz.	East Kent Goldings	4.1% AA	15 minutes
1 oz.	East Kent Goldings	4.1% AA	0 minutes

YEAST

WY1007 German Ale

WY1318 London Ale III

NOTES

Age for 3 months.

BREWER'S PROFILE

Annie Johnson

Annie won the 2013 American Homebrewers Association Homebrew of the Year with her Light American Lager. (Seriously, who manages that?) She has also been named Pilsner Urquell's Master Homebrewer. Not many people can say that Urquell's Master Brewer—Vaclav Berka—said he felt like he was home when he drank your beer. In addition to all that, Annie spends a lot of time answering questions and sharing her experience with other homebrewers online and works as a recipe developer for PicoBrew.

BREWING SINCE: 1998

BREWING MOTTO: There are no bad beers, only bad processes!

BREWING PHILOSOPHY: Brew because it's fun and satisfying.

FAVORITE BREW STYLES: Belgian, Czech pils and dark lager, American amber

FAVORITE BREWING COUNTRY: Czech Republic

BREWING METHODOLOGY: All-grain batch sparge

BREWING LOCATION: Garage or outside (her stand is on wheels so she can take advantage of nice weather)

BREWING SYSTEM: Her system's big pieces include two 20-gallon Blichmann boilermakers, a trusty Sabco keg/mash tun, three Blichmann burners, and two March pumps. As far as process, Annie gets an inspiration and crafts a recipe, including the mashing schedule and fermentation schedule. She procures all of the ingredients and picks the day to brew. She then goes through the brewing process taking notes along the way. "I don't drink or listen to music while I brew." (By the way, this is the same as Denny: no drinking while brewing. Drew usually waits until the boil is going before pouring a cold one.) Annie says, "I stay focused but I do use the time to read about new methods or beers. I pitch my yeast and put the fermenter to bed. Then I crack a beer, turn on the music, and clean up."

HOW SHE GOT STARTED: Annie always loved beer, and her mom told her, "You can do it, you can brew it." Now that's parental support! Her brewing hobby also goes well with her other hobby, watching her Oakland teams, the Raiders and the A's, with friends.

> **DREW:** Drinking while watching Oakland play? Sounds like a necessity to me!

FANCIEST PIECE OF EQUIPMENT: Her really nice brew pots

FAVORITE INGREDIENTS: Annie is a big fan of Munich malt because she finds it extremely versatile. She says, "I love all the beers you can brew with Munich malt. Even at just a small amount of -0.5 to 2.0 lb. [per 5 gallons], it lends a layer of complexity to the beer as well as adding to the body." Annie is also a big fan of Belgian pils and pale malts because she adores Belgian beers. "I spent three years brewing nothing but Belgians and found you can't brew authentic Belgians without those malts. Some may argue, but that's okay." Annie is a woman who knows what she likes!

She really likes noble hops and some of the new New Zealand hops. The nobles are for her Belgian/German/Czech beers, and for hoppier beers, Annie says, "I'm loving Sorachi Ace and Mosaic/Nelson Sauvin."

FAVORITE YEASTS: Annie is a believer in the entire Fermentis family. "I like how they store well, you don't need a starter, they're affordable, and they work well." On the liquid side, she likes WLP001 California Ale for IPA and WY1056 American Ale for American amber. That's an interesting distinction since both yeasts reportedly have the same origin, but it bears out the thinking that the strains have slightly diverged over the years. She also likes WY1450 Denny's Favorite 50 (what excellent taste!) for its versatility and authenticity when brewing a recipe from Denny. She prefers White Labs strains of Urquell (WLP800 Pilsner Lager) and Budjovice (WLP802 Czech Budejovice Lager) lager yeasts. She says there are subtle differences when making a true Czech pils or dark lager.

MOST UNUSUAL INGREDIENTS AND RECIPES: Lavender, rosemary, rose hips—not all together but as additions to Belgian ales. In the world of unusual recipes, she says, "I have done several historic brews, one with mandrake root and yeast cultivated from bapir bread. I also malted my own grain for this. I was following a recipe sent to me by an Egyptian friend. I was going for a recipe that would have been brewed and drunk 3,000 years ago. I served it at NHC 2007 in Denver. I dressed the keg up as a mummy and served it at room temp. I found the women loved it."

DREW: Allow me a moment of shameless self-promotion: Annie also brewed Brut Du Faucon (a champagne beer). She credits the videos my club made as a key to success for what she calls "one of the hardest and best beers I've brewed."

Annie's Reading List for Better Brewing

My advice to new brewers is to take your time, nail the process down, and get a few good beers under your belt. Then branch out; it makes the process so much smoother. Remain calm. Nail a recipe down and make it your own, as in, have a house beer. From there you will have the skills to move on and up!

Pay homage to the storied breweries of the world even though you may not personally be in love with the styles of beers they brew. Spend time brewing all styles, and it will help you have a full understanding of beer. Study up and become a BJCP judge, but not just any judge—try to be a compassionate and knowledgeable judge because we're all here to brew better beer. Most importantly, have fun! Respect all parts from inception to serving; they all matter.

DREW: Since Annie puts a lot of emphasis and value on studying, we asked her what her brewing library looks like. We particularly agree with her stunningly great choice as her last bookshelf recommendation!

HERE'S WHAT'S ON ANNIE'S BOOKSHELVES:

Every *BYO Magazine* from 2004 to present: "This is where I learned about a lot of different styles and how-tos in making my own homebrew equipment."

Brewing by Dr. Michael Lewis: "I got this textbook from a certificate program I took from UC Davis in 2003. It's super technical, but it was the first real brewing book I ever had. I use it now for calculations and terms. The problem is, when I read it, I hear an elderly Welsh gentleman's voice in my head!"

Sacred and Herbal Healing Beers by Stephen Buhner: "This one is a classic; I love historical styles of beer."

New Brewing Lager Beer by Greg Noonan: "The best book if you want to perfect lagers."

Brew Ware by Karl Lutzen: "I loved this book. It helped me figure out how to make everything and identified what things were when I had no clue."

Brewers Association Belgian Series, including *Brew Like a Monk*, *Farmhouse Ales*, and *Wild Ales*.

BJCP Guidelines: "I use these religiously to formulate recipes."

   "I also constantly surf the Internet and read about breweries here and abroad. I love reading about the background information about breweries. It really is the more you know, the better you will do. I also have favorite blogs like Brulosophy, The Mad Fermentationist, and favorite homebrew clubs sites where I'm constantly checking in, like the Maltose Falcons. Dennybrew.com is where I learned about batch sparging, and it changed my whole homebrewing world.

   "The latest and greatest addition to my bookshelf: *Experimental Homebrewing*, of course."

Read every brewing book and magazine you can get your hands on.

Annie's Recipes

THIS BUDVAR'S FOR YOU

Annie's German background comes out in this delicious beer. She's won so many awards for her pils-style beers that you owe it to yourself to try this one. A bit higher bitterness than a lot of Czech-style pils recipes means that this beer will have the bite to cut through on hot summer days. Or cold winter days. Or whenever you drink it!

FOR 5.5 GALLONS AT 1.051 OG, 2.8 SRM, 43 IBUs, 5.25% ABV

GRAIN BILL
11.00 lb.   2-row pilsner malt
0.34 lb.   Sauer (acid) malt

MASH
Acid rest	99°F	15 minutes
Protein rest	102°F	20 minutes
Intermediate rest	140°F	30 minutes
Saccharification rest	149°F	30 minutes
Mash-out	170°F	15 minutes
Sparge	170°F	45 minutes

HOPS
1.5 oz. Czech Saaz	3.5% AA	60 minutes
1.5 oz. Czech Saaz	3.5% AA	30 minutes
1.5 oz. Czech Saaz	3.5% AA	10 minutes
1.5 oz. Czech Saaz	3.5% AA	0 minutes

YEAST
WLP802 Czech Budejovice Lager

ADDITIONS
1 tsp. Irish moss, added at flameout

NOTES
Infuse all mash water at acid rest step rather than adjusting temperature with multiple water additions.

ATOMIC AMBER
(pictured at right)

Annie's Atomic Amber shows a real Pacific Northwest bent with the hop schedule. This amber will have its malt character well balanced by the hopping. A great interpretation of a style that can be, well, boring. Even if you don't think you like ambers, give this one a try!

FOR 5.5 GALLONS AT 1.063 OG, 17 SRM, 44 IBUs, 6.5% ABV, 90-MINUTE BOIL

GRAIN BILL
12.00 lb.   2-row pale malt
0.50 lb.   crystal 40°L malt
0.25 lb.   crystal 90°L malt
0.50 lb.   Victory malt
0.25 lb.   chocolate malt
0.25 lb.   Weyermann Caramunich I malt

MASH
Rest	154°F	60 minutes

HOPS
0.60 oz. Magnum	13.50% AA	60 minutes
0.75 oz. Cascade	5.75% AA	10 minutes
0.75 oz. Centennial	10.50% AA	10 minutes
0.75 oz. Cascade	5.75% AA	0 minutes
1.00 oz. Centennial	10.50% AA	0 minutes

YEAST
Fermentis Safale US-05

Curt Stock

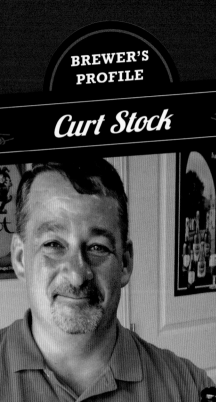

Curt has been brewing for eighteen years and has amassed a huge collection of well-deserved awards for both beer and mead. In fact, he was the American Homebrewers Association Meadmaker of the Year in 2007. He's been featured as a speaker at the National Homebrew Conference, founded the Saint Paul Homebrewers Club (with Gary Hippie), and still brews about forty batches annually.

BREWING SINCE: 1997

BREWING MOTTO: Curt is guided by two mottos in his brewing and meadmaking: "Don't complain about the beer if you didn't bring it," and, "There would be no winners if losers didn't enter."

BREWING PHILOSOPHY: "Homebrewing is the best hobby I've ever had. Not only do you make something that you would normally buy, you can use your brain, your brawn, your expertise, and passion to make something special. You will make great friends and grow your family. Still, know your system and be proficient. Become consistent with your brewing system before getting creative with ingredients, recipes, and techniques."

FAVORITE BREW STYLES: Light German lagers, IPAs, English bitters and porters, cream ale

FAVORITE BREWING COUNTRY: Germany

BREWING METHODOLOGY: "I prepare yeast ahead of time by making a 1.5-liter yeast starter. On brew day, I go to the basement, fill the liquor tank and mash tun with proper volumes of water, and begin heating. I adjust the liquor water with 10 percent phosphoric to a pH of 5.6-ish. Then I head to the garage to measure the grains and run them through a three-roller mill. After all the appropriate rests are complete, using low direct heat and recirculation, I bring the mash to 165°F, and once it's clear I begin the fly sparge with 168°F water. I run off 13.5 gallons of water into my brew pot. I start heating the boil kettle when 4 gallons are collected. I bring it to a boil and boil at least ninety minutes following the appropriate hopping schedule. I use a Whirlfloc tablet with twenty minutes left in the boil. At flame-out, I whirlpool and settle. I chill the wort with a counterflow chiller into a stainless 13-gallon fermenter. I oxygenate with pure oxygen and a boiled aeration stone. When it's time, I pitch the yeast and ferment at the proper temperature—leaving the beer in the fermenter for about two weeks. I rack to 5-gallon kegs. After two weeks, I cold condition and filter from keg to keg using a plate filter, and then force-carbonate and serve."

BREWING LOCATION: "Down a steep flight of gray, wooden stairs, take a right at the sauna, proceed past the poker table and bar, go left at the lager freezer, and arrive at the brewery." Also located in the basement is Curt's treasured Miller Chill sign.

> **DENNY:** I've been in Curt's basement, and the collection of awards he has there is overwhelming: ribbons everywhere for beer, cider, and mead! I couldn't even count how many. Despite his highly awarded brewing prowess, Curt is one of the most down-to-earth people you could ever meet. He's great example of what homebrewing is all about.

BREWING SYSTEM: Key pieces include three burners hooked to natural gas, a 10-gallon liquor tank, a 14-gallon mash tun, and a 15-gallon boil kettle. He has dedicated water taps with carbon block filters. A copper hood hangs over the boil kettle to pull out the moisture and keep the basement safe. He also has two pumps, a counter flow chiller, and miscellaneous tubing and fittings.

HOW HE GOT STARTED: Curt got into brewing because of friends at work who brewed. As he lives in the Minneapolis area, he stopped by Northern Brewer and bought an extract kit. He brewed with extract for about a year before going to all grain.

FANCIEST PIECE OF EQUIPMENT: The aforementioned Miller Chill sign. Obviously, Curt is a guy who has his priorities in order!

FAVORITE INGREDIENTS:
- Saint Paul water: "It tastes good. The pH is typically 8+, but it is very soft and buffers easily. It can be made into almost any regional brewing water by using salts and minerals."

- German Pilsner malt: "I love the clean flavors and the taste of it when it's decocted."

- Flaked corn: "You can't fake the flavor it gives a beer. There is no substitute to replicate the character you get from it."

- Centennial hops: "I love the flavor, and they work very well when paired with other hops in IPAs. They're also a favorite of mine when used in hoppy dark ales. (Note: I did not say Cascadian dark ale or black IPA.)"

FAVORITE YEASTS:
- WY1028 London Ale and WY1056 American Ale: "A reliable alcohol maker while giving a touch of ester."

- WY1098 British Ale: "It makes a great strong bitter by letting the malt and hops shine."

- WY1318 London Ale III: "It makes the best robust porter you'll ever taste: malty, fruity with a touch of sweetness for balancing the roast."

- WY2000 Budvar Lager: "I use this yeast for classic American pilsners."

- WY2206 Bavarian Lager: "It's a popular yeast for a reason—it's good. It's versatile and my favorite for helles. I also like to split a batch of helles and ferment the other half with Budvar!"

MOST UNUSUAL INGREDIENTS: Although Curt says he doesn't brew too much that's "unusual," using a blackberry mead to make a blackberry cream ale was an experiment that paid off for him. (Also, see the recipe for Lime Cream Ale, which follows.)

WHERE CONVENTIONAL WISDOM IS WRONG: "I say fly sparging over batch sparging is the way to go—sorry, Denny!"

Curt's Method for Filtering with a Plate Filter

YOU WILL NEED:
- Filter assembly

- 2 filter pads (coarse pads should be fine for any beer; for instance, the GF1 Coarse pads common to homebrew plate filters at 2 to 7 microns)

- 2 kegs (one with beer to be filtered, one clean/sanitized/oxygen-free)
- CO_2 Cylinder
- 2 ball lock fittings (beer side)
- 2 worm clamps

Filtering beer with a plate filter can be worth it: you can dramatically increase clarity.

INSTRUCTIONS

1. Chill beer (approximately 35°F) to be filtered for at least 2 days. Do not carbonate the beer. That makes filtering much more difficult.

2. Purge tube (ball lock for beer side with 3 feet of $5/16$-inch ID tubing connected). Sanitize filter assembly and filter pads in Star San.

3. Put filter assembly together. Lay each plate, grooved side up, on a flat surface. Place a filter pad on each plate, rough side up. Place the center ring on one of the plates to secure the filter pad. Holding the ring and plate (keeping the pad in place), flip onto the other plate and pad. Align the barbs on each plate and position the barb on the ring 180 degrees from the plate barbs. Using the bolts, secure the plates together. Leave each bolt snug but loose until all six are in place. Tighten each bolt to hand tight. Using an adjustable wrench, tighten each bolt one complete turn. *Note: this is not recommended by the manufacturer. Do at your own risk. If over-tightened, the filter assembly may break.*

4. Hold the filter assembly upright with the plate barbs pointing toward the floor and allow excess sanitizer to drain.

5. Hook up the "Y" and tubing to the plate barbs. Connect an 18- to 24-inch hose to the single post of the "Y" and a swivel nut and barb on the other end. (Do not connect the ball lock fitting at this time.)

6. Connect a $5/16$-inch tube, 24-inches in length, to the ring barb on the filter assembly and a swivel nut and barb with ball lock on the other end. Use a worm clamp on each end of the tubing to prevent leaking. This section will have significant pressure.

7. Move the chilled keg to the filtering area. Take care to not disturb the sediment in the keg. Place the filter assembly next to the beer keg (use an

extra keg to set the filter assembly on) and place the clean/sanitized keg on the other side.

8. Set the CO_2 cylinder to 6 psi. Pressurize the beer keg.

9. Using the purge tube, run off about a cup of beer into a waste container to get the initial sediment that will come out. This will eliminate some of the cake that will shorten the life of your filter pads.

10. Remove the purge tube and place the "filter in" ball lock (tubing hooked to the inner ring barb of the filter assembly) loosely on the out post of the beer keg. Do not engage beer flow at this point.

11. Position the "filter out" tube (single tube from the "Y" fitting) over the waste container (it should not have a ball lock fitting on it yet). Push the ball lock onto the beer keg to start the beer flowing through the filter assembly. Liquid will start to flow from the filter. It will be mostly sanitizer at first and the beer will smell like paper filter. Run about 3 to 4 cups of liquid into the waste container. Then stop the flow by disengaging the ball lock on the beer keg. This should be enough to clear the filter of oxygen, sanitizer, and filter paper taste.

12. Connect a ball lock to the "filter out" tube. Open the pressure relief valve on the clean/sanitized keg (receiving keg). Attach the ball lock to the beer out post so the keg fills from the bottom.

13. Reattach the ball lock to the beer keg to resume beer flow. Increase the pressure on the beer keg if the flow slows. Filtering should take 10 to 40 minutes, depending on the clarity level of the beer being filtered.

14. Once the beer keg is empty and gas begins to enter the filter assembly, the beer will stop flowing through and gas will start bubbling into the receiving keg. A couple pints are still in the filter assembly. If you want to recover that beer, you'll have to find something to clamp off the tubing coming from the upper plate. That way the beer

will be forced through the lower pad. A needle-nose vise grip (or locking pliers) works well for that. The tubing will be cold and hard to pinch off.

15. If your beer to be filtered is fairly clear, you can filter multiple kegs with a single set of pads. You'll have to keep the beginning sludge (what you removed with the purge tube technique) and ending sludge (what will come out when the beer keg goes empty) from entering the filter assembly and coating the pads with excess yeast. It's easy, but you have to pay attention and stop the flow from the beer keg before it goes empty. Be ready when the keg is almost empty: once you start to see the very cloudy stuff come from the keg, remove the ball lock immediately. Then go on to the next kegs. I've filtered up to 25 gallons with a single set of pads. When filtering multiple kegs, start with the lightest, least-hopped beer.

Curt on Staggered Nutrient Additions for Mead

A real advance in mead-making in recent years is called Staggered Nutrient Additions (SNA). Instead of adding all the nutrients at once, the same amount is staggered over several days. SNA promotes yeast health and helps ensure a fast, clean, and healthy fermentation. One thing I like is that you can drink the mead sooner because it doesn't require as much aging, depending on yeast choice.

SNA was developed by the commercial wine industry as a way of supplying nutrients as the yeast needs it during the growth phase—kind of a just-in-time delivery. Healthy yeast is essential for a clean fermentation with less chance of off-flavors or the production of higher alcohols (fusels) which can give mead a burning sensation on the back of the throat—the "rocket fuel" sensation.

I prefer to use Fermaid-K (yeast energizer) and diammonium phosphate or DAP (yeast nutrient) for adding the additional nutrient requirements of the yeast during fermentation. One teaspoon of Fermaid-K and

2 teaspoons DAP should be adequate for a 5-gallon batch. You can mix them together for a stock blend and add them using the following schedule:

- Add ³/₄ teaspoon yeast energizer/nutrient mix immediately after pitching yeast.

- Add ³/₄ teaspoon yeast energizer/nutrient mix 24 hours after fermentation begins.

- Add ³/₄ teaspoon yeast energizer/nutrient mix 48 hours after fermentation begins.

- Add ³/₄ teaspoon yeast energizer/nutrient mix after 30 percent of the sugar has been depleted.

Anyone who has ever stirred a fermenting beverage knows the foaming, triggered by the release of CO_2, can make one heck of a mess! To help minimize this, you should mix the nutrient blend into ¹/₂ cup of must and add it back to the fermenter. Then begin to slowly stir the must to release the main portion of the CO_2 gas. After the foaming has subsided, you can begin to stir more vigorously. Mix the must well enough to introduce plenty of oxygen. Oxygen is needed by the yeast throughout the growth phase. Oxidation is not a concern until you get past 50 percent sugar depletion. SNA serves many purposes for yeast health. Abundant CO_2 is toxic to yeast, so mixing while adding the nutrients will release the gas. Vigorous mixing introduces oxygen needed by growing yeast. The mixing also disturbs the fruit cap (or floating fruit). Punching down the cap should be done at least three times a day during the period of vigorous fermentation.

Curt's Recipe

LIME CREAM ALE

Denny: When I saw Curt drinking Miller Chill out of a bottle at the National Homebrew Conference, I thought I had somehow slipped into Bizarro World. I guess I should have realized that at the world's largest homebrew festival, there would be some "unusual" tastes. But far be it from me to judge anybody by what they drink! At least Curt has come up with a recipe to make his own lime beer!

FOR 5 GALLONS AT 1.055 OG, 4 SRM, 13 IBUs, 5.5% ABV

GRAIN BILL

8 lb.	German pils malt
2 lb.	flaked corn
1 lb.	flaked rice (optional)

MASH

Rest	150°F	60 minutes

HOPS

0.75 oz.	Hallertauer	4.8% AA	60 minutes
0.25 oz.	Hallertauer	4.8% AA	0 minutes (optional)

YEAST

WY1056 American Ale

ADDITION

4 limes, juiced and zested; add to secondary.

NOTES

"After primary rack to secondary (I like to rack to keg), I cold condition for a few days and then run through a plate filter into another keg. I just like clear beers and kegs that don't have a pile of yeast in the bottom."

Joe has been brewing a long time and has won some impressive awards, including two Ninkasi Awards from the American Homebrewers Association's National Homebrew Competition and the Sam Adams Longshot competition. It's a rare thing now to not hear Joe's name called at these events.

BREWING SINCE: 1987

BREWING MOTTO: Brew hard, brew big, and brew consistently.

BREWING PHILOSOPHY: Know your system.

FAVORITE BREW STYLES: Czech and German pilsner

FAVORITE BREWING COUNTRY: England

BREWING METHODOLOGY: Joe brews all-grain batch sparge batches in his basement kitchen. He mashes in a kettle kept warm in a low temperature oven. For lautering, he uses a double bucket system. Joe usually does decoction mashes, noting, "Decoction delivers desirable complexity in most any high malt brew." He chills using a homemade counter-flow chiller and ferments in 12-gallon Pyrex fermenters, then racks to a 5-gallon fermenter for secondary. Joe is proof that the brewer makes the beer, and the equipment is less important.

HOW HE GOT STARTED: Joe majored in biology at the University of Minnesota. He took a tour at Summit Brewing in 1987 and became inspired. He's also full-blooded Czech and says he was born with beer in his veins. Remember that Czechs to this day have the highest per capita consumption of beer on this planet.

FANCIEST PIECE OF EQUIPMENT: A stainless steel conical fermenter that he rarely uses.

BREWING INSPIRATION: Joe is inspired by brewing tradition. When he decided to brew a classic American pilsner, he spent time researching the style to make sure it was as close to the original pre-Prohibition beer as he could make it.

FAVORITE INGREDIENTS: Joe uses 2-row malt from Canada Malting as his general base malt. "It has clean flavor, good amylase activity, and low astringency. I use this for many of my beers. If I am looking at adding more malt character, I do use Maris Otter from Simpsons. For certain English styles, I might go straight Maris Otter. Biscuit and aromatic malts are also my friends to help complete the overall malt flavor profile in paler as well as darker beers. I am a fan of the Cara and chocolate wheats for darker beers when used in conjunction with standard Cara and chocolate malts to again give more background complexity in my darker beers, mainly the exports and the Russian imperial stout."

Joe's brewing equipment is made to use whole hops. He says that the screens he uses in the system clog easily when using pellets. Centennial and Willamette hops are the base hops for his American styles, with other hops such as Cascade, Simcoe, or Citra added, depending on the beer. For British styles he prefers "good old UK Goldings and Fuggles," while Hallertauer shows up in his German-style beers and Saaz in the Czech styles.

FAVORITE YEASTS: Joe likes using WY1272 American Ale II "because of the ester profile that it produces, the consistent level of attenuation, and the solid flocculation. WY1056 [American Ale] is a great clean workhorse that isn't too sensitive to temperature variations and produces a clean brew in which you can highlight the ingredients used. I see it as being similar to using sweet mead yeast in meads: if I have a great flavored varietal honey, I want that profile to be demonstrated in the finished product without a lot of fermentation products mudding up the character."

MOST UNUSUAL INGREDIENTS: This would have to be bananas (see below).

Joe Goes Bananas

Many homebrewers don't consider using bananas even when they're thinking about adding fruit to a beer. Yet bananas can deliver both body and richness to a beer in addition to flavor, which means they can work particularly well in a darker, roasty beer. I once won best-of-show at a homebrew competition for a banana imperial stout, so I'm not the only one that thinks it can work!

Try mashing with bananas before you write it off. The results might surprise you!

Bananas in a blonde ale? Yep! Check out the recipe on the next page.

DREW: Why do we have an Old-School Master talking about a decidedly not European Old-School ingredient like bananas? Because it's fun! Also, depending on which brewing tradition you're looking at—bananas have a long history in beverage production—look no further than Kenya, Uganda, and other East African nations where banana beer is still made today. Stop being so Euro-centric in your traditions, people!

I've experimented with the use of bananas for years in a wide range of styles though, from that imperial stout to blonde ales. Here's what I've found:

You need to use quite a bit of fruit (10 pounds or so in a 5-gallon batch) to get noticeable banana character in the finished beer.

The bananas need to be very ripe but not overripe. It's best when the skins have black streaks but are not completely black.

My rule of thumb is that you remove about half the weight of the base malt per pound of bananas used to achieve a similar OG. So if you use 10 pounds of bananas, take 5 pounds of grain out of the recipe if you want to keep the same or similar OG.

As far as process goes, start by peeling the bananas, then liquefy them as much as possible. I follow a process similar to a traditional American double mash (a.k.a. cereal mash) procedure, where I use two kettles. One kettle is for the main mash and the other is for the bananas. Depending on how thin the liquefied banana slurry is, I might add a little water to that kettle. Then I add 2 pounds of base malt to the slurry and hold at 156°F for thirty minutes. I'll then mash out at 175°F for two to three minutes.

Meanwhile, the other kettle containing the remainder of the grain is going through a standard mash procedure depending on the style of beer being made. This mash then goes into the lauter tun, and the banana mash is layered on top of this to allow for a good grain filter bed to be established and minimize the incidence of a stuck mash due to the gums/polysaccharides in the bananas.

BANANARAMA BLONDE ALE

Banana beer? It sounds really strange until you realize that there's a centuries-old tradition in Africa for brewing banana beer (also known as "Mpahe" and a few other names). In this case, Joe has created a blonde-esque beer to feature the bananas and included an ingredient that we usually leave to the winemakers: tannin. It helps bring an additional level of mouthfeel and structure to the gussied-up banana wine.

FOR 5 GALLONS AT 1.052 OG, 3 SRM, 18 IBUs, 5.5% ABV

GRAIN BILL

5.0 lb.	Canadian 2-row malt
10.0 lb.	slightly overripe bananas (unpeeled weight)
0.5 lb.	German pale wheat malt

MASH

Rest (including bananas)	156°F	90 minutes
Mash out	170°F	10 minutes

HOPS

0.33 oz.	Centennial 9.0% AA	60 minutes
0.25 oz.	Centennial 9.0% AA	10 minutes
0.25 oz.	Willamette 5.2% AA	10 minutes

YEAST

WY1056 American Ale

ADDITION

1 tsp. gypsum/5 gallons filtered water

½ tsp. Brewtan B (tannic acid), last 16 minutes of boil

1 tsp. Irish moss, last 15 minutes of boil

½ tsp. yeast nutrient (rehydrated), last 10 minutes of boil

NOTES

Read "Joe Goes Bananas" on pages 61 to 62.

Boil 75 minutes

Primary: 6 days at 65°F

Secondary: 7 days at 65°F

VARIANT:

For a Blackened Banana Blonde Ale, add 0.5 lb. each of Weyermann Carafa III and Caravienne.

Joe's Recipe

HANNAH BANANA IMPERIAL STOUT

If you're a homebrewer, what's the sense of not going all in on a lunatic idea? In this case, it's Joe taking banana beer and combining it with everyone's favorite ceiling-staining brew—Russian imperial stout—for a crazy banana split of a beer.

FOR 5 GALLONS AT 1.108 OG, 65 SRM, 106 IBUs, 12% ABV, 75-MINUTE BOIL

GRAIN BILL

10.00 lb.	Simpsons Maris Otter malt
10.00 lb.	slightly overripe bananas (unpeeled weight)
1.25 lb.	English roasted barley
1.25 lb.	Dingemans Chocolate malt
1.25 lb.	Dingemans Aromatic malt
1.00 lb.	German white wheat malt
0.50 lb.	German caramel wheat malt
0.50 lb.	German chocolate wheat malt
0.50 lb.	Dingemans Biscuit malt
0.50 lb.	Dingemans Black Patent malt
0.25 lb.	Dingemans Caravienne malt
0.25 lb.	Dingemans Special B malt

MASH

KETTLE #1: BANANA MASH

1. Add 3.0 lb. Maris Otter malt and 10.0 lb. peeled and puréed bananas to 2 gallons 162°F water.

2. Rest at 156°F for 90 minutes

3. Mash out at 170°F for 10 minutes.

KETTLE #2: MALT MASH

1. Add remaining grain to 3 gallons of 130°F water.

2. Ramp to 155°F over 15 minutes. Hold 60 minutes until converted.

3. Mash out at 170°F for 10 minutes.

Layer contents of Kettle 1 over those of Kettle 2 in lauter tun. Sparge with 3 gallons of 175°F water.

YEAST

WY1450 Denny's Favorite 50 (2L starter)

ADDITION

2 tsp. $CaCO_3$ per 5 gallons of filtered tap water

½ tsp. Brewtan B (tannic acid), last 16 minutes of boil

1 tsp. Irish moss, last 15 minutes of boil

½ tsp. yeast nutrient (rehydrated), last 10 minutes of boil

NOTES

Read "Joe Goes Bananas" on pages 61 to 62.
Primary: 12 days at 65°F
Secondary: 30 days at 65°F

BREWER'S PROFILE

Amanda Burkemper

Amanda is a dedicated and talented homebrewer who brews classic beer styles and dabbles in sours. Yet the thing that truly makes Amanda a star is her passion when she's not behind the kettle. She's dedicated to helping other homebrewers grow their skills both online and off. She is active on discussion forums and has spent countless hours organizing and running competitions. Although she's been brewing for just five years, she's a BJCP Master Judge and on the board of the Kansas City Bier Meisters.

⭐

BREWING SINCE: 2010

BREWING MOTTO: If you're going to do it, do it right.

BREWING PHILOSOPHY: Brew with the best ingredients, to style (to an extent), and practice perfect procedures.

FAVORITE BREW STYLES: ESB, Munich dunkel, saison, funky sours

FAVORITE BREWING COUNTRY: America

BREWING METHODOLOGY: All-grain batch sparge

BREWING LOCATION: Garage

BREWING SYSTEM: Amanda's favorite piece of equipment is her Sabco Brew Magic system. As she puts it, "For me, consistency is the best thing about the Sabco. Not only are all of the vessels and hoses/lines in the same spot each time, but the way it regulates temperature is the same each time as is the way it recirculates, and so long as you take notes, everything is totally repeatable. 'Brew. Drink. Repeat,' as they say, and it is actually true. I love knowing that I can brew the exact same Munich dunkel tomorrow as I did last year, with almost no effort. Oh yeah, and the clean-in-place portion of it is pretty dang sweet!"

HOW SHE GOT STARTED: Amanda's dad was a home winemaker. One of his friends gave Amanda a copy of Charlie Papazian's *Complete Joy of Homebrewing*. She read it in two days and bought her first kettle the same week.

FANCIEST PIECE OF EQUIPMENT: 2009 Sabco Brew Magic system

BREWING INSPIRATION: Amanda is inspired by various brewing traditions. For example, she's currently "obsessed" with Firestone Walker Pivo pils, so she's planning on brewing 10 gallons of a German pils, splitting it post fermentation, and dry hopping one half with Saphir hops and the other with "a more American type" dry hop. She's considering the flavor of Pivo pils and looking back to its roots in a traditional German style—but not necessarily staying constrained by that classic style.

FAVORITE INGREDIENTS: For the beers she makes, Amanda has a distinct preference for continental malts over domestic malts. She uses very little American pale malt and prefers German and Belgian pilsner, Munich and Vienna malt, and English crystal malt. She cites the "intensity of flavor" in continental malts. Amanda says that "German Munich malt" blows American Munich malt flavor out of the water. I find that European styles made with American ingredients are fine, but I don't want to make beer that is just fine. I want to make excellent beer." Amanda's most prized ingredients are Best Malz Munich I and II, Dingemans Pilsen malt, and Amarillo hops.

FAVORITE YEASTS:

- WLP565 Belgian Saison I: "When it's treated right, it will drop a saison wort to 1.004 in eight days. Also, I do not like clove in saisons; I like them to be fruity and citrusy with a hint of pepper. I find that other saison strains throw too much clove for my liking, so I've always come back to WLP565.

- WY2308 Munich Lager: "It's between this and WY2206 Bavarian Lager for my favorite German lager strain. Both retain a lot of the malty side without leaving too much sweetness."

MOST UNUSUAL INGREDIENTS AND RECIPES: "My sours have to be my most unusual beers. I like to try out different strains of bacteria and *Brettanomyces*. I really like the combination of Wyeast's *Pediococcus* and Wyeast *Brettanomyces lambicus*—pitching that into the secondary of a darker-colored beer tends to produce a cherry pie aroma and flavor. It's awesome."

Becoming a BJCP-certified judge is a sure path to becoming a better brewer.

Amanda's Competition Tips

RUNNING COMPETITIONS

It all starts with judges, judges, judges! Recruiting judges is the most important thing on your to-do list. Make sure you have more than you think you need, and make sure they're happy or they won't come back next time you ask. Without judges, there are no competitions. Judges love short flights, good food, and a good organizer. Plan for more judging sessions than you think you'll need. You probably won't get as many judges as you need to do it all in one go, so this is a good way to cut down on flight size and increase the amount of points a judge can receive. Short flights equals less than ten per flight, ideally around eight. Here are some other important considerations:

- Register the competition with the BJCP so BJCP judges can get points: www.bjcp.org/apps/comp_reg/comp_reg.php

- Find competent stewards. A bad steward will cost the organizer time. Well organized and instructed people will save you hours on comp day. Understand that just one steward screwing up one set of paperwork or one judge writing a snarky comment on a sheet (or barely filling one out—we've all seen that) can have a negative effect on that competition.

- Get going with the competition software package Brew Competition Online Entry & Management. It's a huge time-saver.

- Swag can help with recruiting entrants/judges, but let's be honest: we all have too many shirts, glasses, hats, etc.

- You need refrigerator space for all of your entries. Keep this in mind.

- Plan to have all your entries delivered two weeks before judging. You'll be running around doing last-minute things, and sorting is not something you'll want to rush through.

- Develop a scoresheet sorting strategy before you start sorting and labeling.

- Provide judges with name tags for the score sheets.

- Have sufficient supplies (cups, score sheets, cover sheets, mechanical pencils, water cups, water pitchers, dump pitchers, staples, bottle openers, and so on).

- Have your stewards keep every entry packet (cover sheet and score sheets) in numerical order according to the table. Trust me, this will save you time when it comes to stuffing envelopes.

- Make sure the room or building you use is not smelly, dusty, gross, full of dogs, or whatever.

- Report the results the next day to the entrants via your competition website.

- Report the BJCP points to the BJCP within two days.

- Mail the score sheets back within five days.

ENTERING COMPETITIONS

My advice is to figure out the beers you want to brew, brew them, taste them as they age, and take tasting notes throughout the aging process. Review the tasting notes and then rebrew them for a competition. I know that the BGSA (Belgian golden strong ale) recipe that I provided for the book is a six-months-to-perfect recipe. I also know that a saison-Brett clone that I make is best at six to eight months from brew day. I like my IPAs around one to two months, but no longer. I do drink my German pilsner during lagering (so three weeks from brew day) but it drinks better at two months from brew day. If you're brewing for competition, you need to know this.

There can be other considerations as well, based on the style. For an IPA, are you avoiding oxygen pickup? Are you bottle conditioning or force-carbing in a keg?

For a classic American pilsner, are you able to get clear beer prior to lagering or did you use a really low flocculent east strain?

DREW: I'll chuck my two cents in here. People get obsessive about their beer age when, in my opinion, they should be obsessive about their beer storage. I've known several people, including Ninkasi winners, who've won the big prizes with standard gravity beers that were one or two years old. Their secret is a combination of near-perfect sanitation, oxidation minimization, and continuous cold storage.

I also don't recommend brewing beers stronger than the style calls for just because it's being judged against many other beers at once. This "strategy" is why I have to drink what is basically a porter in the Schwarzbier category on a regular basis! Sure, an inexperienced judge might reward bigger beers than the category allows, but more experienced judges will call your BS and will bounce the beer by mini-Best of Show. I judged IPAs at NHC this past year, and everything at the mini-BOS table was an excellent, middle-of-the-road (by the guidelines) IPA. The thing that made a beer stand out was the technical aspect of the beer—as in, how well-executed was this beer?

As far as crowded and uncrowded categories, in an open competition, the pale ales and IPAs are usually the most crowded. However, that does not mean that they have a ton of great beers in them. Every time I judge pale ales or IPAs, I wish I had entered the category. I don't think that many experienced brewers enter pale ales or IPAs much anymore because of the high entry counts—yet they really should because what is being sent in is everyone's first or second attempt at an IPA, which is not that enjoyable.

In the Belgian world, 16E Belgian specialty is usually the winner of Category 16, so keep that in mind. Lagers generally have the lowest entry counts, but that has been shifting in recent years.

DREW: When I first started dealing with competitions, the hot categories were APA, blonde, stout, and porter. It almost always seems to track to commercial trends. There are lots of saisons these days and, for a while, a ton of black IPAs. It's not just the categories themselves; oftentimes, the specialty categories are overrun with trends. Currently, the wood-aged category feels like it should be renamed to the "Bourbon Barrel-Aged Russian Imperial Stout" class. You'd have to be brewing a stellar BB-RIS to stand out from the bourbony miasma wafting across the table.

Taste your beers regularly as they age so you know when they're at their best.

Amanda's Recipes

EIN PROSIT
(BELGIAN GOLDEN STRONG ALE)

Amanda and Myles brewed this beer for the toast at their wedding. We had the pleasure of trying it at the 2015 National Homebrewers Conference. It was dry, just a bit tart, and totally delicious. As simple a recipe as the style calls for, there's nothing simple about the complex flavors in this beer.

FOR 5 GALLONS AT OG 1.070, 4 SRM, 25 IBUs, 8% ABV

GRAIN BILL
12.00 lb.   Dingemans Belgian Pilsner malt
1.25 lb.   table sugar

MASH
Rest   149°F   90 minutes
Mash out   168°F   10 minutes

HOPS
0.5 oz. Warrior   16% AA   60 minutes

YEAST
WLP570 Belgian Golden Ale

WATER
Target "Yellow Balanced" in Bru'n Water (see page 100) with mash pH of 5.4

NOTES
Pitch at 64°F. Hold for 2 days, then ramp up to 80°F over the course of 2 weeks.

Cold crash 1 week after terminal gravity is reached to help flocculate the yeast.

Drinks best after 2 months of age but is quite tasty when younger.

DUNKEL DOO BALLS
(MUNICH DUNKEL)
(pictured at right)

Another wedding beer, we don't know where the name came from, and we're not sure we want to! However, Amanda's dedication to style and real love of German beer make this a recipe a must-brew.

FOR 5 GALLONS AT OG 1.050, 17 SRM, 18 IBUs, 4.75% ABV

GRAIN BILL
11 lb.   Best Malz Munich II malt
2 oz.   Weyermann Carafa II malt

MASH
Rest   145°F   45 minutes
Saccharfication rest   160°F   30 minutes
Mash out   168°F   10 minutes

HOPS
0.3 oz. German Herkules   17% AA   60 minutes

YEAST
WY2308 Munich Lager

WATER
Target "Brown Malty" in Bru'n Water (see page 100) with mash pH of 5.3

NOTES
Pitch at 48°F.

Ferment at 50°F.

Kent Fletcher

Fletch, also known as the Brewgyver, is a monster brewer and a monster builder. He's been a speaker at multiple NHCs and once built a slot machine that pays out in beer. When he joined Drew's club in 2001, they allocated him a small amount of funds (about $300), and he built a brand-new 20-gallon system with electronic controls that he plumbed into the homebrew shop's natural gas lines. The kettles were made of one of Southern California's favorite scrap products—stainless steel pool filters. A little nip, a little tuck, a little welding, and they had a system ready and waiting for whatever a homebrewer will throw at them.

BREWING SINCE: 2001

BREWING MOTTO: Everything works . . . if you let it.

BREWING PHILOSOPHY: "Complexity of equipment is a matter of personal taste, but I advise new brewers to do anything possible to make the brew day easier, either with less labor or better control of the process. Making the brew day easier will lead to brewing more often, which will, in turn, lead to brewing better beer."

FAVORITE BREW STYLES: American wheat, American brown, American IPA, saison, tripel, doppelbock

FAVORITE BREWING COUNTRY: Belgium

BREWING METHODOLOGY: Fletch is an automated kind of guy, and it shows in his typical brew day. It all starts the day before with a filling of the HLT and setting of automated timers. At the appropriate hour, while he's still asleep, the system turns on and begins heating strike water. When Fletch wakes up, the water is set perfectly for the grain. He crushes the grain and mixes it into the mash tun with a custom-built malt augur. When brewing on the club system, rice hulls are always added to prevent a stuck lauter caused by the sheer mass of grain.

From there the HERMs takes over with pumps automatically powering on to move the wort through an HLT-mounted copper coil to maintain or boost the mash temperature as desired. The HLT automatically maintains temperature with an electronic pilot light to strike a natural gas burner whenever the temperature dips too far.

When it's time for mash out, the new temperature is dialed in, and the HERMs takes care of the rest. What's interesting is that even with all the automation, Fletch tends to stick to single-infusion, single-temperature mash regimes with a mash out.

Fletch uses traditional fly sparging and calculates appropriate sparge volumes to hit the boil kettle volumes exactly. He's also a big fan of starting the boil kettle fire the second the wort covers the kettle floor. Boil times and hop additions are adjusted based on pre-boil refractometer readings to help Fletch hit his numbers.

The brew is chilled with a massive copper immersion coil with the wort recirculating to speed the chilling process and reduce water usage. From there it's to the fermenters with doses of pure oxygen and plenty of yeast. The wort is then fermented in a temperature controlled fermentation chamber he built as a garage addition.

BREWING LOCATION: Backyard (and the Home Beer Wine Cheesemaking Shop where the club system is stored)

BREWING SYSTEM: A semi-automated 10-gallon keggle system at home and a 50-gallon single tier brew stand with HERMs coil and automatic pilots and pumps at the shop.

HOW HE GOT STARTED: Fletch didn't get started brewing until he hit his 40s, but like a good number of fermentation obsessives, he'd got his first inkling that this was something he wanted to do all the way back in high school. Maybe it was something about his Jesuit teachers that inspired the need to brew.

FANCIEST PIECE OF EQUIPMENT: More than anything else, Fletch loves the automated HLT temp control he built out of a thermoprobe, a simple temperature controller, and a scavenged electronic pilot light and gas solenoid from a water heater.

FAVORITE INGREDIENTS: On the hop side of the equation, he loves the combination of Amarillo and Columbus for any of his hoppy beers. With regards to grain, ready access to Weyermann Carafa III malt, the German dehusked, "debittered" chocolate malt, had a universal impact on his brew design so that he always uses it as a substitution when a recipe calls for Black Patent malt.

FAVORITE YEASTS:

- WLP565 Belgian Saison I and WY3724 Belgian Saison: He says they produce dry, incredibly drinkable, and interesting saisons out of simple ingredients.

- The Trappist yeasts such as WY3787 Trappist High Gravity: He loves their complexity and interesting fruity aromas.

- WLP001 California Ale and WY1056 American Ale: He relies on the clean, neutral all-American character they provide.

MOST UNUSUAL INGREDIENTS: He says as weird as he's ever gotten is probably using sorghum and spelt in a novelty 9-Grain Ale he made with a friend. He added, "Oh, and armadillo in my Remember the Alamo Red." (You may now have a better clue as to why he and Drew get along so well.)

DREW: Let me state this quite plainly: without Fletch, a lot of the things I've written about don't happen—the Brut beers, the Strut Stand, the Randall Bar, the Slot Machine, etc. So here's to the irascible ones, the men and women, like Fletch, who are happy grumps armed with wrenches and welders and big hearts full of daring-do. Without Fletch's real-world skills of making things happen, I'd just be a guy with a bunch of goofy ideas. May you be so lucky as to have a Brewgyver in your life!

Check out Drew's Unistrut stand in action.

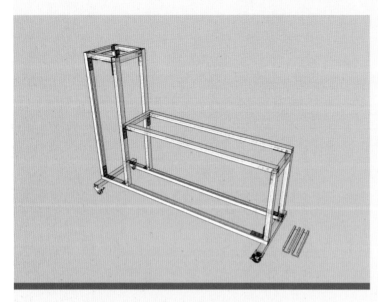

Fletch's rendering for the Unistrut brew stand.

The Scrapyard and Strut

Fletch is big on creative and adaptive reuse of materials that people don't normally know about or see. Remember that automated HLT system that he's proud of? All the parts were originally scavenged from water heater systems. Fletch is fortunate that he's a chief building engineer—a.k.a. the guy who keeps everything in the building operational. That means he has lots of opportunities to scavenge from items being scrapped.

And then there's the scrap yard. If you've never been to a scrap yard, you're probably still thinking something like the TV show *Sanford and Son*. Okay, if you're not as old as us, then maybe, just maybe, you're thinking *Junkyard Wars* (a.k.a. *Scrapheap Challenge* in the UK). Actually, we'd prefer for you to think of the latter, rather than the former. The TV show involved teams of engineers, mechanics, and designers let loose in a junkyard with two days to build a machine that would, say float on a lake and fight a house fire on shore. If that show were still running, you could have no better partner than someone like Fletch. On his

first iteration of the Maltose Falcons' brew stand, he and another equally handy club member found stainless steel pool filter housings at the scrap yard to use as kettles.

Sometimes, though, it's not just about scrap yards: it's also about understanding the materials available to you in the big box hardware stores that litter the American landscape. One of his favorites is called Unistrut, a cheap and supremely sturdy steel tubing system that is extremely easy to use. A 10-foot piece is less than $20 and works with a variety of connectors to assemble anything you need. In my case, Fletch helped me build a two-tier, three-vessel brew stand.

All you need are six pieces of Unistrut, some strut braces, spring nuts, two wrenches, and a chopsaw (or a hacksaw and a ton of patience/arm endurance). For about $300, you can put together a stand that if welded would be over $600.

The spring nut (or channel nut) is the other piece of magic to this whole thing. It's the secret sauce that turns your steel channel into a sturdy beast you could park a car on. It looks a little strange, like a steel mini-chocolate bar with teeth and a giant spring hanging off of it.

Counterintuitively, the nut doesn't affix in the way it goes in easiest (nut against the channel's front edge). Instead you install the nut by feeding the spring into the channel and compressing it until the bar pops into the channel. Give it a twist to lock into the channel. Slide the nut into place, feed a bolt through your bracket and into the nut, and tighten. That's it! If a spring pops out of the slots, just tuck it back in. Once the nut is tightened, the spring's job is done. The nut grips the bent lip of the strut channel and won't move.

To build a stand out of this stuff, all you need to do is figure out how much strut you need and measure everything out.

DREW: I was sitting one day at an AHA conference with Fletch and lamented that I didn't have a proper brew stand. Go look at my photos online—you'll see that I've always rigged things on the fly, this propped up on that, one burner, picking things up and moving them mid-brew, etc. He had just given a talk and demonstrated the flexibility of Unistrut during his lecture. He immediately offered to come build me a stand out of strut. A few weeks later, he arrived at my house armed with some socket wrenches and a chop saw. We went to the big box hardware store, bought about $220 worth of strut and fasteners, and in a few hours put the whole thing together from a drawing done on a napkin. Amazing!

I guess what I'm saying is, you don't need to know how to weld or sweat pipe to be a brewer, but you do have to have knowledge of all the wondrous toys you have available to you.

DENNY: Fletch is pretty much the diametric opposite of my "cheap 'n' easy" philosophy, but that doesn't mean I can't appreciate his skill and creativity. And in a way, his repurposing of so many materials fits in exactly with the way I think. It doesn't get much cheaper than recycling things that might otherwise have no value. And while I can look at a lot of stuff he builds and think "I don't need that," it doesn't mean that those same things aren't a real source of enjoyment and (hopefully) improved beer for him.

Fletch shows off the Unistrut brew stand's load-bearing ability.

Fletch's Recipes

WELL OIL BEEF HOOKED DOPPELBOCK

(A.K.A. PRECIOUS BARLEY FLUID)
(pictured at right)

A homebrewer's sense of humor never stops, and Fletch certainly isn't one to pass up a jokey name. If you don't get the joke, say the name with a bad Irish accent. Even if you still don't get the joke, enjoy the heck out of this very complex doppelbock.

FOR 5 GALLONS AT 1.086 OG, 20 SRM, 29 IBUs, 8.8% ABV

GRAIN BILL

13.75 lb.	German pilsner malt
0.66 lb.	German Munich malt
0.66 lb.	Canadian dark Munich malt
0.33 lb.	British crystal 80°L malt
0.33 lb.	British crystal 105°L malt
0.25 lb.	Weyermann Carafa III Special malt

DECOCTION 1

147°F 20 minutes. Boil for 15 minutes, return to mash at about 145°F for 30 minutes.

DECOCTION 2

168°F 15 minutes. Boil for 15 minutes, return to mash to mash out at 168°F.

HOPS

1 oz.	Magnum (pellets)	14% AA	60 minutes

YEAST

A good German Lager strain, such as WY2206 Bavarian Lager or WLP833 German Bock Lager

NOTES

From Fletch: "If you don't have the time—or are just too lazy—for a double decoction, add about 3 to 5 percent Melanoidin malt [0.5 to 0.75 lbs.] to the grain bill and use a simple infusion mash schedule. Even if you do this, you should still employ a mash out step."

ELKWOOD BROWN

This is one of Fletch's constant recipes, and he's won quite a few awards for it. It's also his test recipe for any new or revised brew system; he knows how well everything is working based on how this beer turns out. It's beautiful American brown ale with just enough hop kick to remind you that, hey, bitterness is a good thing! Despite the high IBU level, this is a real easy drinking beer that makes you go back to the tap.

FOR 5 GALLONS AT 1.062 OG, 23 SRM, 60 IBUs, 6.5% ABV

GRAIN BILL

8.750 lb.	Maris Otter pale malt
0.500 lb.	Simpsons Pale Chocolate malt
0.375 lb.	Baird's British Crystal 105°L malt
0.375 lb.	Baird's British Crystal 55°L malt
0.375 lb.	Scottish crystal 90°L malt
0.375 lb.	Dingemans Aromatic malt
0.190 lb.	Franco-Belges Kiln Coffee malt
0.190 lb.	roasted rye

MASH

Rest	153°F	60 minutes
Mash out	168°F	10 minutes

HOPS (PELLETS)

0.50 oz. Columbus	15.7% AA	60 minutes
0.25 oz. Columbus	15.7% AA	30 minutes
0.25 oz. Amarillo	8.4% AA	30 minutes
0.25 oz. Columbus	15.7% AA	15 minutes
0.25 oz. Amarillo	8.4% AA	15 minutes
0.25 oz. Amarillo	8.4% AA	5 minutes
0.25 oz. Cascade	5.0% AA	5 minutes

YEAST

WY1056 American Ale

CHAPTER 4

The Scientists
(and Process Nerds)

*S*cience has been perhaps *the* major force influencing Western development for the past few hundred years. Of course, science and beer have a long shared history. In the 1700s when the rest of the world was trying to figure out what all of these "natural philosophers" were on about, brewers were grabbing hold of developments like the hydrometer and thermometer to improve their beers (and profits). That relationship has continued on with later developments that lead to an understanding of fermentation, yeast, and more. As you can see, the scientist brewer has a long and proud history to tap into.

Still, it wasn't that long ago that being a nerd was a deeply uncool thing that would get you pantsed rather than praised. But times change. With the whole computer-driven world raging around us, now science rules and jocks drool! (At least that's what the nerd in us fervently hopes).

The Positives

The Scientists are the people to whom we turn when we want an answer that goes beyond "because tradition," or "dunno, but it works for me." For these brewers, the driver is knowledge. How does their mash tun react when given 20 pounds of grain and 25 quarts of 165°F water? How do the WY3724 Belgian Saison and WLP565 Belgian Saison I strains react to different fermentation profiles? The best of the Scientists also share their knowledge and welcome your questions. In the pages that follow, we'll visit with brewers like Marshall Schott and Nathan Smith who have made names for themselves by openly challenging us all to be more thoughtful and precise brewers.

We'd do well to remember that few homebrewers are going to have the necessary control over their processes to do perfect universally accepted science. But the strength of science has always laid in the endless repetition and reproduction of results. Our "citizen scientists" may not be perfect, but in numbers their results can be mighty.

DREW: Another thing I admire with this profile type is the dedication to "dialing in" their recipes. This is the home of the obsessive tweakers who endlessly rebrew just to nail the absolute perfect flavor profile. I have a number of "house recipes," but they usually drift. I abhor repetition, so this behavior is alien and beyond my scope of understanding, but I admire and approve of it. Brew on, you crazy diamonds.

DENNY: I hear what Drew and some others are saying: "There are too many beers to brew for me to brew the same one over and over," "I don't have many chances to brew so I want to brew something different," or my favorite, "It's *so boring* to brew the same beer again." OK, I get it. However, I've found that the best way to improve your brewing skills is to have a target and to repeatedly try to hit that target until you get a bull's-eye. It improves your understanding of the

★ SCIENTIST SUB-ARCHETYPES ★

- **The Death Ray Guru**: Walk into his space and you'll never know if you're looking at a brewery or a mad scientist's workshop. There will be electronics, spiffy thermometers, microscopes, stir plates, pressure cookers, pH meters, and maybe a spectrophotometer to measure IBU levels.
- **The Lab Rat (a.k.a. the Journaler)**: Never to be found without their brew log, a pencil, refractometer, hydrometer, and so on. Want to know what batch number 174 was and how it tasted? They can tell you! This is Denny's tendency to the extreme.

   DENNY: Batch number 174 was a North German pilsner, brewed January 23, 2004. OG was 1.054, with 40.7 IBU of noble hops. Single infusion mash at 148°F for 75 minutes. Nice and dry, but could have used a bit more sulfate to dry it out. Neener neener.

- **The Sharpshooter**: The Annie Oakleys of the brewing world, their whole process is angled to the improbable trick shot of always hitting their gravities, temperatures, and any other brewing number, no matter the grain lot or changes to their equipment. To them, missing the gravity is on par with a Shakespearean tragedy (or at least an opportunity to consider the whole effort an unfortunate failure in need of rescue).
- **The Speed Racer**: A firm believer in *more speed*. These brewers are obsessed with their lag time from pitch to full fermentation. Listening to them, you'd think they were talking about how fast they could hit the quarter mile in their custom hotrod. (Glad they're paying attention to yeast health, but we can't endorse the obsession with fast starts since much of your flavor and aroma is generated at the beginning of fermentation.)

Do you have a thirst for knowledge and a mind for numbers? You're probably in the Scientist archetype!

process, which is also really valuable for those one-off beers you won't brew again. You can keep moving on if that's what works for you. Me? I'll keep rebrewing until it's perfect.

The Negatives

Okay, we've established that science is good and wonderful as long as it's in the hands of brewers and not megalomaniacal despots. So what could possibly be negative about the Scientist archetype? To answer that, we have to remember that brewing is a craft—a form of practical magic that blends know-how with artistry. Go too far into one of those extremes and everything becomes off-kilter.

As an example, the need to explore ingredients pops up in every brewer's life. In the past, the answer was "make a simple beer and use it to explore the ingredients." Nowadays, anything less than a SMaSH (Single Malt and Single Hop) style approach of extreme simplicity is almost derided as overly complex and supposedly renders the taster incapable of determining an ingredient's impact.

DREW: I think SMaSH, and to a lesser extent, my Brewing on the Ones method of exploration, misses out on the critical factor that context plays for an ingredient. For instance, how do different ingredients play together? A SMaSH recipe may be very far from the recipe you'd actually use your tested ingredient in.

LIKELIHOOD OF BREWING A PREVIOUSLY BREWED RECIPE BY SCIENTISTS

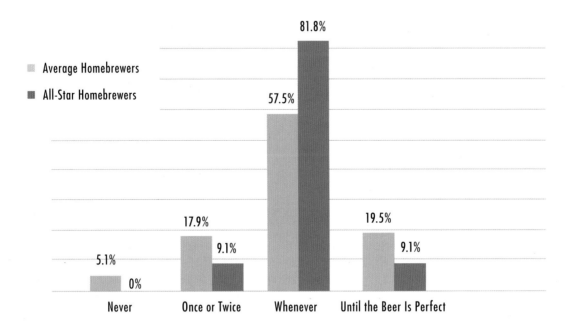

Legend:
- Average Homebrewers
- All-Star Homebrewers

Category	Average Homebrewers	All-Star Homebrewers
Never	5.1%	0%
Once or Twice	17.9%	9.1%
Whenever	57.5%	81.8%
Until the Beer Is Perfect	19.5%	9.1%

★ OUR SCIENTIST SIDES ★

DREW: Since this is Denny's chapter (see 84), here's my two cents. Of all of the sciencey subtypes we've defined on page 80, I can definitely say I've drifted through most of them over the course of my brewing career. Early on I was the Lab Rat and the Sharpshooter, fretting over every number and step along the way. My computer is still filled with notes from those first years of brewing. Now the notes only really come out in force when dealing with something new and different. I did enter the manhood measuring world of the Speed Racer for a while until I realized it was silly and pointless and a lousy indicator of beer quality. I will confess, I'm still something of a Death Ray Guru because I have three refractometers (one fancy digital one), two stir plates, a vacuum setup, microscope, etc. My spectrophotomer and gas chromatograph are currently on back order. Unfortunately, due to federal regulations, a death ray is still out of the question.

Okay, now here's the other thing we see go terribly pear-shaped with our sciencey types— the nerd bludgeon. This is the officious twit impulse in some Scientists that leads to arguments and derisive statements like, "You're doing it wrong because you're not following my process!" You have our permission to finish your beer and then smack this brewer upside the head with your now empty glass.

Scientists by the Numbers

When looking at the data for the Scientists, it's clear this is a group that cares about accuracy. The average homebrewers who fell into this type were some of the most accurate of all surveyed and heavy on repetition. However, the All-Star Scientists did deviate from this norm on repetition: they are more likely to repeat their recipes when the mood strikes rather than as a rule. The average homebrewer in this type said that he or she would repeat the brew until the beer was perfect almost 20 percent of the time, and another 17 percent would repeat a brew at least once or twice. For the All-Stars in this type, only 9 percent said they would repeat the brew until it was perfect and another 9 percent would repeat it once or twice. However, we think the differences can be accounted for in the staggering difference in years of experience: where our General Scientists have been brewing for 6.7 years on average, our All-Stars have been brewing for an average of 14.2 years. At this point in their brewing careers, the All-Stars have their recipes down cold and have become focused on the things they consider most important.

Choice Quotes from Scientists

We asked all of our survey respondents to provide us with some thoughts about homebrewing. Collected here are some of the best responses we received from the regular brewers. For the All-Stars, read on for their profiles. (Yes, we know some of the quotes throughout the book are contradictory, but that's what you get when it comes to homebrewers.)

- "Equipment changes will alter your brew day drastically compared to your ingredients."
- "Even when mistakes are made, chances are the beer will come out just fine."
- "It is super easy to make okay beer and much harder to make really good beer."
- "You can make great beer paying attention to only the things that matter. Pumps, fancy kettles, and powerful burners are great, but it's the little things that differentiate *great* beer from mediocre beer."
- "It's just like lab work, but you get beer out of it!"
- "The thing that surprises me most is to see how much the brewing process is reproducible and predictable once you start doing things seriously (i.e., when you control your parameters)."
- "Most people scoff when I say that I go grain to glass on average in two weeks. However, it's not that hard to do if you have your process down."
- "Racking to secondary doesn't do a damn thing."
- "In my process, I need to secondary. I find that it helps prevent stuck fermentation and help clear the beer faster. It probably compensates for yeast pitching and oxygenation issues."

Denny Conn

Denny has not only brewed about 500 batches of beer, but he's also a tireless resource for other brewers. He learned much of what he knows about brewing online, and he pays it forward in the forums. In real life, Denny has served for nine years on the governing committee of the American Homebrewers Association and he founded their AHA discussion forum. Denny is a BJCP national ranked beer judge and has judged many homebrew competitions, including four final rounds of the National Homebrew Competition. He's a frequent presenter at the National Homebrewers Conference, the inventor of the "Cheap 'n' Easy" batch sparge brewing system, consults for commercial breweries . . . and he's the only homebrewer with a yeast named after him (WY1450 Denny's Favorite 50—though he swears he begged them not to call it that).

BREWING SINCE: 1998

BREWING MOTTO: You never know 'til you try it.

BREWING PHILOSOPHY: Homebrewing is a chance to play with flavors and explore chemistry, and you get to drink the results!

FAVORITE BREW STYLES: American IPA, Belgian tripel, Belgian dark strong ale, Belgian golden strong ale, Altbier, German pils

FAVORITE BREWING COUNTRY: Belgium, closely followed by the United States and Germany

BREWING EQUIPMENT: "I use a 7-gallon aluminum kettle to heat water; either a 13-gallon or 15.5-gallon converted keg kettle for boiling (depending on batch size); a 48, 70, or 152 cooler mash tun (depending on batch size); a 50-foot, 3/8-inch immersion chiller; a March 809 HS pump with the 815 impeller upgrade; and buckets to ferment. For yeast starters, I use a stir plate and a 1-gallon glass jug." Denny sometimes uses a Picobrew Zymatic to brew, also.

BREWING METHODOLOGY: "I start the yeast in an appropriately sized starter—usually 2 to 3 quart for most of my beers—about five days before brewing. I let it ferment to completion—thirty-six to seventy-two hours— then refrigerate it to drop the yeast. My typical mash is about 1.65 quarts per pound, although it can be more or less depending on how much grain I'm using. Before I brew, I use Bru'nwater software (by Martin Brungard— see page 100) to calculate any water salt additions I may want to make. I close the cooler and let the mash rest sixty to ninety minutes.

"After the mash rest is complete, I vorlauf until the wort is free of pieces of grain (about 1 to 2 quarts), then run off the mash into a converted keg kettle. As I do that, I'm heating sparge water in my kettle to about 185 to 190 degrees Fahrenheit.

"Once the mash has run off, I take a specific gravity sample to check my conversion efficiency and then measure the volume from my first run off. Then I thoroughly stir the sparge water into the mash, vorlauf again, and run the sparge into the kettle. I once again measure the volume so I know how much I have in the kettle.

"I boil to OG, not time or volume, so about twenty minutes before the anticipated end of boil, I'll take another gravity reading to see if I'm on track to add my finishing hops. If so, I'll go ahead with the hop schedule. If the gravity is lower than where I think it should be at that point, I'll continue to boil before I add my finishing hops.

"With ten minutes left in the boil, I add $1/2$ teaspoon of Wyeast yeast nutrient per 5 gallons. At five minutes to end of boil, I add $1/2$ Whirlfloc tablet per 5 to 6 gallons. I chill the wort to a few degrees below my intended fermentation temperature, then pump it into a sanitized fermenting bucket that's marked in $1/2$-gallon volume increments so I know my finished volume.

"I pull my yeast from the fridge, decant the spent wort on top of the slurry, and immediately pitch it into the wort without waiting for the yeast to come to room temperature first. I ferment anywhere from one to three weeks with temperature control depending on what the beer needs. I almost never use a secondary. I usually dry hop in the serving keg and leave the dry hops in one to two months until the keg is empty."

BREWING LOCATION: About half of a 400-square-foot detached garage.

HOW HE GOT STARTED: "Living in the Pacific Northwest, I developed a love of good beer. I also developed a real 'do-it-yourself' attitude, and I've been cooking since I was twelve years old. Brewing seemed like the perfect combination of all of those interests, plus a chance to use the knowledge I developed as a chemistry major in college. My wife bought me a kit of equipment and ingredients as a birthday present. I still recall opening the first bottle of beer, hearing the 'pssshhhh' as I popped the cap, and tasting that pale ale. It was delicious, and a brewer was born!"

FANCIEST PIECE OF EQUIPMENT: Auber TD-100 (temperature controller for a chest freezer)

BREWING INSPIRATION: "Creating the flavor I have in my mind. Sometimes that comes from a great commercial beer, sometimes from a recipe I read, sometimes it's purely inspiration."

FAVORITE INGREDIENTS: "Rahr 2-row pale malt is my favorite of all the domestic pale malts I've tried. It has a rich, full malt flavor that I haven't found in other domestic base malts. And it has a lower pH than other malts, which helps me to get the correct mash pH.

"I've tried just about every brand of continental malt and finally settled on Best Malz as my preference. Like the Rahr malt, I find Best malts to have a much bigger malt flavor that really enhances my beers. In addition, they're highly modified which makes them easy to work with. I especially like their pils and Munich.

"My preferences in hops run to pretty standard American and German varieties: Columbus, Cascade, Centennial, Amarillo, and Simcoe are the varieties I use most often for the styles I brew. For my German and Belgian styles, I turn to Hallertauer and Tettnang most often, although I always use Spalt for altbier."

FAVORITE YEASTS: "Is this a trick question? WY1450 Denny's Favorite 50—what else? It's an all-purpose yeast for most American styles. It's a clean yeast, not quite as clean as WY1056 American Ale, but it leaves a full, smooth mouthfeel that I haven't found in other American strains.

"For Belgian styles, I like WY3787 Trappist High Gravity and WY1762 Belgian Abbey II. I like WY3787 because it ferments well at temperatures in the low 60s, so I can get phenolics from it without overwhelming fruit. WY1762 is Rochefort yeast, and I love it when I want a bit more fruitiness in my beers without going too far into fruit land.

"For lagers, I like WY2206 Bavarian Lager or WY2124 Bohemian. WY2206 leaves a lot of body and is great for styles like bock and Maibock. It also makes a great pilsner. It's very clean and easy to work with and seldom throws diacetyl. For a really crisp German pils, I turn to WY2124."

MOST UNUSUAL INGREDIENTS: "Chanterelle and matsutake mushrooms add flavors that I haven't been able to get any other way. Both add a subtle earthiness and mouthfeel. The chanterelles add in some apricot-like flavors that really complement a wee heavy. The earthy funk of matsutakes gets tamed just enough to make them a wonderful addition to a Belgian Golden strong ale."

MOST UNUSUAL RECIPES: "I don't brew a lot of really unusual recipes. Any unusual ingredients I use need to complement the beer flavor, not define it. With that in mind, my most unusual recipes are a wee heavy with chanterelle mushrooms and a Belgian Golden Strong ale with matsutake mushrooms."

All About Malts with Denny

"Over the course of nearly five hundred homebrew sessions, I've designed a lot of recipes. Some were good enough that other homebrewers and commercial breweries used them, to my great honor. Others were so bad that I've never mentioned them (that's a good way to make people think you're a great brewer!). But whether they were good or bad, they were all learning experiences. Some of the biggest lessons are about how to use grains . . . the combinations, the processes, and the effect they have on your beer's flavors, body, and mouthfeel."

ALTERNATE BASE MALTS

"One of the first things I learned is that you can use a lot more than pale or pilsner malt for a base malt. An American IPA made with an all-Munich malt base can be a great way to bump up the malt character to match the intense hopping many people do. Even splitting the base malt 50/50 between pale and Munich can make a big difference."

DREW: Personally, I prefer my blend of American Pale Malt and Maris Otter Malt, but I do live closer to San Diego than Denny does, so . . .

"Don't overlook Vienna or Special aromatic malts as a base for your beer. Despite the fact that they're kilned to a darker color than pale malt, they lend a dryness to your beer that can be desirable in an easy drinking beer for hot weather. You get not only a dry, drinkable beer, but it will also have a nice toasty character from the malt.

Sure, wheat malt is traditionally a base for hefeweizen, but why stop there? If you like the bready character with a bit of spice that it gives you, try a wheat IPA for a change. You may want to add a bit of crystal malt for body and flavor, or you can just go with all wheat. Here's a tip: many people who use all (or large amounts of) wheat in their beers report lower than normal extraction efficiency. That is usually due to a poor crush. Wheat has a smaller kernel than barley so your mill gap may be too wide to get a good crush with wheat. If you use a lot of it without crushing it well enough, your efficiency will suffer. You can reset your mill gap to be narrower, or you can just run the wheat through the mill twice. Depending on how your lautering system is designed, you may need to add rice or barley hulls to your mash to aid runoff in a mash with a lot of wheat. Know your system."

DREW: Another alternate malt that hangs out there with enough diastatic power to convert itself is oat malt. I've seen people do 100 percent oat malt beers before, but usually the reports back are less than stellar. However, I do have a fantastic tripel-like beer that basically uses 50 percent oat malt and 50 percent pilsner. It's rich without being cloying and is very interesting.

DENNY: Same thing with rye malt. It has enough diastatic power that theoretically you could use it at 100 percent as a base malt. But I doubt you'd like the thick, oily mouthfeel. However, 50 to 60 percent rye malt makes an interesting and distinctive beer.

CRYSTAL MALTS

When it comes to using crystal malts, there are a lot of "rules" out there: don't use more than 5 percent, don't use more than 10 percent, don't use them at all—just manipulate your mash temperature or boil down some wort to get the same effect. I hate rules! I believe in common sense. The key lies in knowing what the crystal malt brings to the beer and integrating it properly. Use it for the deep, rich flavors you can get from it. Boiling down wort or raising the mash temperature will not give you the same flavors. A light crystal malt in the 20 to 40°L range will bring a subtle sweetness to your beer. The most commonly used crystal malt like 60°L adds a deeper sweetness with malty notes and produces a beautiful red/amber hue in the beer. A dark crystal like 120°L or Special B adds an almost rum- or raisin-like character to the flavor. The key with all of these is to use them appropriately and balance them with the other ingredients. Use hops to

Don't be afraid to break the "rules" with crystal malts.

cut through some of the sweetness (if that's your goal) while still getting the flavor from the malt.

The other thing to keep in mind when using crystal malts is that they will increase, or "thicken," the body of your beer. Sometimes that's perfect. Otherwise, you have a couple of options. You can replace some of your base malt with sugar. That will reduce the body of the beer coming from the base malt to compensate for the added body coming from the crystal. Yeah, I know they seem at odds with each other, but that way you can get the flavor and complexity from the crystal without thickening the body of the beer. Try this for starters: for each pound of crystal you add to a beer over 1.065 OG, drop 1/2 pound of base malt and replace it with 2.5 ounces of plain old table sugar—nothing fancy needed. That's a starting point. Adjust as you feel it fits your goals.

The other thing you can do is mash at a lower temperature for a longer time. That helps produce a more fermentable wort, which can help to compensate for the body added from the crystal malts. If you use a lot (that's the subjective "lot") of crystal, try mashing at 148°F for ninety minutes. I can hear Mike Karnowski (page 148) screaming since he's not a fellow believer in mash temperature affecting body, but for me it works.

DREW: Anyone else thinking, "Two brewers enter, one brewer leaves?" Just me?

ROASTED MALTS

Dark malts, like chocolate, black patent, roasted barley, or even Carafa, can be problematic for a few reasons. Too much black patent, for instance, can make your beer taste like an ashtray. And all of them will reduce the pH of your mash, which can lead to astringency if not accounted for. My preference is to add them directly to the mash and account for that pH effect by using pickling lime (calcium hydroxide) to raise the pH. I use the Bru'n Water spreadsheet developed by Martin Brungard (page 100) to figure out how much to add.

The possible harshness from dark malt has led homebrewers to solutions like using Carafa, a dehusked dark malt, in the place of other dark malts in an effort to get a "smoother" flavor in dark beers. Sinamar is another option. I, too, went through this phase—seeking smoother and smoother. I took my basic house porter recipe (Nick Danger Porter; recipe follows) and started gradually increasing the amount of Carafa in it to replace the chocolate malt I had previously used. When I reached the point where all the dark malt was carafa, I realized I'd gone too far. The beer was now smooth almost to the point of being insipid and flavorless. I went the other direction—back to using chocolate malt. I added in crystal 60°L, Munich, and Special B to add some sweetness to balance the chocolate malt. And because I wanted a bit of bite to it, I added in some black patent. The result was a beer that hasn't changed since. To me, it's my "perfect porter."

Consider your choice of base malts as carefully as you consider your crystal and roasted malts.

Denny's Recipes

NICK DANGER PORTER

"Nick Danger is my assistant brewer—a little black cat named after the Firesign Theater character. He always shows up in the garage when I brew, so I decided he needed a beer named after him. This beer is almost as dark as he is, so it seemed like the right one."

FOR 5.5 GALLONS AT 1.061, 32 SRM,
49 IBUs, 6.3% ABV

GRAIN BILL

10.00 lb.	2-row pale malt
1.50 lb.	Munich malt
1.00 lb.	crystal 60°L malt
0.75 lb.	chocolate malt
0.50 lb.	Dinegmans Special B malt
2.00 oz.	black patent malt

MASH

Rest   154°F   60 minutes

WATER

Adjust water to the Bru'n Water (page 100) "Black Balanced" profile and keep the pH around 5.4.

HOPS

0.6 oz.	Tettnanger	5.2% AA	First wort hop
0.9 oz.	Magnum	12.0% AA	60 minutes
1.0 oz.	Cascade	6.0% AA	10 minutes

YEAST

WY1450 Denny's Favorite 50 or WY1056 American Ale

ADDITIONS

0.5 tablet	Whirlfloc, 5 minutes
0.5 tsp.	yeast nutrient, 5 minutes

NOTES

Ferment at 63°F until complete, about 10 to 14 days.

NOTI BROWN ALE

(pictured at left)

"This was the first beer I ever entered into a contest, about six months after I started brewing. It took first place and even won a ribbon for the label. That was all the encouragement I needed: a monster was created! Ferment at 63 to 65°F."

FOR 5.5 GALLONS AT 1.063 OG, 23 SRM,
48 IBUs, 6.5% ABV

GRAIN BILL

8.00 lb.	2-row pale malt
3.75 lb.	Munich 10°L malt
1.25 lb.	crystal 60°L malt
0.50 lb.	chocolate malt 350°L (Chateau, also called Castle, recommended)

MASH

Rest   153°F   60 minutes

HOPS

0.50 oz.	Magnum	13.70% AA	60 minutes
0.20 oz.	Columbus	17.50% AA	45 minutes
0.50 oz.	Willamette	5.10% AA	45 minutes
0.25 oz.	Willamette	5.10% AA	30 minutes
0.25 oz.	Willamette	5.10% AA	15 minutes
1.00 oz.	Chinook	12.00% AA	0 minutes

YEAST

WY1450 Denny's Favorite 50

OTHER INGREDIENTS

0.5 tablet Whirlfloc, 5 minutes

NOTES

Ferment at 63°F until complete, about 10 to 14 days.

Denny's Recipes

SANTA'S HELPER

(pictured at right)

"Another early medal winner for me was my interpretation of a German altbier that I called "Milo's Alt" after a beloved, departed cat. At that point in time, it was commonly thought that altbier should have a large percentage of Munich malt. I later discovered that wasn't how traditional altbier is made, but hey, I loved my version and it won awards. One year I decided to make a bigger version—which I call an uber-alt—as Christmas gifts for friends, and Santa's Helper was born. Big and malty, with enough bitterness to cut through, this beer will definitely help you survive the holiday madness. Ferment this beer at 58 to 60°F and cold-condition it at 35°F for at least a couple months. It will be worth the wait."

FOR 5.5 GALLONS AT 1.076 OG, 15 SRM, 57 IBUs, 8% ABV

GRAIN BILL
16.0 lb.	Munich 10°L malt
0.5 lb.	Weyermann Caramunich I 80°L malt
2.0 oz.	Weyermann Sinamar malt (added to the boil or 1 oz. Carafa III malt to the mash)

MASH
Rest	150°F	90 minutes

HOPS
1.1 oz.	Spalter Select	4.8% AA	First wort hop
3.3 oz.	Spalter Select	4.8% AA	60 minutes
1.0 oz.	Spalter Select	4.8% AA	0 minutes

YEAST
WY1007 German Ale

ADDITIONS
0.5 tablet Whirlfloc, 5 minutes

NOTES
Ferment at 55 to 58°F until complete, usually 10 to 14 days.

BATCH 400 QUADRUPLE

"For my 400th batch of homebrew, I knew I wanted to make something special for it, something that would age for years, assuming I could keep my hands off of it. About that time, I was sent some samples of dark candi syrup by Candi Syrup Inc. I'd tasted Belgian candi syrups before, but this stuff had the most flavor and complexity of any I'd tried. I knew it had to go into Batch 400. The beer turned out as well as I had imagined. It was brewed in May 2011, and as I write this in January 2015, I'm pleased to report that I still have four bottles left, and it continues to improve with age."

FOR 5.5 GALLONS AT 1.103 OG, 30 SRM, 26 IBUs, 12% ABV

GRAIN BILL
15.0 lb.	pilsner malt
2.0 lb.	Munich 10°L malt
0.5 lb.	Weyermann Caramunich I 80°L
1.0 lb.	turbinado sugar
2.0 lb.	D-180 candi syrup

MASH
Rest	147°F	90 minutes

HOPS
2.5 oz.	Hallertauer	3.9% AA	60 minutes
1.0 oz.	Strisselspalt	2.5% AA	0 minutes

YEAST
WY3787 Trappist High Gravity.

ADDITIONS
0.2 oz. coarsely cracked coriander seed, 5 minutes

0.5 tablet Whirlfloc, 5 minutes

NOTES
Pitch 3 quart starter off at 63°F. Begin fermentation at 63°F. After 5 to 7 days, increase temperature to 70°F and let ferment 2 more weeks.

BREWER'S PROFILE

Marshall Schott

Marshall is the man behind Brulosophy.com. He's made his name challenging conventional wisdom through rigorously controlled exbeeriments. To say the results have had an impact in the homebrew community is an understatement. In addition to debunking myths like "it's very important to avoid rust in your fermenter," he's promoted a better understanding of how to explore the world of brewing techniques.

BREWING SINCE: 2004

BREWING MOTTO: Question convention and don't fear change.

BREWING PHILOSOPHY: Simplify without sacrificing quality.

FAVORITE BREW STYLES: Pilsner, helles, schwarzbier, California common, APA

FAVORITE BREWING COUNTRY: Germany

BREWING METHODOLOGY: Single infusion/batch sparge

BREWING LOCATION: Garage

BREWING SYSTEM: Two 70-quart cooler mash tuns, two 15-gallon kettles, two 10-inch burners, JaDeD Brewing King Cobra immersion chiller, plastic carboy fermenters

HOW HE GOT STARTED: Marshall became interested in beer the month he turned 21 and began frequenting a local brewpub. After a colleague talked to him about making beer at home, he bought a kit, enjoyed the science-y feel of the process, and really enjoyed the fruits of his labor. His annoying obsession with efficiency and simplification, mixed with a healthy dose of optimistic cynicism, led him down a path of experimentation, mainly with process variables.

FANCIEST PIECE OF EQUIPMENT: That would be his JaDeD Brewing King Cobra immersion chiller. Marshall started out using a well-known brand of plate chiller, but was frustrated by having to set up a pump and tubing to use it and found it difficult to clean to his standards. He researched immersion chillers and came across the JaDeD chiller, which claimed to have even better chilling time than his plate chiller did. He found he could chill 5.5 gallons of wort from boiling to 65°F in less than four minutes. Between that and the easy set up and cleaning, he was sold.

BREWING INSPIRATION: Experimentation. Almost every batch he makes is an experiment in some way. One example: He made two 5-gallon batches of the same wort and beat the living hell out of one during all parts of the process prior to it being chilled, basically exposing it to as much air as possible, while the other was treated as gently as possible. He learned from this that hot-side aeration doesn't appear to be something homebrewers need to worry much about.

FAVORITE INGREDIENTS: Belgian pils malt from Dingemans or Malteries Franco-Belges gives Marshall a "rich bready/ cracker character" that he prefers to German pils malts.

Honey malt is an ingredient Marshall feels doesn't get the attention it deserves. He prefers it to most crystal malts and uses it for up to 12 percent of some grain bills. He finds it imparts a nutty-sweet character that's not cloying, and it contributes to body and head retention.

Centennial hops are Marshall's favorite of the classic American hops. He uses them for the "predictable clean citrus character" they add to styles from session pale to IPA. Tettnanger, on the other hand, has a "fairly distinct pungency" that he feels complements his lagers. He calls Saaz "recognizable and predictable."

Mosaic hops are Marshall's new hands-down favorite hop. He loves the blend of "juicy passion fruit with danky/resinous character." He says it's one of the few hops he finds that can be used alone in a beer and still produce a layered complexity.

FAVORITE YEASTS:

- Yeast Bay's Vermont Ale yeast: "Peachy, juicy, and unique" are the words Marshall uses to describe this yeast. He says it "does something magical when used in highly hopped beers."

- WLP090 San Diego Super yeast: Marshall grew bored with the "Chico" strain of yeast so often used in popular American ales and started looking around. He found the San Diego yeast produced a beer with good malt character while still allowing the hops to shine through. It ferments and drops clear quickly.

- WLP029 German Ale/Kölsch yeast: It ferments quickly and cleanly at 58°F. He's found that he actually prefers it to some lager strains.

- WLP830 German Lager yeast: It has a classic, crisp character and clears quickly. It's ideal for fast lager fermentation schedule

MOST UNUSUAL INGREDIENTS: Marshall doesn't stray too far from traditional ingredients. He says honey malt is about the most exotic ingredient he's used so far but has plans to branch out in the future.

The Dry Yeast Exbeeriment

When Marshall brews, the purpose is as much to learn something about brewing as it is to make beer. He tests conventional wisdom as he compares different ingredients, equipment, and techniques in his "exbeeriments." Then he publishes the results on his website. That means you can dig deeper or brew them yourself if you want to verify them.

Note: Depending on the particular experiment and his beer inventory, Marshall will brew either two 5-gallon batches, a single 10-gallon batch, a 10- and a 5-gallon batch, or up to two 10-gallon batches simultaneously. For 5-gallon batches, he almost exclusively brews no sparge, while larger batch sizes warrant batch sparging. Marshall always collects his brewing liquor and mills his grains the night prior to a brew day, then wakes up very early (4 a.m.) to get started. He staggers the start time of each batch by thirty minutes to keep things less hectic, plus it allows him to use the same chiller in each one. He prefers a 1-gallon pitcher and a little elbow grease to pumps, high-quality immersion chillers to counterflow/ plate chillers, and a 6-gallon plastic bucket to tiered gravity setups. Simplicity without sacrificing quality is the name of his game. He can usually hammer out a dual-batch, 10-gallon brew day in a hair under five hours, flame-on to all cleaned up.

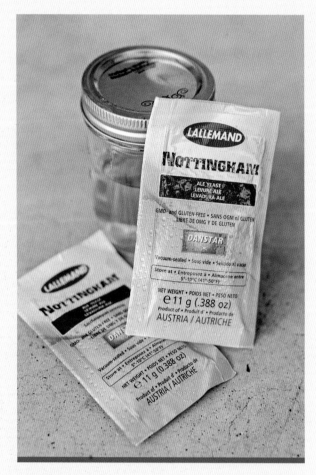

Does dry yeast need to be rehydrated? See what you think and try the "exbeeriment" for yourself.

DO YOU NEED TO REHYDRATE DRY YEAST?

Okay, let's take a look at one of Marshall's "exbeeriments" to see how he conceptualizes it, makes the beers, and evaluates them. This is an experiment that focuses on a question that seems to be ever-present in homebrewing discussions: do you really need to rehydrate dried yeast before pitching it in your beer?

Most dry yeast manufacturers recommend rehydrating the yeast in water before it goes into the wort. The idea is that this increases the chance of yeast surviving the shock of pitching and will result in pitching more healthy

yeast cells that are ready to go to work turning your wort into beer. But many homebrewers (Denny included) have noticed that they get great results by simply pouring dry yeast into the fermenter without rehydrating it first. Their thinking is that while you may end up pitching fewer healthy cells, there is enough yeast in a dry yeast packet that losing part of it won't really affect your beer in a negative way.

To put an end to the debate, Marshall brewed an 11-gallon batch of wort and split it between two fermenters. After both fermenters were cooled to pitching temperature, Marshall rehydrated one pack of Danstar Nottingham ale yeast per directions in 93°F water for fifteen minutes, then cooled it to within 10°F of the wort temperature before pitching it. The other fermenter got a pack of Nottingham, added dry. (Denny's note: Although Marshall doesn't mention it in his blog, in an experiment where you're using dry yeast, it's really important to make sure that the date codes on the packs are the same. Often, there will even be a time code in addition to the date code. You might be able to pick up packs of yeast dated only minutes apart.)

Both fermenters went into a temperature-controlled fermentation chamber and fermented for a week, then cold-crashed for four days. Both batches reached the same final gravity (FG) of 1.013. There was no significant difference in appearance. The beers were carbonated and allowed to condition for two weeks before tasting.

THE TRIANGLE TASTE TEST

Marshall decided to use a blind triangle test to evaluate the beers. He found thirteen tasters to participate. The procedure went like this:

STEP 1: A piece of paper with a three shapes (triangle, square, star) on it was placed on a table.

STEP 2: A clear plastic cup was placed on each shape.

STEP 3: Prior to the participant entering the room, the dry-pitch beer was added to two cups (square, star) and the rehydrated beer was added to one cup (triangle).

STEP 4: Participants were then asked to enter the room and complete a brief online survey that asked them to consider which of the beers was different, then choose one of four options: triangle, square, star, or no detectable difference.

STEP 5: Once the participant submitted his response, he informed Marshall (privately) what he chose. Those who were incorrect were dismissed, and those who were correct were asked to complete a more detailed survey comparing the differences between only the two different beers while still blind to nature of the "exbeeriment." At this point, the rehydrated beer was relabeled "Sample A" and the dry-pitch beer became "Sample B."

The results? Only five of the thirteen testers were able to identify the different beer, so only 40 percent got it right. Upon further questioning of those five people, the majority of them noted no real difference between the beers. When queried about general characteristics of the beers, the comments were pretty evenly split. For example, two tasters thought that the dry-pitched beer was more malty, while two others thought that the rehydrated pitch had more malt flavor and aroma. In the triangle testing world, this pretty much comes down to the fact that if there is a difference, it's so slight as to be inconsequential.

And that's the purpose of experiments like this. We're not trying to come up with big, universal truths: we're just trying to make better beer at home. This is an easy experiment for you to recreate at home. You don't necessarily have to brew two 5-gallon batches. Brew a batch of whatever size your equipment makes easy and split it into two different fermenters—carboys, buckets, gallon glass jugs, whatever you have around. Then apply an objective tasting method like the triangle test and make your own decision.

Oh, and as for Marshall? He admits that while the results surprised him, he still rehydrates dry yeast because he feels that he can tell a slight difference.

Blind triangle testing is a good way to remove potential bias in a tasting.

A LIL' SLACK IPA

"This IPA blends pungent new world hops with popular American varieties to create a balanced profile with notes of citrus, tropical fruit, and a subtle dankness."

FOR 5 GALLONS AT 1.062 OG, 7 SRM, 60 IBUs, 6.6% ABV

GRAIN BILL
10.13 lb. 2-row pale malt
1.75 lb. Munich 10°L malt
0.75 lb. honey malt

MASH
Rest   154°F   60 minutes

HOPS
0.4 oz. Simcoe   13% AA   60 minutes
0.5 oz. Simcoe   13% AA   30 minutes
0.5 oz. Mosaic   13% AA   20 minutes
1.0 oz. Mosaic   13% AA   Whirlpool (15 to 20 minutes)
0.5 oz. Simcoe   13% AA   Whirlpool (15 to 20 minutes)
2.0 oz. Mosaic   13% AA   Dry hop #1 (5 days)
0.5 oz. Columbus/Tomahawk/Zeus
                   14% AA   Dry hop #1 (5 days)
1.0 oz. Nelson Sauvin
                   12% AA   Dry hop #2 (3 days)
0.5 oz. Simcoe   13% AA   Dry hop #2 (3 days)

YEAST
WLP090 San Diego Super

NOTES
Pitch at 66°F and ferment for 3 to 4 days before raising to 72°F.

Add the first dry hops in primary after the first 4 to 5 days of fermentation.

Add the second dry hops 2 days later.

Cold-crash to clear haze when fermentation is complete.

MAY THE SCHWARZBIER WITH YOU
(pictured at right)

"A traditional German dark lager fermented with a clean kölsch yeast strain, this beer is not only easy to make, but it's delicious and insanely drinkable."

FOR 5 GALLONS AT 1.052 OG, 26 SRM, 27 IBUs, 5.2% ABV, 90-MINUTE BOIL

GRAIN BILL
7.33 lb. German pilsner malt
2.00 lb. Munich 10°L malt
0.50 lb. Weyermann Carafa II malt
0.50 lb. crystal 60°L malt
0.25 lb. chocolate malt

MASH
Rest   152°F   60 minutes

HOPS
0.33 oz. Magnum   14% AA   60 minutes
1.00 oz. Saaz   4% AA   15 minutes

YEAST
WLP029 German Ale/Kölsch

NOTES
Pitch and ferment at 58°F for 4 to 5 days, ramp to 65°F over 3 days.

When fermentation is complete, cold-crash for 2 days to clear the beer.

BREWER'S PROFILE

Martin Brungard

Beer is at least 90 percent water, and Martin is the water man. He is a professional engineer dealing with water and wastewater issues for municipal and industrial clients. He also runs a consulting practice advising brewing industry clients on water and wastewater issues. Of course, he does plenty for homebrewers as well. He is the author of the Bru'n Water spreadsheet for adjusting brewing water, he was a technical editor for the *Water* book from Brewer's Publications, and he is a frequent contributor to the AHA discussion forum. In addition, Martin's articles on water for brewing around the world have brought a wealth of water knowledge to homebrewers and helped them brew better beer by teaching them about what matters with water.

BREWING SINCE: 2000

BREWING MOTTO: Learn, create, enjoy.

BREWING PHILOSOPHY: You have to be in the ballpark if you want to hit a home run.

FAVORITE BREW STYLES: American pale ale, American brown ale, mild, porter

FAVORITE BREWING COUNTRY: England

BREWING METHODOLOGY AND SYSTEM: Martin has an almost all homemade, all electric RIMS brewery in a dedicated basement space. It's run by a control panel that he built. He brews 5-gallon all-grain batches and fly sparges. He starts with RO water and adds minerals as needed for each particular brew. He's precise with his mash temperature steps and always does a mash out since it's easy to perform that step with his system. He uses a plate chiller and an inline oxygenation system to prepare the wort for the fermenter. He uses both liquid and dry yeast, but uses dry more often. The wort ferments in a thermostatically controlled fermentation chamber. The only time Martin bottles his beer is when he enters it into a competition. Otherwise, he kegs.

HOW HE GOT STARTED: Martin and his wife attended a small homebrew tasting event that introduced him to the fact that he could brew his own beer. His wife bought him a homebrewing kit for a Christmas present, and that's all it took.

FANCIEST PIECE OF EQUIPMENT: He's one of only a few All-Stars who finds the sport of collecting and creating gear as much fun as the brewing (or at least he's one of the few who is honest about it). His favorite piece is his homemade electric brewing control panel.

FAVORITE INGREDIENTS: Martin likes Rahr 2-row because it's a "good clean malt" that is more acidic than typical malt. He says that is more likely to provide better results to most brewers "since we more often need more acid in our mashes to bring mash pH into the proper range. That advantage is mostly to those brewers who don't treat their water—they should though!"

Another favorite is Simpson crystal malts. He says they have a "richer and broader caramel flavor than American crystal malts. I think the broadness in flavor comes from the variability in the kilning and that is probably the reason that Simpson reports its crystal malts with a range of color, due to its kilning variability."

Martin also likes Simpsons' pale chocolate malt. He says it has a nice light chocolate and coffee flavor that's perfect in smaller beers like a mild.

When it comes to hops, Martin likes the classics. He says that Cascade hops have citrus notes that are the "epitome of what American ales are. It is a flavor I want in my American ales: pale, amber, brown, and stout." Centennial hops also get the thumbs up from Martin. He says it's "a great hop that has a broader flavor and aroma than Cascade, more floral. Great as a dry hop."

He enjoys trying out older hop varieties such as Brewers Gold as well, an English hop that was very common in the past but is seldom seen now. He enjoys it for the black currant flavors it brings to his English-style beers. If you want to try a classic American hop that provides a very black currant/blackberry flavor, the classic go-to would be Cluster.

FAVORITE YEASTS: Again, Martin goes for the classics. He likes WY1056 American Ale, saying it's a good, clean yeast. He also uses WY1028 London Ale. It's one of the key components of his American brown ale (even though it's a British yeast). He uses it because of "minerally flavor" it provides.

Martin also uses dry yeast, specifically Fermentis Safale US-05. He says it is like WY1056 but easier to use since it's dry. "I've had great success with this yeast in a broad range of beers where yeast character is not needed or desired—that is, clean," he says. "It's produced great APA and IPA for me, but it has also produced great malty, lager-like performance in Munich helles at 52°F and clean Scottish beers at 60°F. It's even finished out a Berliner weisse that had been soured to a pH of 3.1 before the yeast fermented it. This is a trooper of a yeast and one that should be in every brewer's refrigerator to serve as backup whenever their primary yeast doesn't work out."

Martin on the Importance of pH in Brewing

After you get comfortable with brewing and have proper fermentation temperature control, managing your water should be the next step. (Unless your water is too unsuited for brewing, which can be the case even if the water still tastes good. In that case, a brewer may have to learn how to manage their brewing water as their first step.) In any case, you can't create great beer if your water is in the way.

When addressing your wort, pH is always the main and central focus. Mash and kettle wort pH affect so many things throughout the brewing process: body, fermentability, astringency, hop utilization, bitterness, flavor, crispness and dullness, and so on. Get the wort pH in the correct range, and the rest of the beer's flavor and perception has a chance to fall in line. Get the pH wrong, and you will beat your head into the ground trying to get a beer right.

The primary interest to brewing is the pH of wort during mashing. Yet the pH of the raw water you use to mash is not a major factor. It's actually the water alkalinity and mash grist composition that have a greater effect on mashing rather than the pH of the raw water. The resulting pH of the mash influences a number of factors in brewing including fermentability, color, clarity, and the taste of the wort and beer.

A slightly acidic mash pH of between 5.2 and 5.8 (measured at room temperature) improves the enzymatic processes during mashing. The lower end of that range produces more fermentable wort and thinner body. It also produces better extraction efficiency, lighter color, and better hot break formation, plus the resulting beer will be less prone to form haze. However, allowing the mash pH to fall below this lower boundary increases the potential to solubilize excess protein into the wort (De Clerck,

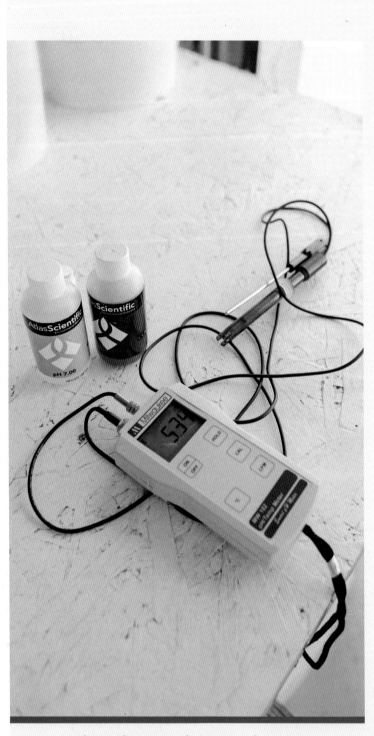

Always make sure you take your pH readings at room temperature, between 68°F to 77°F.

1957). The upper end of that range produces less fermentable wort and more body (Briggs et al., 1981). Tailoring the mash pH helps a brewer create the wort character desired for the finished beer. In most cases, narrowing the target mash pH range to between 5.3 and 5.5 is recommended. Reducing sparging water pH to between 5.5 and 6.0 can help avoid a rise in pH during sparging.

Minor increases in wort or beer pH above that threshold can create problems in the finished beer. It makes the perception of bitterness more coarse, which is generally less pleasing. (The isomerization of alpha acids during the boil increases slightly as wort pH increases, which may add to the coarseness.) Another problem is that increased pH in wort and the finished beer slows the reduction and removal of diacetyl from beer during maturation. During mashing, a pH greater than 6.0 can also leach harsh-tasting silicates, tannins, and polyphenols from the grain into the wort (Briggs et al., 1981).

Mash pH measurements vary with the temperature of the mash. There are two components to this pH measurement variation. The first component is a chemical change caused by the change in the energy in the water that makes it easier to split hydrogen protons from acidic molecules in the mash. A hotter mash is therefore a bit more acidic. The second component is due to the change in electrical response of the pH meter probe electrodes with temperature. These two factors produce a mash pH measurement when using a pH meter that measures about 0.2 to 0.3 units lower at 150°F than at room temperature. Therefore, it is important to standardize the temperature at which mash pH is measured. All pH readings mentioned here assume measurement at room temperature, between 68°F to 77°F (20°C to 25°C).

Note: Brewers should know that Automatic Temperature Compensating (ATC) pH meters only compensate for the response of the pH meter's electrode at varying temperature. That feature *does not compensate for the actual pH shift produced chemically in the mash* as mentioned. Thus, all mash pH measurement should be performed at room temperature. Another consideration is that most pH probes use a thin glass bulb that will be subjected to more thermal stress when inserted into a hot mash, and the probe is more likely to fail prematurely. Therefore, ATC-equipped pH meters are not necessary for brewing use since it is important to cool the sample to room temperature to avoid the chemical mash pH variation and damage to the pH probe.

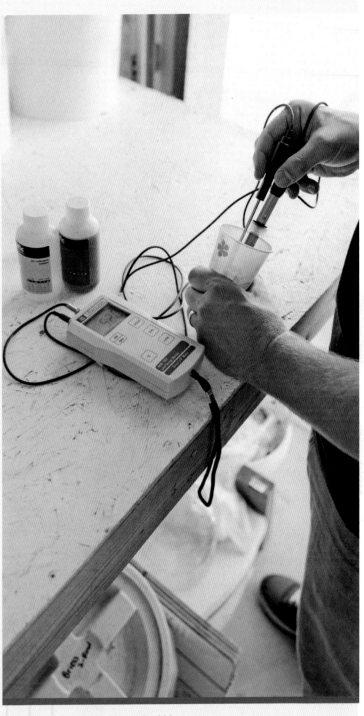

The pH of wort during mashing should be your primary concern.

Martin's Recipe

★

AMERICAN BROWN ALE

"This recipe was originally created by Matt Cole who was then at Rocky River Brewing in Rocky River, Ohio. I've tweaked it since then to meet my expectations and goals. My wife and I enjoyed many of Matt's beers at that place and his subsequent brewery, Fat Heads. This beer was developed by Matt to be similar to the original Pete's Wicked Ale. This beer displays the woody, citrusy hop flavor and aroma that is supported by a broad array of malt flavor. The minerally notes from the London ale yeast are a critical and desirable addition. Matt was adamant about that yeast character, and I agree. This is a well-bittered beer (36 IBU) and should not be targeted to be a malt bomb or the flavors won't work. The dry hopping with cascade and northern brewer is a perfect complement to the very modest chocolate notes in the beer. With just over 10 percent crystal malts, this recipe is at the upper range of crystal 'tolerance' for me, but it's not overly sweet. The flaked wheat produces a large head. This is about a 1.060 OG beer. This is a short-lived beer since it is best when the hop flavor and aroma are high. It has scored as high as 42 in the Florida State Fair and has been a favorite in my household for over a decade."

FOR 5.5 GALLONS AT OG 1.060, FG 1.015, SRM 36, 27 IBUs, 6% ABV

GRAIN BILL

7.00 lb.	2-row pale malt
0.75 lb.	flaked wheat
0.66 lb.	Vienna malt
0.50 lb.	biscuit malt
0.33 lb.	cara-pils dextrine malt
0.25 lb.	chocolate malt
0.25 lb.	crystal 60°L malt
0.25 lb.	crystal 75°L malt

MASH

Rest	152°F	60 minutes

NOTE

Shoot for a pH of about 5.4 to 5.5.

HOPS

0.5 oz. Northern Brewer	11.0% AA	70 minutes
1.0 oz. Hallertauer Mittelfruh	3.2% AA	15 minutes
1.0 oz. Cascade	5.3% AA	5 minutes
0.5 oz. Northern Brewer	7.4% AA	Dry hop
0.5 oz. Cascade	5.3% AA	Dry hop

YEAST

WY1028 London Ale

WATER

Gypsum ($CaSO_4$) to achieve 70 to 80 ppm sulfate

Calcium chloride ($CaCl_2$) to achieve 50 ppm chloride

Chris Colby

BREWING SINCE: 1990

BREWING MOTTO: Think for yourself.

BREWING PHILOSOPHY: Be clean. Pitch big.

FAVORITE BREW STYLES: Berliner weisse

FAVORITE BREWING COUNTRY: America

BREWING METHODOLOGY: Single-infusion fly sparge

BREWING LOCATION: Outdoors or kitchen

BREWING SYSTEM: Chris uses a MoreBeer 1550 tippy dump brewing system. It has three 15-gallon brewing vessels, and the mash tun tips to aid in cleaning it out. Chris says he got the version without electronics. "I didn't want any switches or sensors to do anything automatically and steal my brewing fun from me," he says. His brewing process is variable, but he typically uses an infusion mash and fly sparge. He's a believer in pitching with the optimal number of yeast cells (as estimated by starter volume), holding fermentation temperatures constant, and paying very close attention to cleaning and sanitation. And lest you think he's all about brewing big, he still brews partial mash in his kitchen as well.

HOW HE GOT STARTED: "I started in graduate school, because brewing."

FANCIEST PIECE OF EQUIPMENT: The MoreBeer tippy dump system, of course.

FAVORITE INGREDIENTS: "I really like Cascade hops, plus most of the other 'old school' American hops. There are a lot of new and interesting hop varieties out there, but I keep coming back to Cascade. I think it pairs well with Amarillo and Centennial, two of my other favorite hop varieties. In fact, I think it blends well with a wide range of hops, yet is still interesting enough to stand on its own in a beer.

"I also am a big fan of black patent malt in dark beers. I think it got a bad rap in the early homebrewing literature as lending 'burnt' or 'acrid' flavors to beers. It doesn't. Black malt is roasted, not burned, and there's a difference. Black malt adds color and foam to beer but also adds a fairly neutral roasted flavor in higher doses. I find this flavor works great to round out the flavor profile in beers with more flavorful dark grains in the mix."

> **DENNY:** I have gone back to using a bit of black patent as well, after giving it up for years. I kept trying to make my porter smoother and smoother and finally reached the point where it was insipid. Adding just an ounce or two of black patent added a "zing" to my porter without a major change in flavor.

FAVORITE YEASTS: Chris's favorite yeast is WY1056 American Ale. His reason? "It's a clean ale yeast, and I know it well. I've used both Wyeast's and White Lab's versions of this, which are very similar, as well as [Fermentis Safale] US-05, which I find slightly different, but still suitable for any clean ale.

"I also like WY1968 [London ESB], especially for my porter. The character this yeast lends to beer depends on the pitching rate and temperature, and you can brew a lot of different beer with this single strain. Plus, it flocculates like a rock, which can be nice."

Taking Notes and Repeating Brews with Chris

I'm a huge believer in learning everything you can about brewing, then brewing yourself and taking good notes. You can learn the general aspects of brewing from books but need experience to get the most from your equipment and local water. Taking good notes in a brewing notebook means you will never lose any of the lessons you learn and keep you on a track of improvement.

Also, for brewers who are serious, I strongly recommend picking one—or at most a few—beers and brewing them over and over until you perfect them. My porter is one such beer I've refined by repeatedly brewing it, taking notes, and tweaking it next time based on my previous results.

Even if you don't want to log everything on the computer, keep a pencil and paper around on brew day to record important details.

DREW: Chris walks the walk when he's talking about his notes. He'll make sure to take notes to compare the end results and figure out what affected the beer. While he believes that brewing is a hardy and resilient process that's tolerant of mistakes, he'll record things like "no hot break in the boil" so he'll have the note to check when it's beer-tasting time. As for repeating recipes, just check out pages 109 and 110—he's brewed both those beers with slight tweaks more than twenty-five times!

DENNY: Okay, so maybe this lesson isn't as exciting as starting a Solera (page 143), but there's a reason it's in the book: knowing your own brewery is the foundation of so much other knowledge. Sure, some of the beginning brewing books tell you to take notes. But what notes should you be taking?

Even if you don't want to record every little detail, we recommend writing down the following:

1. The recipe (obviously)

2. Yeast strain, starter size (if used), the date on the yeast package if you don't use a starter

3. Temperature of your strike water and the temperature your mash settles at. That will help you determine how much heat your mash tun and grain are taking away and help you hit your mash temperature more accurately in the future.

Note: Calibrate that thermometer! I'm gonna say that again—calibrate that thermometer! You can find instructions all over the Internet about how to use boiling water and ice water as standards for calibration. But if you want it to be the most accurate it can be, calibrate it at mash temperature (around 150°F) using a certified lab thermometer as a standard. Yeah, lab thermometers can be expensive, but I've seen brewing thermometers that were perfect at boiling and freezing temperatures but way off at mash temps. Unless you mash at 32°F or 212°F, calibrating at 150°F will always be more accurate.

4. Water volumes into the mash and sparge, and wort volumes out: that will help you get a handle on losses in your mash. That, in turn, can help you figure out why your efficiency may not be what you'd like.

5. The gravity of your mash and sparge runnings. The mash runoff gravity can be used to give you conversion efficiency figure based on the maximum concentration of sugar in the wort. That can help you find out if you are having problems with conversion. The gravity of the sparge runoff can help you find overall mash efficiency problems you may be having. For more information, check out this link: www.braukaiser.com/wiki/index.php?title=Troubleshooting_Brewhouse_Efficiency#Determining_Conversion_Efficiency.

COLBY HOUSE PORTER

"This is an all-grain porter I have brewed, in one form or the other, over 25 times. It is a robust porter with a hint of molasses. If you don't tell anyone about the molasses, they probably won't pick up on it. In some previous incarnations of the recipe, I also added brewer's licorice. The first time I brewed it, back in 1991, the recipe was a slight alteration of a bock recipe from Charlie Papazian's book. From there I've tweaked and retweaked it to my liking. [Author's note: If you want it to compete at a BJCP contest, boost the OG and IBUs to the top of the category limit, or maybe 10 percent over.] The dark grains and hops are nicely balanced for a delicious aroma, full-flavor, and a very drinkable beer. This and my pale ale are my go-to beers that I try to have on tap as often as possible. My local water is high in carbonates, and this is one of the few beer recipes I have that don't require 'cutting' my tap water with lots of distilled water."

FOR 5 GALLONS AT 1.048 OG, 58 SRM, 45 IBUs, 5% ABV, 90-MINUTE BOIL

GRAIN BILL

5.5 lb.	Maris Otter malt
1.0 lb.	Munich 10°L malt
1.0 lb.	crystal 40°L malt
7.0 oz.	chocolate malt
6.0 oz.	black patent malt
3.0 oz.	roasted barley

MASH

Rest	153°F	45 to 60 minutes
Mash out	168°F	10 minutes

HOPS

1.2 oz. Northern Brewer	9% AA	60 minutes
0.5 oz. Fuggles	5% AA	15 minutes

YEAST

WY1968 London ESB or WLP002 English Ale

WATER

100 ppm calcium (Ca+2)

20 ppm magnesium (Mg+2)

300 ppm carbonate (HCO_3-)

ADDITION

12 fl. oz.	molasses (boiled for 15 minutes)
1 tsp.	Irish moss (boiled for 15 minutes)
½ tsp.	yeast nutrients (boiled for 15 minutes)

NOTES

Stir the mash a couple times if you can do so and maintain temperature (via heating mash tun or adding hot water). Sparge steadily over 75 to 90 minutes to collect about 7 gallons of wort. Vigorously boil wort for 90 minutes to yield post-boil volume around 5.5 gallons. Add hops, Irish moss, molasses, and yeast nutrients at times indicated. Chill wort, then rack to fermenter. Your yield should be about 5.25 gallons. Aerate wort thoroughly and pitch sediment from yeast starter. Ferment at 68°F.

Chris's Recipe

★

PATRICK HENRY PALE ALE

"This is my basic American-style pale ale. I've brewed this recipe—slightly tweaking it every time—over 30 times, and it's a great go-to beer. I really like the combination of Centennial, Cascade, and Amarillo late hops, and I use this combo in most of my other pale ale-like beers, including my sweet potato ESB. The only non-standard part of this recipe is the tiny amount of chocolate malt added. This changes the hue of the beer slightly and can be omitted if you want."

FOR 5 GALLONS AT 1.052 OG, 1.011 FG, 11 SRM, 44 IBUs, 90-MINUTE BOIL

GRAIN BILL

9.500 lb. 2-row pale malt
0.500 lb. crystal 40°L malt
3.000 oz. crystal 60°L malt
0.125 oz. chocolate malt

MASH

Rest	152°F	45 minutes
Mash out	168°F	10 minutes

HOPS

0.375 oz.	Simcoe	13% AA	60 minutes
0.500 oz.	Centennial	10% AA	30 minutes
0.660 oz.	Cascade	7% AA	15 minutes
0.250 oz.	Amarillo	8% AA	15 minutes
0.660 oz.	Cascade	7% AA	0 minutes
0.250 oz.	Amarillo	8% AA	0 minutes
0.750 oz.	Cascade	7% AA	Dry hop
0.500 oz.	Amarillo	8% AA	Dry hop

YEAST

WY1056 American Ale, WLP001 California Ale, or Fermentis Safale US-05

1.5-qt. yeast starter for liquid yeasts

WATER

50 ppm carbonate (HCO_3-)

~125 ppm calcium (Ca+2); use 3:1 ratio of gypsum ($CaSO_4$) to calcium chloride ($CaCl_2$)

ADDITIONS

1 tsp. Irish moss (boiled for 15 minutes)

¼ tsp. yeast nutrients (boiled for 15 minutes)

NOTES

Make yeast starter 2 to 3 days ahead of time.

Heat 12.7 quarts of brewing liquor to 163°F and mash in grains. Mash at 152°F for 45 minutes, stirring every 15 minutes if you can do so without losing too much heat from your mash tun. Sparge steadily over 90 minutes to collect about 7 gallons of wort.

Vigorously boil wort for 90 minutes, to yield a post-boil volume around 5.5 gallons. Add hops, Irish moss, and yeast nutrients at times indicated. Chill wort, then rack to fermenter.

Your yield should be about 5.25 gallons. Aerate wort thoroughly and pitch sediment from yeast starter.

Ferment at 68°F. After fermentation stops, rack to secondary fermenter with dry hops.

Dry hop for 5 to 6 days.

John Palmer

John is best known for his book *How to Brew*, which is generally recognized as the book that every homebrewer needs to read. Seriously. It covers the gamut of homebrewing for beginners, but it also tackles advanced topics—and it contains some great recipes. Oh, then there's *Brewing Classic Styles* and *Water*, also penned by John. John now travels the world, talking about beer and advising brewers amateur and pro. Not bad for a man who started with a little website and a self-published manuscript.

BREWING SINCE: 1995

BREWING MOTTO: Brew unto others as you would have them brew unto you.

BREWING PHILOSOPHY: Brewing is cooking.

FAVORITE BREW STYLES: Vienna lager, IPA, sweet stout

FAVORITE BREWING COUNTRY: America

BREWING METHODOLOGY AND SYSTEM: John brews all-grain fly sparge beers using a multistep mash on a Blichmann Top Tier system. He mashes in at beta rest temperatures (146 to 150°F), then ramps up to an alpha rest (154 to 160°F), and finally mash out (165°F+). He uses first wort hops, multiple kettle additions, and often runs his wort through a hopback at the end of his brew. He chills the wort to around 75°F and puts it in his temperature-controlled refrigerator/fermentation chamber overnight to finish cooling to pitching temperature and pitches his yeast starter the next day.

BREWING LOCATION: John brews in a dedicated brew shed in the middle of the Angeles National Forest borderlands.

HOW HE GOT STARTED: It's pretty simple: John craved dark beer in a lite beer world.

FANCIEST PIECE OF EQUIPMENT: Blichmann Top Tier with an automated RIMS. (John also belongs to the "hey, gear is fun" crowd.)

FAVORITE INGREDIENTS: When you ask John about his favorite malts, the first one he mentions is Briess Dark Chocolate malt. He says, "I think dark chocolate malt has a sharper, more accented chocolate/cocoa note than regular chocolate or pale chocolate malt. Sometimes the chocolate notes in a beer can be dull or seem to oxidize quickly, and I perceive a better chocolate/cocoa flavor and aroma from this malt. It's more mocha-like." John also likes Briess Special Roast. He says that its unique toasty, dry cereal character adds complexity to brown ales and porters.

Next on John's list is Vienna malt because it "has a warmth and a rich malty flavor that other base malts lack. Also, Munich malt tends to bring too much of a bread crust or stewed flavor for my taste. I like using Vienna along with my base malt for pale styles and to give more warmth to my pale ales."

Pale ale malt gives John "a warmer, richer version of pilsner base malt with less dimethyl sulfide (DMS), a chemical with an aroma reminiscent of cooked canned corn—think Rolling Rock. It is not as rich as Vienna malt, and that can help produce a drier-tasting beer without the sulfury, grassy notes that can come from pilsner-type malts."

When it comes to hops, John's pick is good ol' Cascade. "Perhaps it's simply what I grew up on, but the signature aroma of Cascade makes American pale ale; if it's not a good American pale ale, then it better be recognizable as a British pale ale or it's simply bad homebrew in my book. It may not be realistic, but that's how my opinions run."

Also, not surprisingly for a "water" guy, a water adjustment lands as one of his most important ingredients: gypsum is something he can't imagine brewing without.

FAVORITE YEASTS: John has similar opinions about classic American and British yeasts. He notes, "I sometimes wonder if I have gotten too used to the clean character of American ale yeast; other brewers may say that I have a limited palate if I can't accept high levels of esters or phenols, but to me those flavors typically indicate lack of fermentation temperature control. A good British pale ale has more esters than American ale, but those esters should be balanced by richer malt character as well. I like British ale yeast for fermenting a dry yet richer tasting beer."

MOST UNUSUAL INGREDIENTS: "I am not very avant garde when it comes to beers. I once brewed a Christmas spice beer that I found to be unpalatable. The most unusual beer I have brewed was a sour cherry beer, using tart cherry juice concentrate and oak chips that had been soaked in the dregs of Russian River Brewing Company's sour beer. It turned out very nice, fermented first with Trappist Ale yeast and followed up with the chips for a secondary fermentation."

DREW: The tart cherry beer that John's talking about is the first beer I've ever tasted from him. Now, keep in mind, I've lived less than 10 miles from John for years, and we've gone out for lunch a bunch. It took almost six years before that first taste. It was awesome, and I'm just sitting here thinking either John is shy or very jealously guards his beer. Regardless, that cherry beer was pretty damn awesome.

Palmer's Top Five

The first and most important lesson from John is, "You should take Palmer with a grain of salt." Remember that a good portion of this book's purpose is to reinforce that idea. We should all remember that there's a ton of ways to do this whole thing. Even someone as lauded as Palmer isn't an expert on your system and needs. Still, to brew great beer the Palmer Way:

STEP 1: Clean and sanitize.

STEP 2: Control fermentation temperature.

STEP 3: Manage your yeast (starters, pitching rates).

STEP 4: Control your recipes (sense of proportions, not too many malts/flavors, don't go overboard on any one ingredient).

STEP 5: Understand how water chemistry affects beer flavor. The minerals in water affect the mash pH and malty-to-hoppy flavor balance. The mash pH affects conversion and wort properties, including lauterability and fermentation. The wort pH affects fermentation. Fermentation affects beer pH, and beer pH affects beer flavor. Water may only account for 10 percent of a beer's overall character and flavor, but it is the 10 percent that make the difference between a bad beer and a good beer, or a good beer and a great beer. Often, close enough may be good enough, but if you are looking for that missing piece, that icing on the cake, look at the water.

John on Fermentation Temperature Control

Fermentation temperature control is critical to achieve the proper balance of beer flavors across the alcohol, esters, and so on. If the temperature is too warm, the beer flavor may be too estery, too phenolic, or too solvent-like. If the temperature is too low, the beer character can have acetaldehyde (think green apple, cut pumpkin, or even cidery) or can have yeast stress notes such as phenols. Temperature control means the difference between the beer singing or complaining.

Some advise brewing Belgian styles during warm weather, supposedly because they perform better at warmer temperatures. I don't necessarily agree with that. My feeling is that you're almost always better off starting a fermentation at, or even a bit below, the minimum temperature recommended by the yeast manufacturer. Hold that temperature for seventy-two to ninety-six hours, then start letting the beer warm up. After the first few days, the chances of generating excessive esters and fusels is greatly lessened, so you can raise the temperature to ensure that fermentation is fully complete. This kind of strategy works for lagers as well as ales. (See the Mike McDole profile on page 186 for information about a fast lager fermentation schedule).

> **DENNY:** John has touched on a subject that Drew and I both believe in strongly. If you can't control the temperature of your fermentation, at least for the first few days, all the other work, time, and money you've put into your beer will be wasted. You can buy the freshest, best quality ingredients, you can do a triple decoction mash, but if you can't control the fermentation temperature, it will all be for nothing. Here are some ideas you can use to make sure you have a great fermentation:

- The "Cheap 'n' Easy" fermentation control system is nothing more than a big tub of water that you put the fermenter into. The extra mass of the water buffers thermal swings and helps maintain a reasonably steady fermentation temperature. You can add ice packs to the water to cool things down, or put in an aquarium heater to warm it up. I've even put the heater on a timer so it comes on only at the coldest times of day. To increase the cooling effectiveness, you can put a piece of wet cloth (a T-shirt is often used) over the fermenter and blow a fan onto it. The evaporation will help cool the fermenter.

- A refrigerator or freezer with a temperature controller is the most common way home-brewers control fermentation temperature. If you live in a warm climate, you might be able to use a single-stage temperature controller for cooling only. But most people will want to use a dual-stage controller, so you can both heat and cool. The fridge or freezer plugs into the "cold" side of the controller, and you plug some sort of heater into the "hot" outlet. For heating, I like to use a terrarium heater bulb. It emits heat but not light, so you don't have to worry about light-struck beer.

- If you're the DIY type, you can build a box out of rigid insulation or foam core. You put frozen containers of water in the box, then install a muffin fan to circulate cold air. You'll need to change out the frozen water once or twice a day.

- If you're a deep-pockets brewer, you can use a conical fermenter that uses either a glycol jacket or a Peltier cooling module—very easy and effective but not so cheap.

COWABUNGA IPA

In this recipe, the malt takes a back seat to the hops. The use of sugar dries out the beer so the hops can really come through. Some people say that you need a "big malt backbone" when you use a lot of hops in order to have a balanced beer. We say, "Always remember, balance is a subjective state of mind."

FOR 6.0 GALLONS AT 1.066 OG, 1.011 FG, 70 TO 110 IBUs, 7.25% ABV

GRAIN BILL

12.25 lb.	2-row pale malt
1.00 lb.	Caravienne malt
0.66 lb.	sucrose or dextrose

MASH

Rest	152°F	60 minutes

HOPS

1.00 oz.	Summit	16% AA	60 minutes
0.75 oz.	Simcoe	12% AA	30 minutes
1.50 oz.	Amarillo	8% AA	15 minutes
1.25 oz.	Cascade	6% AA	Whirlpool (30 minute stand)
1.25 oz.	Centennial	9% AA	Whirlpool (30 minute stand)
1.25 oz.	Cascade	6% AA	Dry hop (3 days)
1.25 oz.	Centennial	9% AA	Dry hop (3 days)
0.33 oz.	Amarillo	8% AA	Dry hop (3 days)
0.33 oz.	Simcoe	12% AA	Dry hop (3 days)
1.25 oz.	Cascade	6% AA	Dry hop #2 (3 days)
1.25 oz.	Centennial	9% AA	Dry hop #2 (3 days)
0.33 oz.	Amarillo	8% AA	Dry hop #2 (3 days)
0.33 oz.	Simcoe	12% AA	Dry hop #2 (3 days)

YEAST

WY1056 American Ale or WLP001 California Ale (2 vials in 3L starter)

WATER

Calcium: 100–150 ppm

Magnesium: 10–20 ppm

Total alkalinity: 40–80 ppm as $CaCO_3$

Sulfate: 200–500 ppm

Chloride: 50–100 ppm

Residual alkalinity of ~50–30 ppm as $CaCO_3$

John's Recipe

BLACK BEAUTY STOUT

Although there's quite a list of malts in this recipe, don't let that throw you. You need them to get the complexity this beer exhibits. The relatively low bitterness really lets all the malts come through to make a roasty black stout. Note John's use of residual alkalinity, one of the techniques that he has talked at length about in his books.

FOR 5.5 GALLONS AT 1.055 OG, 1.016 FG, 55 SRM, 36 IBUs, 5.15% ABV

GRAIN BILL

7.0 lb.	Briess 2-Row malt
1.0 lb.	roasted barley
1.0 lb.	Briess Carapils (Dextrine) malt
0.5 lb.	caramel 40°L malt
0.5 lb.	caramel 80°L malt
0.5 lb.	special roast malt
0.5 lb.	dark chocolate malt
0.5 lb.	black malt

MASH

Rest	152°F	60 minutes

HOPS

1.5 oz. Challenger	7% AA	60 minutes
0.5 oz. East Kent Goldings	5% AA	15 minutes

YEAST

WY1056 American Ale or WLP001 California Ale (2 vials in 1L starter)

WATER

Calcium: 50–100 ppm

Magnesium: 20–30 ppm

Total alkalinity: 120–200 ppm as $CaCO_3$

Sulfate: 50–100 ppm

Chloride: 100–150 ppm

Residual alkalinity: 150–200 ppm as $CaCO_3$

Janis Gross

Janis is the project coordinator for the American Homebrewers Association. What that innocuous-sounding title really means is that she runs the National Homebrew Competition, the world's largest homebrew competition. In that position, she has a chance to monitor trends in homebrewing, like the popularity of various styles, ingredients, and techniques.

BREWING SINCE: 1993

BREWING MOTTO: Go with the flow.

BREWING PHILOSOPHY: "My creation is what it is, regardless of what I thought I was brewing. Sometimes what you brew doesn't come out like you planned. When that happens, adjust to fit the reality."

FAVORITE BREW STYLES: ESB, American pale ale, fruit beer, porter, altbier, kölsch

FAVORITE BREWING COUNTRY: England

BREWING METHODOLOGY: Janis is an extract/specialty grain brewer who uses single-infusion mashing for her grain. "Being short on time, it's usually an extract and partial grain brew. I try to have all equipment cleaned and sterilized ahead of time. I also measure out the hops and adjuncts ahead of time. I use carbon-filtered water, and usually there are several other brewers setting up in the backyard as well. Naturally, I use my cell phone timer for all of the hop and adjunct additions. As all of the brews finish their boils, we move the same immersion chiller from pot to pot to cool down the wort. Typically, I do a full boil and don't need to top up the volume, but if needed I add filtered water. We transfer all brews to their carboys, take temp and OG measurements, and then pitch the yeast if the wort is cool enough. I add some adjuncts to the primary, but add most adjuncts to the secondary."

BREWING LOCATION: Outside

BREWING SYSTEM: Besides all the little bits and bobs that homebrewers use, Janis' main equipment consists of two Cajun Cooker propane-powered burners that she uses outdoors. She also utilizes both 4- and 7.5-gallon kettles. This lets her demonstrate her commitment to homebrewing by loaning out the spare equipment during Big Brew or Learn to Homebrew Day sessions.

HOW SHE GOT STARTED: "I first learned one could brew beer when I was fifteen, and I bought my first how-to brew book when I was seventeen, but it wasn't until I was out of college that I started brewing. The idea of brewing was magical, and I never lost the desire to brew, even though I waited so many years to start."

FANCIEST PIECE OF EQUIPMENT: Janis feels that the gear is secondary to the beer so her fanciest gear is a refractometer.

FAVORITE INGREDIENTS: "I'm continually amazed at the flavor and aroma adjuncts you can use and the variety of methods to accomplish the best results; coffee, rose petals, orange zest, spruce tips, red bell pepper, garlic, etc."

FAVORITE YEASTS: Janis says she seems to have settled on WLP002 English Ale and WLP005 British Ale, as well as WY1968 London ESB and WY1335 British Ale II as her favorite yeasts.

MOST UNUSUAL INGREDIENTS: "I have used spruce tips in a kölsch, which turned out great, and I use a combination of ginger root, cinnamon sticks, orange zest, and honey in Ednarae's Orange Ale (page 120). In mead, I have used plums, cherries, rose petals, orange zest, cranberries, blueberries, huckleberries, coffee, apple juice, raspberries, and boysenberries."

Janis on Extract Brewing

I can make excellent beer with extract and other ingredients that are widely available today. For the most part, it's a time consideration. Since I like to hike, bike, kayak, backpack, etc., it's important that I use my brewing time efficiently, and brewing partial grain extract batches works for me in this regard.

DREW: You want to know why extract has a bad reputation? In this day and age, it's super easy to find super-fresh extract, so it's really not the ingredients—it's the brewer. Don't believe me? Give this experiment a try. Some random weekend, break out the old pots and make a quick extract batch. Do everything right (full boil, chill, proper pitch of yeast, etc.) and let it ferment. I guarantee you'll be pleasantly surprised when you discover you can make excellent beer from a

much-maligned ingredient. You may not be able to bang out a perfect pilsner, but you can make a bunch of great beers in less time.

Typically, I don't use the late addition method of adding extract. For me, this technique is only needed for high OG brews with a concentrated boil so that you don't have to add more hops. I usually do not brew high-gravity beers, and also I don't tend to brew hop-heavy beers. When it comes to extract type, I like to use pale liquid extract and get the color from steeping specialty grains. I steep grains in a grain bag as I heat the water, then hold at about 150°F for twenty or thirty minutes. I then remove the bag and shut off the heat while I stir in the extract. The only exception to this is when I need Munich malt for German styles. I try not to use dry extract, because it is light, fluffy, and tends to make everything sticky; however, I do use dry extract when needed (and when making malted ice cream).

Once the extract is dissolved, I crank up the burner and continue as normal. When it comes to boil size, I can do either partial or full boil. Usually it is dictated by someone else using some of my equipment at the same time that I am brewing (usually happens during Big Brew at my house). If I am brewing by myself, it's easier and slightly less dangerous to use the smaller kettle and do a partial boil. The issue is with my somewhat petite size and reduced grip strength, it can be tough to pour the cooled wort into the funnel on top of the carboy. The smaller kettle with less liquid is easier to handle. Otherwise, when I do a full boil, I need someone to help with pouring the wort into the carboy. I don't notice any difference in the quality of the end product.

DREW: Janis isn't alone in being concerned about the weight of large volumes of liquid. We've seen this echoed several times in our research for this book and other efforts. Turns out, not everyone has the inclination to move 40-plus pounds of liquid around.

EDNARAE'S ORANGE ALE

Oranges and amber beers just seem to work so well together. Maybe it's the wintery spirit of the brew or just that combination of warm cinnamon heat and the brightness of the orange peel. Regardless, enjoy this beer in a nice hearty pint and let it envelop you.

FOR 5 GALLONS AT 1.047 OG, 9.5 SRM, 28 IBUs, 4.9% ABV

GRAIN BILL
6.5 lb.	pale malt extract (liquid)
4.0 oz.	English 40°L crystal malt
4.0 oz.	torrified wheat
1.0 oz.	chocolate malt
1.0 lb.	orange blossom honey at flame out

STEEP
Heat water to 150°F and steep the grains in it for 20 minutes. Filter and add the extract.

HOPS
1.0 oz.	Mt. Hood	5.1% AA	60 minutes
1.0 oz.	East Kent Goldings	5.7% AA	15 minutes
1.0 oz.	Cascade	5.8% AA	0 minutes

YEAST
WLP002 English Ale

ADDITIONS
¾ tsp. Irish moss (rehydrated), boiled for 15 minutes

1.5 oz. fresh, thinly sliced ginger root, boiled for 15 minutes

6 3-inch cinnamon sticks, boiled for 15 minutes

1.5 oz. fresh orange zest (about three Valencia oranges; use a vegetable peeler), added for one
week during primary

NOTES
Chill to 67 to 70°F and pitch yeast.

After 1 week, transfer to a secondary with the freshly peeled orange zest and age for another week.

Keg and carbonate to 2.5 volumes of CO_2.

Nathan Smith

Nathan has been homebrewing since 1998, winning more than his fair share of awards along the way. He's shared what he's learned with homebrewers around the world as a presenter at the National Homebrew Conference, the Australian National Homebrewers Conference, and the Bluebonnet Homebrew Contest. You also may know him as a frequent host on the Brewing Network podcasts.

BREWING SINCE: 1998

BREWING MOTTO: Have a good time, all the time.

BREWING PHILOSOPHY: Know your ingredients. Simplify your recipe.

FAVORITE BREW STYLES: American pale ales of all types, saison, kölsch, pilsner, helles, Scottish Light 60/-

FAVORITE BREWING COUNTRY: America

BREWING METHODOLOGY AND SYSTEM: Nathan brews 15-gallon batches, usually no sparge, in his garage, a rickety seventy-year-old structure he suspects will fall apart in the next earthquake. He uses a system that he describes as "a cobbled-together mess of little bits and pieces from here and there that would absolutely, positively never scale to any commercial level. Nor would it be efficient, time saving, or cost saving. Thank goodness I don't care about any of those things when I'm homebrewing." Nathan is a guy who cares more about the result than the equipment.

His brewing process is straightforward: "Clean everything the night before. Everything that's going to touch prefermented, chilled wort gets a Powdered Brewery Wash (PBW) soak. Everything else gets a once-over to double check for any filth, crust, or dust. Make a yeast starter at least twelve to eighteen hours before expected pitching time. The day of: Mill grain right before mash in. All brewing water gets a carbon block filter—yes, even the sanitizing water. Strike water gets measured, but mostly eyeballed—same for mash volume. Hitting the mash temperature and a mash volume within reason are a lot more important—same for pre-boil gravity. I'm real big on collecting pre-boil gravity and going from there. Pre-boil gravity accuracy is much more important than pre-boil volume. If you're way out of whack on volume, you can always adjust the hopping accordingly, since IBU calculations are mostly just estimations anyway. Start a good, vigorous boil. Hops go directly in the kettle, no bags or anything like that. Whirlpool, and chill with a plate chiller."

HOW HE GOT STARTED: Punk rock is largely responsible for putting Nathan on the road to homebrewing. He says, "There was definitely a DIY philosophy around playing music as a kid in Minneapolis in the late '80s. At the same time, the whole first wave of the microbrewing revolution was just starting to hit in force about the time that I could get into bars, so the two ideas were always inextricably linked in my head. Hellspawn, one of the bands from my high school days, had a song on their 7-inch EP about homebrewing. I still remember one of the lyrics: 'Do it yourself, save the tax, smash the 'ticians, here's an axe.' I think it left an impression!"

FANCIEST PIECE OF EQUIPMENT: MoreBeer temperature-controlled conical fermenter

FAVORITE INGREDIENTS: Nathan likes to use both Weyermann and Castle pils malt. He uses Weyermann when he wants an unmistakable malt foundation with a bready, melanoidin-rich, complex, toasty-but-not-too-toasty flavor. He also says that Durst pils malt is fantastic but harder to find.

He says that Castle pils malt is a bit less complex but very pale (more so than the Weyermann). He adds, "It's slightly more rough around the edges, the kernel sizes slightly less uniform, and a bit more stalk material and even an occasional tiny stone in the grist. It's absolutely packed with enzymes; converts extremely well; and esters, phenols, and all yeast character come forward with less malt presence."

Nate lists American hops as one of his favorite ingredients. "Simcoe/Amarillo is a classic, newer school, simple combination that is tough to beat. It's highly complex when done well. The lemon zest and huge citrus of a 100 percent Centennial IPA is absolutely wonderful, and good 'ol Cascade and Chinook are still a great combination. The very new school American hops that intentionally are built with a one-hop beer in mind are also equally interesting. They have huge oil content and complexity, and are just bred for IPAs: Mosaic, Equinox, Citra."

FAVORITE YEASTS: As you would expect from someone who brews as many styles as Nathan does, he has a wide range of favorite yeasts.

- WLP001 California Ale and WY1056 American Ale: This is the standard for clean, dry American ale fermentation, with just enough slight citrus and mixed fruit ester to accentuate American hops and low intensity malt, but not too much ester to distract from showcasing those two ingredients. On WLP001 versus WY1056: "On my system, with my process they are different yeasts. If I have good temp control for a batch, WLP001 is a better choice, but, if not, WY1056 might be a better choice. Regarding WLP001: If you stress it, there's a higher chance you'll get butter. However, for WY1056, there's a higher chance you'll get green apple paint thinner."

- WLP029 German Ale: "A special strain for clean and dry brewing—there is no equivalent. It's absolutely killer with noble hops and pils malt. However, risks include sulfur. It needs a long, cool fermentation. Give it that time to finish out."

- WY3711 French Saison: "This is a special strain for saison-type yeast character. There is no equivalent elsewhere. It's slightly less complex than 565/3724, but has more dependable attenuation performance (especially on the first pitch). It's absolutely glorious with noble hops and pils malt, or slightly more characterful hops."

- WLP530 Abbey Ale: "This is the most versatile Belgian strain and probably one of the most common ones you'll find in use within Belgian breweries. It has a very different flavor profile at the top and bottom end of its temperature range and pitch rate. It's also a great one to play around with and find a profile that you personally like. Its risk is that it does not like even small drops in temperature. Even a 2-degree temperature drop can cause it to drop out and go home early, refusing to finish out."

- WLP830 German Lager/WLP833 German Bock Lager: "I've always found them to perform more predictably in attenuation and flocculation versus other lager strains that I tried. It goes without saying that lager strains require special attention and care. Once you find one or two that seem to play along favorably in your environment, it seems like the path of least resistance to stick with those instead of wandering into new uncharted territory. The WLP833 is a bit more alcohol tolerant and slightly easier to work with than WLP830, in my opinion, but WLP830's profile can be even more awesome when all of the stars align."

SURPRISING INGREDIENT COMBINATIONS: In his continuing exploration of the surprising complexity that arises from simplicity he's found from combining straight pilsner malt wort and *Brettanomyces*: "Very interesting flavors can be created that way. Or, even that same wort fermented with lager yeast first, and then hit it with Brett after the lager yeast has done its job."

All About Hops with Nathan

Hops are undoubtedly one of the most exciting and unique ingredients for brewers. Hops are also an inexact, highly variable agricultural product. However, with a little knowledge and planning, the brewer can keep hops fun and interesting.

HOP SELECTION

With more than 100 hop varieties available and new varieties becoming available every year, it can be confusing to decide how to use what hop at which stage of the process. Statistics and metrics provided by the growers can help guide us. These, at a minimum, are typically provided: alpha acid, beta acid, oil percentage, and cohumulone.

When we hear these metrics referenced, they are often discussed in the context of:

- Ratios around alpha acid and beta acid percentage by weight

- Total levels of cohumulone

- Total essential oil percentage by weight.

Even when a full set of information is provided, each factor is, at best, a guideline and not a fixed rule. Hops have traditionally been assigned a binary bittering/aroma role for the brewer as a way of summarizing these statistics and sensory characteristics of a hop. Those rules and recommendations have started to break down as homebrewers find creative uses for hops outside of their traditional recommended roles. Many of the innovative American IPA recipes that started to emerge in the early 2000s are great examples of effective and creative use of hops outside of their intended purpose. For example, high alpha hops such as Columbus, Tomahawk, and Zeus originally thought of as bittering-only hops, have now found themselves to be very useful in the late kettle and dry hop.

BITTERING

When considering the bittering hops, use cohumulone as a guideline but not a rule. Cohumulone can be useful as a basic indicator of how rough, or coarse, the isomerized alpha acid bitterness perception will be—yet this perception is highly subjective. As a general rule, when dialing in the use of a new hop or developing a new recipe, avoid higher cohumulone hops in a beer that is intended to have a soft, gentle, or subtle bitterness. But don't be afraid to blend in a small or moderate amount of a higher cohumulone hop (such as Chinook, Columbus/Tomahawk/Zeus, or even Cluster) in a style such as double IPA or American barleywine where you may want to increase the perception of bitterness. When cohumulone is a consideration, don't forget that many of the moderate to higher alpha US signature varieties also have low cohumulone, such as Simcoe. So, in addition to Simcoe's status as a rock-star, highly characterful, signature hop, Simcoe's low cohumulone can make it a versatile bittering hop for many different styles.

FLAVOR AND AROMA

The traditional thinking around flavor and aroma characteristics in hops has been:

• Old-world hops from Germany, Belgium, and the UK as spicy, neutral, floral, and earthy with a gentle, clean bitterness.

• New-world hops from the United States with a citrus and pine character, with coarse, aggressive bitterness.

However, some of the newer hops and many that are just starting to become available blur the traditional lines between simple old-world and new-world regional distinctions. We can now find German landrace varieties cross-bred with American Cascade (Huell Melon and Mandarina Bavaria) and American hops consciously bred to enhance tropical fruit and berry character, bringing the sensory profile closer to New Zealand hops versus traditional American citrus and pine.

New hop breeding is also bringing new hop sensory characteristics to the forefront. Tropical fruit, berry, melon, licorice, cocoa, and coconut have not traditionally been discussed as common hop characteristics, yet showcasing these characteristics is now a focus of new hop breeding. Exotic descriptors aside, these wonderful and interesting characteristics are delivered via hop essential oil. Total essential oil percentage by weight of a specific hop sample is now a more commonly provided statistic, and that percentage can be invaluable when deciding how effective a hop might be at flame-out or dry hop. Two examples of hops that have the potential for very high oil content (over 3 percent) need no introduction as rock star-status late-kettle and dry-hop hops: Citra and Equinox. However, there are other varieties with a very high oil content, such as Polaris (which can be 5 percent total oil by weight!), which are less favorable for use in the same full-on hop-assault way that Citra and Equinox get used in the late-kettle and dry hop.

Note: Terroir and crop year of a hop can also be very important. This is especially true for high character varieties such as Centennial, Amarillo, Simcoe, Citra, and Mosaic. For example, US Hallertauer and US Tettnang are two hops that have very familiar names but are very different than their old-world counterparts. (The latter may be a completely different hop.) If you're looking for a US-grown Tettnang-like character, it's actually better to consider Santiam, a highly underrated

There is a world of flavor and aroma in these tiny hop pellets.

hop. Just as hops vary from region to region, the crop year can be equally as important. Hops are an innately variable agricultural product and can vary a lot year to year even when the hops are grown on the same farm or in the same region. The ADHA hop Summit, for example, had a ton of tangerine when it was introduced in 2008, but in subsequent years was more onion and garlic.

TRADITIONAL HOPPY RECIPE EXAMPLES

BEST WISHES SAISON AND PETITE BOURGEOISE SAISON

www.beersmithrecipes.com/viewrecipe/188663/best-wishes-saison
www.beersmithrecipes.com/viewrecipe/219842/petite-bourgeouisie-saison
Assertive bitterness and late hopping in Belgian styles, especially saison and tripel, can help enhance dryness. Belgian-style beers can and should be more hop-assertive than most American homebrewers realize.

MOSAIC MONSTER IPA

www.beersmithrecipes.com/viewrecipe/462542/mosaic-monster-ipa
Mosaic is a perfect example of a highly complex, very expressive, new variety. One of the more effective ways to use it is to showcase all that it can do, and then out of the way and let it take center stage. Since creating this recipe I have had at least two different wonderful

commercial examples of single-hop, single-malt beers featuring Golden Promise or Maris Otter with Mosaic as the only hop.

CITRUS BOMB IPA

www.beersmithrecipes.com/viewrecipe/291686/citrus-bomb-ipa
Citrus Bomb IPA is an example of layering assertive American hop aroma and flavor. Amarillo, Simcoe, and Citra all have aspects of their flavor and aroma that overlap and interlock with each other. The goal is to show off the citrus, pine and tropical aspects of American hop character, but to create an impact that is greater than the sum of its parts.

DANKNESS IPA

www.beersmithrecipes.com/viewrecipe/462510/dankness-ipa
The use of Apollo in this beer is an example of a coarse, aggressive bittering hop that is so assertive that it can contribute to flavor and aroma in the finished beer. Summit, the other highly aggressive hops in this beer, can also be aggressively dank in its own right, and the whole goal of Dankness IPA is to be unapologetically in-your-face dank. So Apollo can fit right into that plan, even if the flavor of the bittering charge carries over into the finished beer.

LOOSE CHANGE SCOTTISH ALE

"As fun as it is to go crazy on hop selection and usage by translating American IPA brewing techniques to other styles, sometimes a simple approach is best: one classic variety, one bittering addition only. This idea can be especially effective when you want to showcase non-hop aspects of the beer, malt, and yeast. When attempting to brew this beer with a traditional flavor and aroma kettle addition, it never turned out as well. One simple addition always worked better."

Denny: *This particular recipe won a Silver medal in the second round of the National Homebrew Competition, and that's as big of an endorsement as anything we could say.*

FOR 6.5 GALLONS AT 1.036, 21 SRM, 16 IBUs, 2.8% ABV

GRAIN BILL
10.00 lb.	British pale malt (Maris Otter/ Golden Promise)
0.75 lb.	crystal 55°L malt
0.50 lb.	crystal 120°L malt
0.50 lb.	Munich 10°L malt
0.33 lb.	chocolate malt

MASH
Rest	154°F	45 minutes
Mash out	168°F	15 minutes

HOPS
0.88 oz. East Kent Goldings
  5% AA 60 minutes

YEAST
WLP001 California Ale

WATER
2.25 grams $CaCl_2$

ADDITIONS
1 tablet	Whirlfloc	30-minute boil
1.0 gram	*Servomyces*	10-minute boil

Nathan's Recipe

BELMA KÖLSCH

"This is an example of how to break some traditional rules about selecting old-world versus new-world hop varieties while still respecting the original style boundaries. It is also a reminder that some new hops, such as Belma, work best in a subtle capacity. Just because new hops have the potential to present tropical, berry, and melon complexity, it does not mean that they can do that in an American IPA context."

FOR 6.0 GALLONS AT 1.051 OG, 4.6 SRM, 24 IBUs, 5.4% ABV

GRAIN BILL
12.0 lb.   German pilsner malt
0.5 lb.   Vienna malt

MASH
Rest   148°F   75 minutes
Mash out 168°F   10 minutes

HOPS
0.5 oz. Simcoe   13% AA   60 minutes
2.0 oz. Belma   13% AA   0 minutes

YEAST
WLP029 German Ale

WATER
2.25 grams $CaCl_2$ (mash)

ADDITIONS
0.5 tablet Whirlfloc for 30 minutes

1.0 grams *Servomyces* for 10 minutes

NOTES
Boil wort for 90 minutes to avoid DMS.

Gary Glass

Gary is the director of the American Homebrewers Association. In that capacity, he's been responsible for creating and implementing policies and actions that directly affect all homebrews. He's been instrumental in getting homebrewing legalized in all fifty US states, as well as overseeing changes to the AHA website to make homebrewing information more readily available to all of us. Yeah, he's a big deal!

BBREWING SINCE: 1992

BREWING MOTTO: Gary doesn't have a brewing motto, but he's got a theme song: "Thick Ass Stout" by Skankin' Pickle. Seriously, he says that his motto would probably be, "There's no such thing as the perfect beer. There's always room for improvement." We suspect there may be something more in the Colorado air than alpine breezes and snow!

FAVORITE BREW STYLES: Pilsner, maibock, saison, porter

FAVORITE BREWING COUNTRY: America

BREWING METHODOLOGY AND SYSTEM: Gary brews 10-gallon, all-grain batches, fly sparging on a two-tier system. He usually boils for 75 minutes.

BREWING LOCATION: Outside (we're not sure how that works during the long, snowy season, but when you're the director of the AHA, you probably find a way).

HOW HE GOT STARTED: "My sophomore year of college, a friend brought over a homebrew to my apartment—I think it was a strawberry wheat or something. I was already a big fan of craft beer—before anyone called it that—but the thought of making beer had never occurred to me. I think I bought my first homebrew equipment kit within a week of that first taste of homebrew."

FANCIEST PIECE OF EQUIPMENT: A stainless steel conical fermenter that was a gift from his wife, Erin (who happens to be the membership coordinator of the AHA's parent organization, the Brewer's Association)

BREWING INSPIRATION: Gary says, "I'm not talented enough to make flavorless beer, so an appreciation of flavor is pretty important for me as a homebrewer." (Cue Denny falling out of his chair laughing!) "When crafting a homebrew recipe, I create a mental flavor profile that I'm aiming for and choose ingredients accordingly. In my brews, I like to have layers of complexity of flavors, but try to avoid flavors becoming muddled. Thus, while I do tend to use a variety of malts and hops in my beers, I don't particularly like brewing 'kitchen sink' beers that throw together a huge variety of ingredients."

DENNY: This is exactly how I approach recipe design, and I recommend everybody try this approach to see how it works for them. Use whatever you think it will take to make the beer you've envisioned, but make sure every ingredient has its place and makes a definite contribution.

FAVORITE INGREDIENTS: Gary likes to use Centennial hops because they give him the distinct American citrus flavor and aroma along with a nice spiciness that he feels that you don't get from other American hop varieties. He feels like Hallertauer Mittelfruh also gives him some of those same qualities.

Victory malt is another of Gary's favorite ingredients. He says it gives him a roundness of flavor without being overly assertive. "To me, great beers are all about complexity of flavor. If you overdo more assertive malts, like crystal or roast malts, you can end up out of balance or with a train-wreck of flavor."

LEAST FAVORITE INGREDIENTS: Summit hops: He says he gets "nothing but onion" from them. Along with Denny, Gary is a charter member of the Fuggle Hops Haters club. Their motto is, "If I wanted my beer to taste like dirt, it would be far cheaper to just add dirt."

FAVORITE YEASTS: Gary says he doesn't have a favorite strain, but he does have one axe to grind: "I don't understand why so many people love WY1056 American Ale and WLP001 California Ale, which are not only boring but are really poor flocculators."

MOST UNUSUAL INGREDIENTS: Gary tends to be on the conservative side with his beers but more experimental when he makes mead. He's made a mead with a blend of roasted jalapeño, poblano, and Anaheim peppers. He says "After aging for three years, the heat, which at first was intense, totally dropped out and left the mead with a balance of smoky, roasted chile and sweet honey—it was absolutely fabulous. When blended with a prickly pear mead, it was out of this world." Gary has also used both blueberry juice and rhubarb juice (!) in a mead that he says came out really well.

WHERE CONVENTIONAL WISDOM IS ALL WRONG: "The current convention that says you don't need to secondary is a direct result of most brewers and judges having no clue what autolysis tastes or smells like. It is way too prevalent!" (More on this in a moment.)

Gary's Strong Opinions

Because of his intimate involvement in homebrewing, Gary has developed a lot of strong opinions about things he's done and seen homebrewers do. Here are some of his thoughts.

FLAVORED OPINIONS

Coffee in kölsch: It sounds terrible, but when done right, it is a thing of beauty. On the other hand, personally, I think Belgian IPAs rarely work. The hops and esters tend to clash and come out muddled, almost never better than an IPA or a saison on its own.

DREW: Never done it with a kölsch, but I can wholly endorse the notion of pale beer plus coffee. I first tasted this when we needed to fill out one last Randall on our Randall bar at the Seattle NHC. The only beer we had remaining was Kent Fletcher's Elkwood American Wheat and the only Randall filling we had left was whole coffee beans. We put them together in the spirit of "why the hell not" and were floored at just how well it worked together. On the subject of Belgian IPAs, I was totally in agreement with Gary until the rise of the newer, softer style hops that emphasize fruit, usually marketed as low cohumulone (Amarillo, Citra, Galaxy, etc.). These have worked unusually well for me with my saison-based Belgian IPAs. (I think I just felt Gary shudder.)

DENNY: Maybe the best thing about home-brewing is that since taste is subjective, everybody gets to decide for themselves what they like and want to brew. Like any beer, a poorly done Belgian IPA isn't gonna please anybody. But I have tasted many and brewed a few that I felt really worked and that I completely enjoyed. Gary says he dislikes the clash of hops and esters, and I can agree with that. But a Belgian IPA fermented with something like WY3522 Belgian Ardennes at temperatures in the low 60°F range to limit esters and enhance phenols really works great with American hops, for my tastes at least.

THE JOY OF SCREWING UP

Homebrewing is about experimentation, finding flavors that work well together regardless of tradition. Experiments don't always work out great, but they always teach the brewer a lesson that makes that person a better brewer. As an example, I was brewing a maibock, and after the boil, I was chilling the wort using my roommate's counterflow wort chiller for the first time.

After dialing in the post-chiller temperature, I proceeded to start cleaning up while the wort transferred to the fermenter. A few minutes later I looked up to see hot vapor coming out of the carboy into which I was racking the wort onto a yeast cake. Needless to say, I managed to cook the yeast that was in the fermenter.

I put the carboy into a water bath to cool it down, then after a day or two of zero activity, pitched a vial of Belgian yeast, which was the only yeast I had at the time, into the beer. A second carboy of the maibock made it onto the lager yeast just fine. Both the Belgian version and the maibock came out great, but I think I actually liked the Belgian better. You never know, a total screw-up could turn into a great beer.

ON CLUBS

When I first started homebrewing, it was very much an individual effort. When I joined the staff of the AHA, I suddenly found an amazing community of the best people you could ever hope to meet. Lesson: if you are a homebrewer, don't be a loner. Join a club, join the AHA, go to the National Homebrewers Conference be a part of the broader homebrewing community.

I frequently use one of the National Homebrew Competition gold medal-winning recipes posted in *Zymurgy* magazine and on HomebrewersAssociation.org or Brewing Classic Styles as a base recipe, then tweak it to suit my own personal tastes and brew system.

DREW: I'd make fun of Gary for being such a company guy, promoting organization resources, but in this case, they're good resources to use!

PARTING ADVICE

NEW BREWER: Sanitize everything, and I do mean everything, that touches your wort/beer post boil. But that's the obvious advice that every new brewer gets, and so here's something more unique: despite what many will tell you, don't start homebrewing by brewing all-grain. Take it easy, eliminate as many variables as possible your first time by brewing a simple extract kit. From there you can build your experience and knowledge to confidently try more complex brewing techniques.

EXPERIENCED BREWER: Become a judge. Judging and interacting with other judges has done more to expand my understanding of brewing than I could ever hope to get from books, podcasts, forums, etc.

Oh, and learn what autolysis tastes like before telling everyone and their mother that they're an idiot if they use a secondary fermenter. Too cynical? How about this: don't forget to have fun! That's why you got into homebrewing in the first place, right?

Sanitation may seem like a no-brainer, but hasty or improper sanitation is still a common source of problems for beginning brewers.

Gary's Recipes

★

DAS BOOT PILS

(pictured at right)

We don't know if this beer is named after the movie or the famous crystal drinking glass, but does it really matter? The malt body, the hop schedule, and the smooth German yeast all combine to produce a great version of a German pils. Have a liter or two! Just remember the all-important turn before you get to the toe.

FOR 5.25 GALLONS AT 1.044 OG, 5.4 SRM, 23.1 IBUs, 4.75% ABV, 90-MINUTE BOIL

GRAIN BILL

8.5 lb.	pilsner malt
0.5 lb.	Weyermann Carahell malt
6.0 oz.	melanoidin malt

MASH

Saccharification rest	149°F	30 minutes
Saccharification rest 2	156°F	30 minutes

HOPS

0.75 oz. Magnum	9.3% AA	First wort hop
0.25 oz. Magnum	9.3% AA	30 minutes
0.50 oz. Hallertauer Mittelfruh	4.5% AA	15 minute
0.50 oz. Hallertauer Mittelfruh	4.5% AA	5 minute
0.50 oz. Hallertauer Mittelfruh	4.5% AA	0 minute

YEAST

WY2206 Bavarian Lager

MIA WALLACE MAIBOCK

In the movie Pulp Fiction, Uma Thurman played femme fatale Mia Wallace. How Gary turned that into a beer is beyond us, but who cares when the beer tastes this good? A lot of maibocks are too sweet, but the 35 IBU in this recipe mean that you'll get enough bitterness to keep the malt from becoming cloying. The 2-hour boil means that you'll darken the wort just a bit to end up with the rich golden color that says, "Drink me!"

FOR 5.25 GALLONS AT 1.066 OG, 6.8 SRM, 35.8 IBUs, 7% ABV, 120-MINUTE BOIL

GRAIN BILL

8.50 lb.	German pilsner malt
4.50 lb.	Vienna malt
1.25 lb.	American crystal 15°L malt
1.25 lb.	Belgian caramel pils malt

MASH

Protein rest	127°F	30 minutes
Saccharification rest	148°F	30 minutes
Saccharification rest 2	156°F	30 minutes
Mash out	177°F	10 minutes

HOPS

0.65 oz.	Horizon	11% AA	First wort hop
0.75 oz.	Horizon	11% AA	30 minute
0.25 oz.	Horizon	11% AA	10 minute
0.125 oz.	Horizon	11% AA	0 minute

YEAST

WY2124 Bohemian Lager

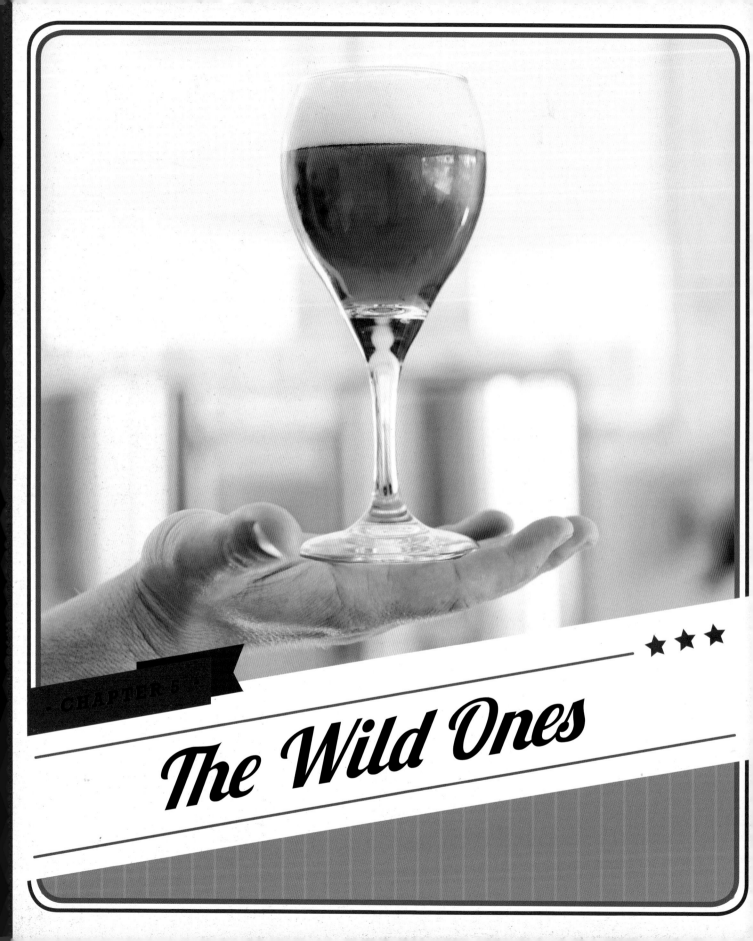

CHAPTER 5

The Wild Ones

*W*hile some brewers are content to watch the world ferment in a clean and orderly way, others watch their carefully constructed wort become the scene of a teenage house party with a mix of savory and unsavory characters. They invite into their fermenters creatures that frighten a normal brewer: *Brettanomyces*, *Lactobacillus*, *Pediococcus*, and more. All of this madness has a goal, of course: unique beers with funky, earthy, and tart sensations.

In our survey, the Wild Ones were the second-rarest category, which makes sense if you think about it. Those who dabble in alternative fermentations invariably start as regular beer brewers. However, the Wild Ones' online presence demonstrates how madly passionate their voices are in the pursuit of sour ales and other strange fermentations. And no doubt there are many brewers who dabble toward or aspire to be a Wild One someday.

If you're drawn to barrels, you might be a Wild One.

The Positives

Not that long ago, if you wanted to have a long pull on a beer mug, you had two choices: really, really young beer or old, sour, and funky beer. Laws even existed to prevent the brewing of beer during the hot summer months in order to prevent the manufacturer of beer that "spoiled" too quickly. Before the competing researches of Pasteur and Béchamp in the late 1850s, people just didn't understand the role of yeast as a microorganism or that there were other critters ("lactic yeasts" in Pasteur's terms) that soured the wort.

Luckily, the beer and wine industry seized on Pasteur's research and ran with it to discover how to eliminate the souring elements from their products. Our Wild One brewers, however, show that the daring pull those elements back into their beer production willingly. It's this sort of daring to bring hardy, potentially beer-destroying creatures into the brewery that really causes people to be surprised and in awe of these brewers.

But they're not going about it haphazardly. The truly dedicated Wild Ones show an amazing amount of patience. Remember that outside of new techniques like kettle souring, wild beer

★ WILD ONES SUB-ARCHETYPES ★

- **Au Naturel**: The best things in life are as free as the wind and are carried into your fermenter on the breeze. These brewers don't mess with expensive cultures, preferring to inoculate their wort via Mother Nature like the lambic producers in Belgium.
- **Barrel Chested**: This brewer may only be into sour, funky beers as an excuse to have a collection of barrels and wood products. Some people just need to live the dream of having their very own medieval cellar.
- **The Bug Hunter**: Some get excited about new grains or hops, but the bug hunter is all about finding and trying anything new with a crazy Latin name: the more obscure, the better!
- **The Dregs Hound**: This brewer buys a ton of sour beer and doesn't let the party stop when the beer runs out. Instead, they carefully decant the beer from the bottle and pitch the bug-laden dregs into their homebrew.
- **The Orchard Maven**: These brewers secretly like fruit beers, but needs to couch them as "sours" so they don't hate themselves in the morning. (But seriously, fruited sours are awesome, and we're just being silly.)

projects usually take months to produce results. Traditional styles like Lambic-inspired beers take years to come together.

Most homebrewers can, perhaps, dedicate themselves to a single long-term project or two, but when you encounter someone like our Wild One All-Stars, you realize that these crazy cats have many, many, many different batches all occurring at once. Even if you're not impressed by their daring or their patience, you're surely agog at the sheer logistical fortitude necessary to manage this much fermentation.

Lastly, with our Wild Ones, there needs to be something said about the skill set necessary to be an All-Star at wild fermentations. No other form of brewing requires so many different skills and touches of artistic flair. You need to start with a knowledge of microbiology to know all the various critters and their needs. Add in a scientist's mind to develop precise schedules

of pitching different cultures and controlling their fermentation environment. Then mix in the vintner's artistic touch of handling barrels and blending different batches together for the perfect final product. It's truly impressive.

The Negatives

With the exception of smoked beers, there's literally no category of beer in the world as polarizing as the sour and funky brews. No matter how serious and dedicated the wild brewer, there's sometimes a sneaking suspicion that they're trying to pass off bad beer on us. Part of that is because we hear *Lactobacillus* and *Brettanomyces* and think, "Hey, these are beer spoilage organisms!" Naturally, we then think the beer is spoiled as well. Not so.

DREW: I've conducted tastings before with otherwise-adventurous beer drinkers who've grumbled and damn near

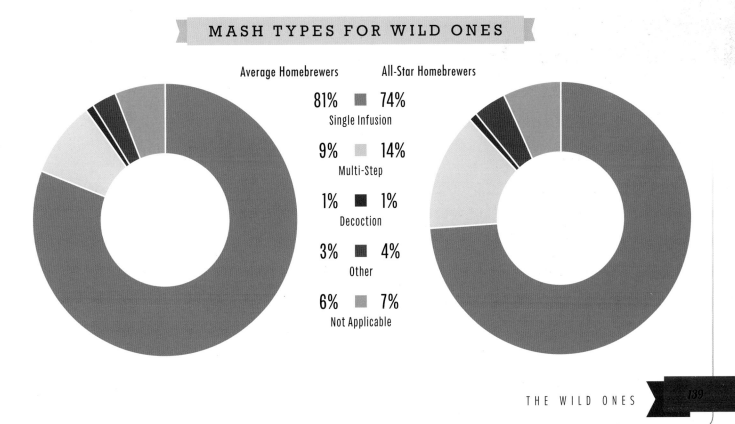

MASH TYPES FOR WILL ONES

Average Homebrewers		All-Star Homebrewers
81%	Single Infusion	74%
9%	Multi-Step	14%
1%	Decoction	1%
3%	Other	4%
6%	Not Applicable	7%

It takes a lot of practice and patience to create tasty sour beers.

walked out when they learned the subject matter would be sour beers.

In truth, we've known plenty of homebrewers who have actually passed off unintentionally infected beer with a casual lie of, "Oh, this is my wild beer." We're very much of the philosophy that you have to accept the beer that you created and not the one you intended to create, but please, for the love of Ninkasi, don't go passing off bad beer as purposely-soured beer. Own the mistake and use it as a teaching lesson for all involved. This also goes for intentionally soured beer that didn't turn out well—in fact, it goes double!

Lastly, there's a weird strain of snobbery that happens with some of the Wild crowd. It's a mix of their own type and the hard-core Old-School Master vibe that believes the old ways are the one true path. In some cases, like for the traditional Lambic producers of Belgium, it's a good thing to defend the elaborate process of a beer style that was rapidly disappearing. However, to get snarky over someone kettle-souring a beer instead of attempting a long, uncertain ferment seems a bit too precious for our taste. (However, in the commercial world, if you're a brewer doing a kettle sour and charging outrageous sums for it as a sour, then a pox on your bottles.)

★ OUR WILD-ONE SIDES ★

DREW: I love funky, odd beers, but I'll admit I often lack the patience to wait out the critters as they do their work. Still, some of the most interesting things I've done have been wild—like my Pasadena wild ale that I made by exposing growlers of wort to the air and letting them grow. Most samples were gross, but one produced something very interesting that I could pitch into a full batch. Good stuff!

DENNY: Like Drew, I admit to not having the patience to go through the sour beer process and wait until the bugs have done their work. I also find that while I enjoy tasting sour beers and investigating the flavors, it would likely take me years to go through a 5-gallon batch. So I'll let someone else brew them and enjoy the fruits of their labor.

Wild Ones by the Numbers

Looking through the data here's what we see: Wild Ones tend to prefer slightly more complicated mashing procedures and care less than average about the overall accuracy with their brewing process. It's the only group where it's clear they're in the game for improved knowledge and having fun with different critters. It's also not surprising that the Wild Ones are more prone to play with alternative fermentations, like kombucha. On matters of brewing gear and space, an interesting thing to note is that almost all of our Wild Ones ferment their wild ales in the same area as their regular beers (about 80 percent), but the average wild brewer is less likely to have separate "wild" equipment than the All-Stars (49 percent versus 60 percent).

Choice Quotes from Wild Ones

We asked all of our survey respondents to provide us with some thoughts about homebrewing. Collected below are some of the best responses we received from the regular brewers. For the All-Stars, read on for their profiles. (Yes, we know some of the quotes throughout the book are contradictory, but that's what you get when it comes to homebrewers.)

- "I don't typically use bittering hops, and I hop heavily near the end, even for sours that I age six months or longer."

- "Producing a bottle of decent sour beer will generally require blending of several batches to get the desired flavor profile. Throwing a vial of souring bugs into a single batch will get you something decent, but it won't really shine on its own."

- "Bottle dregs of sour beers can be way stronger than commercial cultures."

- "Brett can do some great clean-up on already well-done beers."

- "Open fermentation yields a more intense and complex ester profile than closed fermentation, even at lower temperatures."

- "I didn't discover it, but there is a conversion that happens from spicy clove phenolics of 4-vinylguaiacol (4VG) to the barnyard funk of 4-ethylguaiacol (4EG). Using a ferulic acid rest (109–113°F) in my saisons has helped me create the spicy phenols that in time age into unique barnyardy characters."

- "Wild and clean beers can be the same room/equipment. I can make a super-clean Oktoberfest with the exact same wild equipment I've used for years."

- "So you did a 100°F lacto ferment, exposed it to oxygen, and you're surprised it tastes like cheese or baby vomit? Come on now . . ."

Michael Tonsmeire

Most people became aware of Mike's brewing prowess through his amazing website, The Mad Fermentationist (www.themadfermentationist.com). It's a collection of beer recipes, tips, and thoughts on the brewing process that can keep beer geeks like us occupied for hours. The website eventually led to a book, *American Sour Beers*, based on lessons learned, science researched, and interviews with dozens of brewers. But that's not enough for Mike! Beginning in early 2012, he became a consultant for Modern Times Beer in San Diego, California. Working with founder Jacob McKean, Mike helped develop the four core recipes for Modern Times, along with many one-off recipes. He brewed pilot batches, grew microbe cultures, and even did odd jobs like painting. He's now consulting for half a dozen other breweries.

BREWING SINCE: 2005

BREWING MOTTO: I brew the beer I want to drink.

BREWING PHILOSOPHY: The results in the glass are the most important thing.

FAVORITE BREW STYLES: Berliner weisse

FAVORITE BREWING COUNTRY: America

BREWING METHODOLOGY: Single infusion (minimal sparge). Michael has been using a cold-water sparge and found it saves him time without having much effect on his efficiency. He gets an efficiency boost compared to the no-sparge brewing he had tried.

BREWING LOCATION: Garage or basement

BREWING SYSTEM: Mike's equipment will be familiar to most homebrewers, but not his process. "I have two 20-gallon Mega Pots. I fill the mash tun with all but 2 or 3 gallons of the filtered water I'll need. I heat it to the strike temperature and stir in my grains and water salts. I run the pump to recirculate and adjust the temperature as necessary. Then I take a pH reading and add salts or acid if needed. I rest for fifteen to thirty minutes, recirculate for a few more, then start sending the wort to the kettle. Once the liquid is down to an inch above the grain bed, I add the rest of the cold water. This boosts efficiency and cools the grain bed. Then it's boil, chill with a plate chiller, and ferment in two 30L Speidel fermenters."

HOW HE GOT STARTED: "I loved cooking and beer, so homebrewing seemed like a logical step. I took a student-taught class, Beer Brewing and Appreciation, my senior year at Carnegie Melon."

FANCIEST PIECE OF EQUIPMENT: A 60-gallon wine barrel

BREWING INSPIRATION: Mike is inspired by cloning, experimentation, flavors, and the stories and traditions of beer. We asked him for an example of a beer inspired by those traits, and he told us about a Gruit Kvass he brewed. "It was a loose clone of a kvass brewed by East End. My friend Nathan Zeender (now head brewer at Right Proper Brewing Co.) and I experimented by replacing the standard rye bread with homemade pumpernickel, and the caraway seeds with spruce and elderberries. To evoke a Scandinavian winter, we also added a touch of smoked malt. We pitched only baker's yeast, allowing the *Lactobacillus* it contains to sour the unhopped beer."

FAVORITE INGREDIENTS:

- White nectarines: "My favorite fruit to add to pale sour beers. It's juicy, bright, and doesn't dominate a mild beer, and it's so much less common than cherry, raspberry, etc."

- Good tropical Simcoe: "There is some Simcoe that is much more catty; the real good stuff is mango and pine."

  DREW: Mike is drawing the line at the late-harvest Simcoe that develops that pungent cat pee aroma. How to tell? Outside of brewing with a small portion from a provider and giving the beer a sample, I couldn't tell you. But once you find a reputable source (for that one harvest), stick with it!

- CaraVienna: "A nice, all-purpose, crystal malt. The Briess version adds a little stonefruit that is nice in hoppier beers. Malteries Franco-Belge's is cleaner and better in Belgian-style beers."

FAVORITE YEASTS:

- WLP007 Dry English Ale: "Contributes light, fruity esters that work well with hoppy beers; quick, reliable, and strong attenuation."

- WLP833 German Bock Lager: "Beautifully malty flavors, wonderful for any malt-focused lager (from helles to doppelbock)."

- WY3068 Weihenstephan Weizen: "It makes beers that taste like hefeweizen should. Can get too banana-focused (or even vanilla and bubblegum) fermented

warm; perfect around 62°F."

- WY3787 Trappist High Gravity: "Reliable Belgian strain, easy to manipulate the character by changing the fermentation temperature."

- WY1728 Scottish Ale: "My favorite yeast for strong, non-Belgian ales. Tolerant, just enough character, plays especially well with roast and smoke."

- ECY02 Flemish Ale: "I grew enough microbes to start different cultures in about twenty-five red wine barrels at Modern Times between our first two batches of sour base beer (a red and a brown). This culture was the best. It adds layers of tart red fruit and depth without destroying the malt."

Start a Solera with Mike

Have you ever wished your beer was more like a pet? If so, start a solera. The concept, borrowed from sherry producers, is to drain a portion of a batch off for packaging, then refill the fermenter. This creates a constantly evolving blend. It works especially well with sour beers, allowing a pull every six to twelve months of mature blended beer.

A solera can be maintained in a carboy or keg, but it really excels in a barrel. It is the best way for most homebrewers to deal with a commercial-sized, 50- to 60-gallon oak barrel. If you pull one-third of the liquid each year, the blend will approach an average age of three years. I split each 20-gallon pull from the two soleras in my basement four ways: some bottled as is, while the rest is transferred into carboys with fruit, dry hops, or other interesting ingredients, including elderflowers and acorn squash.

It is essential to refill the solera as soon as possible, ideally the same day. You can either use freshly brewed wort or fermented beer. Adjust the top-off beer based on how the solera is doing. Not sour enough? Mash hotter! You can either use the same recipe each time or vary it to change the character of the solera. If you are using a barrel, remember to brew a little more than you pull to compensate for evaporation.

Each solera takes on its own personality: you'll notice the unique flavors it produces. Figure out how often you can pull beer, and learn how quickly it evaporates. If you have one you really love, transfer 10 percent to a vessel with fresh beer or wort to create a daughter. It won't be exactly the same as its parent, but they'll share some family characteristics.

You can keep a solera going until either it turns vinegary from too much air exposure or too much yeast builds up and autolysis flavors appear, although refilling with bright beer will delay this.

DREW: Given the size of the barrels, soleras are a fantastic club project since your group can brew and fill the barrel and then have wort/finished beer ready to go whenever you want to serve the barrel aged. Here's the tricky part when brewing as a club. Make sure you have more beer than you have barrel capacity for and appoint someone the keeper of the barrel. Here's why:

One of the keeper's most important jobs is to test every beer going into the barrel and tactfully prevent any bad beer from going in. It's better to have some tweaked noses than damage everyone's efforts with bad beer. My suggestion is to have the club members deliver their beer and have a little tasting party. Have everyone taste the beers and write down notes and scores. Use those notes and scores to determine in secret what beers are destined for the barrel and in what quantity.

Add the beers to the barrel away from the club members. Here's where having extra beer on hand is crucial: it means you can silently avoid adding any bad beer and still have enough to fill the barrel. If no one's beer is bad, then you have enough beer to top up after evaporation. One advantage of this method is that everyone can happily believe their beer is in the blend and no one gets upset.

If large barrels seem intimidating to fill, team up with friends in your club for a barrel project.

EMPTY HATS

"This is the base beer for Modern Times Empty Hats Oud Bruin (despite the fact that it's just 14 SRM). It is fermented in stainless for a few days with our house saison blend, which is mostly Dupont with a little Westmalle, then transferred to red wine barrels with bugs. An ounce of oak cubes and a cup of Cabernet would be a fine replacement. ECY02 Flemish Ale was the best version, but WY3763 Roeselare would be a suitable substitute, especially with dregs from your favorite sour beer."

FOR 5 GALLONS AT 1.061 OG, 14 SRM, 15.5 IBUs, 7% ABV

GRAIN BILL

3.25 lb.	Munich 10°L malt
3.25 lb.	Vienna malt
3.00 lb.	2-row pale malt
0.75 lb.	Weyermann Caramunich I malt
0.75 lb.	flaked corn
6.00 oz.	Weyermann Special B malt

MASH

Rest   156°F   45 minutes

HOPS

1.00 oz.   Hallertauer   4.8% AA   60 minutes

YEAST

WLP565 Belgian Saison I and WLP530 Abbey
    Ale for primary

ECY02 Flemish Ale and WY3763 Roselare
    for secondary

ADDITION

1 oz.	French oak cubes (see Notes)
1 cup	cabernet sauvignon (see Notes)

NOTES

Soak oak in wine during primary fermentation. Ferment in primary with the saison and abbey ale strains. Add oak, wine, and souring critters to secondary and age for 9 to 12 months before bottling.

Mike's Recipe

★

PERPETUUM SOUR

This is a scaled-down version of Mike's solera project. To fill a full wine barrel, you'll want to scale this up to at least 55 gallons (or brew at least 55 gallons of it). Call breweries and wineries in your area to see if they have used barrels on hand. Soleras work best with barrels that have been used. Since most of the oak character has been expended, you have more time to age the beer without worrying about overwhelming oak flavors.

FOR 5.5 GALLONS AT 1.058 OG, 4.0 SRM, 10.5 IBUs, 6.5% ABV

GRAIN BILL

5.50 lb.	German pilsner malt
5.00 lb.	2-row pale malt
1.00 lb.	flaked oats
1.00 lb.	unmalted wheat
0.75 lb.	wheat malt

MASH

Rest	156°F	90 minutes
Mash out	168°F	15 minutes

HOPS

4.25 oz.	Williamette	3.70% AA	60 minutes
3.00 oz.	Cascade	5.75% AA	60 minutes

YEAST

ECY01 Bugfarm

Dregs from a bottle of Jolly Pumpkin like Bam Biere or La Roja

ADDITION

0.5 tablet Whirlfloc	15 minutes
1 tsp. Irish moss	15 minutes

BREWER'S PROFILE

Mike Karnowski

Mike owned a homebrew shop and brewed twice a week for thirteen years before switching to commercial brewing. He has amassed nearly thirty years of brewing experience, and on the homebrew scale alone has brewed more than two thousand batches. His book *Homebrew Beyond the Basics* covers a wide range of techniques, ingredients, and recipes that will give homebrewers of any level insight into ingredients and processes they may not have thought of or worked with, as well as historical perspectives on beer. As we write this, he has just wrapped up his tenure as the specialty brewer at Green Man Brewery in Asheville, North Carolina—where he was in charge of all beers other than the company's flagship brews and started Asheville's first commercial sour program. Don't worry, though; he left to open his own brewery, Zebulon Artisan Ales!

★

BREWING SINCE: 1998

BREWING MOTTO: Never be satisfied.

BREWING PHILOSOPHY: Beer is meant to be consumed in large quantities, not out of 2-ounce snifter glasses. Make beer that is thirst quenching, not cloying.

FAVORITE BREW STYLES: Farmhouse ales, pilsners, historical stouts

FAVORITE BREWING COUNTRY: Belgium

BREWING METHODOLOGY AND SYSTEM: Mike brews 5-gallon, all-grain batches using a multi-step mash on a basic homebrew rig in his basement. To quote, "If carbon monoxide hasn't killed me yet, it's not gonna.'"

Note: The authors of this book do not endorse Mike's cavalier attitude about the dangers of carbon monoxide. It's to be expected that owning a homebrew shop gave Mike a different perspective on reality!

He mashes in a stainless pot with a Bazooka screen, then boils in a cutoff keg kettle. He chills with an immersion chiller and then ferments in buckets in a temperature-controlled refrigerator.

HOW HE GOT STARTED: When Mike was in the army in Fort Lewis, Washington, he thought it would be fun to try homebrewing. He and a buddy bought a starter kit in Seattle, and he was hooked.

BREWING INSPIRATION: Mike takes his inspiration from history and experimenting with new techniques and flavors. He has made a 5.5 percent ABV, 70 IBU 1805-style porter using 50 percent brown malt, which was the way it was done before black patent malt was invented. He's also become interested in the idea of a "moveable farmhouse ale." He says, "You take a French/Belgian farmhouse brewery and pick it up *a la Wizard of Oz* and put it down anywhere in the world. Then you have to imagine what you'd have to work with. For example, I've done a Thai farmhouse ale with coconut, lemongrass, ginger, and Thai basil with rice in the mash. You could imagine many other scenarios: Tokyo farmhouse, Saskatchewan farmhouse, etc. . . ."

DREW: This same concept was what inspired a number of my saison experiments. Denny loves to talk about the one that convinced him I was a madman—the Saison Guacamole. That beer was inspired by a session of laying in my yard, thinking about the nature of a farm, looking up at my avocado trees, and realizing I had all the parts for a big bowl of guacamole. Now how could that be a beer? Same thing with my tea, wine, and other flavors of saison.

DENNY: It not only convinced me that Drew was a madman, but also that he knew what the hell he was doing. That beer had no reason to be any good at all, and yet it was astoundingly successful.

FAVORITE INGREDIENTS: Mike lists his favorite ingredients as "malt, hops, yeast . . . no wacky stuff." His favorite yeasts are likewise straightforward: WY3726 Farmhouse Ale and WY1318 London III are his go-to yeasts.

MOST UNUSUAL INGREDIENTS: Although Mike stays away from the truly weird, he also doesn't hesitate to experiment with some unusual ingredients. A beer made with a heavy dose of Forbidden Black Rice is a good example.

Mike on Choosing Your "Bugs"

While working as the assistant brewer at Green Man, I took it upon myself to start Asheville's first sour beer program. With an empty and spent rum barrel from my old distilling gig, a variety of commercial sour beer dregs, and five 12-gallon batches on a homebrew system, Green Man birthed Funk #49. From there we bought wine barrels from the local winery and grew the program with dregs from the rum barrel. The next beers, Maceo and Snozzberry, were huge hits—Snozzberry even scored a perfect 100 from the Beer Advocate guys! Then we kept buying new barrels, and the cycle kept moving. My last beer at Green Man was a sour black called Bootsy (see page 152 for the recipe). Many thought it was the best sour I have ever made.

Now that I'm starting my own brewery that will specialize in wild beers, one of the hardest things is figuring out which strains of saison ale yeast, *Brettanomyces*, and *Lactobacillus* to use. Back in the early 1990s when I first started to brew sour beers, your only choice was to special order one of three to four strains from Wyeast. Now there are new "boutique" yeast wranglers popping up right and left with dozens of new, exciting Brett strains and blends.

Still, Brett is what really brings the funk to the party—the almost rotten fruit or barnyardy notes. While there are lots of different strains available, I think it is best to use a Brett blend to get the most complexity and attenuation. Here are a few of my go-to strains:

- Brett Bruxellensis: Usually isolated from the Belgian beer Orval, it has the classic spicy, perfumey Brett character that many find familiar.

- Brett Lambicus: Lambicus has that "cherry pie" character that goes so well in Flanders reds and browns.

- Brett Drie/Vrai: Isolated from Drie Fontaine lambic, Drie/Vrai has a super intense overripe fruit character. It is often used as a primary fermentation strain. Note this is not to be confused with "Brett" Trois, which has a similar flavor but has turned out to be weird ale yeast.

- Brett Clausenii: Originally isolated from English casks, old English beers almost always had this strain of Brett in them.

Any of these strains can be used as your primary yeast, but surprisingly you won't get much funk out of them that way. I have much better luck fermenting with a normal *Saccharomyces* strain then adding the Brett in the secondary. Make sure you give the Brett plenty of time to eat up those sugars that the *Saccharomyces* yeast couldn't or you could end up with bottle bombs. Look for a steady FG of at least 1.004 or lower. (At the time of writing, I have been really enjoying the Amalgamation Brett blend from Yeast Bay if you are looking for a good all-purpose source of Brett.)

DREW: To Mike's point about *Brettanomyces* as a primary fermentation strain, it's a strange quirk, but when forced to tackle the wort from the beginning, Brett ends up acting just like a cranky dose of regular yeast. What I learned to do with Brett was pitch it after the primary is in full swing/ slowing down and make sure to add some fresh wort, sugar, or fruit at the same time to give a little extra bump.

Lactobacillus is what brings the sourness in most sour beers, and it can be sourced from pure cultures, blends, probiotic pills, yogurt, or even malted barley. I haven't had much luck with the pure cultures from the labs. Omega Yeast Labs has a nice blend that works really fast at room temperature, though. I have also had a lot of luck using yogurt as my Lacto source. Just make a starter out of unhopped wort and toss in a tablespoon of a good hippie yogurt, one that is unpasteurized and has lots of different Lacto strains in it.

Pediococcus can also contribute sourness, but you risk diacetyl which can turn your beer into a liquid with snot-like consistency. Eventually those things will go away if you add Brett as well, but it takes a long time. Why would a brewer purposely add Pedio? Many claim it contributes a better sourness than Lacto, and you don't have to keep your IBU close to zero like you do with Lacto. However, personally, I stick with Lacto.

ADVANCED TIPS

While the above will usually make a nice sour beer, there are steps you can take to ensure a good, clean sour consistently:

- Lower the wort pH to 4.5 before adding the Lacto culture. This will keep any spoilage bugs from growing and will help with the head retention in the finished beer.

- Really keep the oxygen out. Racking the beer to a CO_2 purged keg for souring will ensure you don't get any off flavors.

- Pitch a healthy amount of yeast or Brett for fermentation. The yeast aren't going to like being thrown into a 3.2 pH wort, so consider adding some extra nutrients, oxygenate well, and don't plan on reusing the yeast. I have had good luck using California ale yeast. Brett doesn't mind the wort's low pH as much as *Saccharomyces* does, so this would be a good choice for a 100-percent Brett fermentation.

Culturing bottle dregs is a quick way to grow a complex group of organisms to pitch.

Mike's Recipe

★

BOOTSY

"People can't believe how simple the recipe is based on the intense complexity of the finished beer. Brewing the beer is the easy part; getting a good blend of "bugs" and waiting for 12 to 15 months is the hard part." Between the two Wild Mikes—Karnowski and Tonsmeire—we hope you see that there's a real power to keeping your grists simple and letting the creatures do the talking.

FOR 5.5 GALLONS AT 1.075 OG, 28 SRM, 0 IBUs, 9% ABV

GRAIN BILL

13.5 lb.   Thomas Fawcett Pearl Malt
1.0 lb.   Carafa Special II

MASH

Rest   155°F   60 minutes

HOPS

Add a few hop pellets to satisfy governmental regulations and "the hop gods."

YEAST

A blend of your favorite *Lactobacillus*, *Brettanomyces*, or *Saccharomyces*.

NOTES

Brew, chill to 75°F, and ferment with your magic blend of critters. Wait 12 to 15 months for them to chew through all the sugar and fully attenuate the beer before bottling and enjoying.

Brandon Jones

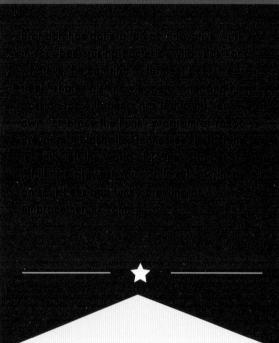

BREWING SINCE: 2001

BREWING MOTTO: Embrace the funk.

BREWING PHILOSOPHY: Brew what *you* like.

FAVORITE BREW STYLES: Wild ales, saisons, and specialty beers

FAVORITE BREWING COUNTRY: America

BREWING METHODOLOGY: All-grain fly sparge, single infusion (with or without mash out)

BREWING LOCATION: Garage

BREWING SYSTEM: Blichmann Top Tier 2 burner, Therminator counterflow chiller, O_2 tank with diffusion stone. "I use an electric heat stick to preheat my strike water. It's on a timer to cut on five hours prior to brew time."

HOW HE GOT STARTED: "My wife bought me a Mr. Beer kit. The beers sucked and went sour. That's how I discovered sours. I went on to learn everything I could about funky beer."

FANCIEST PIECE OF EQUIPMENT: TriClamp ½ barrel conical fermenter (15.5 gallons)

FAVORITE INGREDIENTS: Lacto, some of his own cultured Bretts, specialty citrus, hops with a research number (unnamed ones), Cara Ruby malt, and Golden Naked Oats.

FAVORITE YEASTS: *Brettanomyces claussenii* (WY5151PC/WLP645), *Brettanomyces custersianus* (ECY19, WY3726 Farmhouse)

Sour Beer Advice from Brandon

When I first started brewing wild and sour beers, there were many myths about these styles, such as that *Brettanomyces* will sour a beer or that you will need a different carboy to ferment sour beers. A lot has changed since then. We now know that some strains of saison yeast can be more invasive than *Brettanomyces*, bacteria is what sours beer, and really, you just need to dedicate "soft" pieces of equipment to these styles.

I have never encountered an issue fermenting an IPA using a properly cleaned and sanitized glass carboy or stainless vessel that previously held a Flanders Red. However, soft equipment can pose a risk of cross-contamination. So a good rule of thumb is to remember that anything that is pliable, plastic, or silicone will be porous. This includes airlocks, stoppers, and even fermentation buckets. These items should be clearly marked with red tape to prevent accidental usage on "clean" beers.

When you are first starting down the path of brewing sour and wild brewing, remember that in many cases the process is very similar to brewing most other styles of beer, with the biggie being to pitch a healthy count of microbes at the proper temperature. When in doubt, contact the manufacture to determine the proper temps.

I usually suggest a Berliner weisse as the first beer style a new sour brewer attempts. This is a fantastic style to get comfortable with: the turnaround can be as little as one month, it is a fairly inexpensive style to brew, making a fruited or oaked variation is simple, and you will end up with a nice fresh, funky slurry to use on your next batch.

FOUR YEARS' WORTH OF EMBRACETHEFUNK.COM KNOWLEDGE

- Make sure the stars are what you aim for. You will make mistakes, but don't worry. It's a journey—enjoy the ride.

- Use lager or hybrid pitching rates when brewing 100-percent Brett beers.

- Kettle souring and natural souring can both make yummy beers.

- You must have a way to test gravity and pH or Titratable Acidity if you are feeling adventurous.

    DREW: Titratable Acidity is a measure of how much acid is actually present—it has a larger correspondence to a sour beers organoleptic sensation than pH; pH is just 100 times easier to measure.

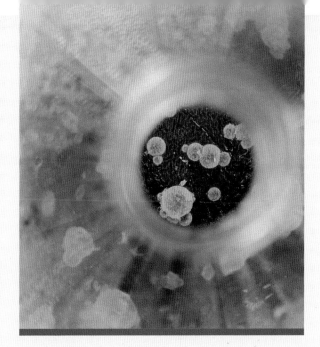

Don't fear the funk—embrace it!

- Your barrel-aged beer will often take more time than you expected.

- Your barrel-aged beer will often take less time than you expected. Have beer ready to fill the barrel.

- Use 17 percent more CO_2 to purge than you think is necessary (this number may or may not be exact; the point is, when dealing with sour beer, don't skimp on CO_2).

- Temperature has a lot to do with how good a spontaneously fermented batch ends up. With the exception of some warmer-weather states in the United States, ask yourself, "Is Cantillon brewing now?"

- Even a few hours of spontaneously inoculated wort or isolated local wild yeast is a great way to add a twist on your beer.

- Err on the side of less than what you expected when dealing with new microbes. Most will continue to develop into something more. It's okay to take your time.

- Revisit your "perfect" recipes and techniques often.

- Investigate and employ techniques that make the best beer possible in your garage, kitchen, patio, or brewery. Don't just buy into one-thing-fits-all. I assure you techniques that work at one world-class brewery do not directly translate to another world-class brewery.

THE FUNKY PATH BERLINER WEISS

"There are two options for brewing this recipe: natural sour development in the fermenter or kettle sour/boil. I would recommend the natural sour method of pitching your bacteria and yeast into the fermenter to constantly develop. Kettle souring is a slightly more advanced technique where a brewer will keep the wort in the boil kettle at 95 to 100°F overnight with a pitch of Lacto. When the desired sourness is achieved—usually within 24 hours—the wort is brought back up to a boil for 15 minutes to kill off the Lacto. This allows the brewer to use his or her normal equipment including the 'soft equipment' I mentioned earlier without the risk of clean side contamination. Again, I recommend the natural sour development method."

FOR 5.5 GALLONS AT 1.030 OG, 0 IBUs, 3.1% ABV, 0–15 MINUTE BOIL

GRAIN BILL

4.0 lb.	pilsner malt
2.5 lb.	white wheat malt

MASH

Rest   150°F   60 minutes

HOPS

None

YEAST

Choose a *Lactobacillus*: WY5335 *Lactobacillus* / WLP67 *Lactobacillus delbrueckii*

Choose a yeast: WY1007 German Ale / WLP036 Dusseldorf Alt / Fermentis Safale US-05

Choose a *Brettanomyces*: WY5526 *Brettanomyces lambicus* / WLP653 *Brettanomyces lambicus*

NOTES

Do not oxygenate the wort. I would advise against putting 95°F wort into a glass carboy; a bucket or "PET style" carboy is safer. Pitch the Lacto culture *only* into the wort, and let the bacteria work overnight. If you have a pH meter or strips, try to target 3.5 pH before moving on to the next step. Once the wort has soured, cool to 70°F using an ice bath and pitch the ale yeast. When the high krausen begins to fall, you can optionally pitch the *Brettanomyces*. Let the beer ferment in primary for one month, then carbonate to three volumes.

VARIANTS

Add tropical aroma hops, such as Citra, to dry hop.

Add tart cherry juice and lime peel.

Try using orange liqueur-soaked oak chips.

DARK FUNK

Brandon brings the funk in this recipe with a more complicated base wort that's still focused on providing structure for the big bugs coming later in the brew. The currants add a fresh "zing" to the top of the acid, and earthiness is provided by the Brett and souring bacteria.

FOR 5.5 GALLONS AT 1.078 OG, 24.5 SRM, 42.6 IBUs, 60-MINUTE BOIL

GRAIN BILL
10.0 lb.	Belgian pale
1.5 lb.	Munich 10°L malt
0.5 lb.	Special B malt
1.0 lb.	dark candi sugar crystals

MASH
Rest	150°F	60 minutes

HOPS
0.5 oz.	East Kent Goldings 5.2% AA	60 minutes

YEAST
WY3787 Trappist High Gravity

WY3763 Roeselare or ECY02 Flemish Ale

WY5526 *Brettanomyces lambicus*

ADDITION
1 oz. merlot-soaked French oak wood chips, added dry to primary fermenter, 7 days

6 oz. black currants (late aging addition)

NOTES
Pitch an active starter of WY3787 Trappist High Gravity at 68°F.

When gravity reaches 1.050, pitch WY3763 Roeselare or ECY02 Flemish Ale.

When gravity reaches 1.015, pitch WY5526 *Brettanomyces lambicus* and age for a minimum of 6 months.

After the minimum 6-month aging period, add 6 oz. of dried black currants and age for 30 days.

Mary Izett

Mary specializes in wild and sour brews and freely shares what she learns, both on the podcast *Fuhmentaboudit!* with her husband Chris Cuzme as well as in her book *Speed Brewing*. Additionally, she and Chris have founded a gypsy brewing company in New York called Cuzett Libations (the first letters of his last name and the last of hers). Beers like the Cuzet Grisette and the Australian Galaxy-infused Australian sparkling ale, Revenge of the Emu, have received rave reviews.

BREWING SINCE: 2006

BREWING MOTTO: Fuhmentaboudit! (Or, Just Ferment It!)

BREWING PHILOSOPHY: "Why not?"

FAVORITE BREW STYLES: Sour beers, herbal beers, fast-fermenting beers, sessionable beers, and anything interesting, intriguing, and/or weird.

FAVORITE BREWING COUNTRY: Too many to list!

BREWING METHODOLOGY: Mary brews all-grain brew in a bag (BIAB), 2.5-gallon batches using a single infusion mash in the kitchen of her Brooklyn loft. Mary found great advantage to switching to a smaller brew setup because it required less space (don't be fooled by television: New York City apartments are tiny!); less strength to handle everything; and, most importantly, ferments finish faster which allowed her to tackle more variety with less overall risk.

Using BIAB, she mashes in her oven to maintain mash temperature and drains over a perforated pizza pan (ingenuity!). She might dunk the bag to do a "sparge," then boil and chill with an immersion wort chiller before pitching her yeast and fermenting in a thermostat-regulated chest freezer.

She's much more concerned about the finished product than the equipment that produces it, as evidenced by the fact that she lists a 1.75-gallon keg as her fanciest piece of equipment.

HOW SHE GOT STARTED: Mary has a bachelor's degree in biology, plus graduate studies in horticulture. While studying the bulb-to-bulb variations of *Allium cepa* (the common onion to normal folks), she discovered she really enjoyed craft beer. Brewing was a natural next step.

FANCIEST PIECE OF EQUIPMENT: "1.75-gallon keg? I'm not really into fancy."

> **DREW:** It may not be fancy, but Mary introduced me to the reCAP, a plastic lid for mason jars, nominally for drinking, that perfectly mounts an airlock. They're great for all your mason jar

ferments! Also, she swears by a good digital thermometer and scale.

BREWING INSPIRATION: Mary gets her inspiration from finding new flavor combinations, playing with new and exciting "critters" to ferment her beers, and acquiring knowledge. The drive for new flavors and techniques has sent Mary well beyond the standard world of beer and even beyond the world of "beer normal" wild critters into non-beery fermentations that involve SCOBYs, tea, kefir, bananas, saps of various varieties, and more.

> **DREW:** A SCOBY isn't a misspelling of everyone's favorite cartoon dog detective. It's an acronym that stands for "Symbiotic Culture Of Bacteria and Yeast." A great many traditional ferments revolve around SCOBYs. They almost always form puck-like rubbery groupings and disks that the brewer can simply scoop up and move to the next fermentation. Though it varies, all sorts of critters are found in the colony including *Acetobacter*, *Lactobacillus*, *Pediococcus*, *Brettanomyces*, and strange alternative yeasts such as *Schizosaccharomyces* and *Zygosaccharomyces*. It's truly wild stuff.

FAVORITE INGREDIENTS: One of Mary's favorite ingredients is rice, more specifically rice solids, a powdered rice product like dried malt extract. She praises their ease of use and says, "They lighten the body of a beer and can add depth in aroma and flavor."

> **DENNY:** In my opinion, rice in beer has been given a bad name due to the flavorless light lagers that use it as an adjunct. Like Mary points out, it's a great way to lighten the body of a beer if used as you would sugar. And the subtle flavor addition can really complement the other ingredients in something like a cream ale.

Another favorite ingredient is tea—all sorts of tea. Yes, tea is a fundamental ingredient of kombucha, but Mary's love of it goes beyond that. (We're not sure, but she might be secretly British.) She says, "Teas come in so many different flavors and combinations of flavors. They ferment out absolutely fabulously with honey or sugar substrates and can work well with malty worts, though I find them a bit trickier in beers, particularly the more tannin-filled varieties. I find tea shops so inspiring, packed full of predesigned flavor combinations. And white, green, and black teas can add a tannin depth and balance. Seriously, one of my favorite beverages of all time is a fermented jasmine green tea. So. Delicious."

Additionally, Mary has been championing the rise of local and regional ingredients in her brewing efforts—think local maltsters and the resurgence of local hop growers in the traditional New York hop-growing region.

FAVORITE YEASTS: For someone playing out there on the raggedy edge of microbiology, Mary's favorite yeasts are surprisingly low key. For regular beery yeast, she likes Fermentis Safale US-05. The dried yeast is easy to work with for her smaller batches, cleans up well, and provides a neutral character that allows her to spotlight other characteristics.

If she needs an aggressive fermenter, she breaks out the Champagne yeast. She appreciates its incredible tolerance of temperatures, pH, and nutrient-deficient sugar musts (honey, sugar, fruit juice). Many of her favorite ciders, short meads, and sugar ferments take advantage of the tolerance and give her the ability to push the ferment quickly without producing overwhelming off characters.

Lastly, on the funky side, Mary's been playing around with a lot of *Lactobacillus*-based ferments. Instead of sourcing a cultured version of Lacto, she's been grabbing her critters from natural colonies found on grain and in whey.

> **DENNY:** Another example of Mary's creativity, like her brewing system and recipes!

KEEPING THINGS SEPARATE: While Mary mostly is brewing with funky creatures, she doesn't maintain separate anything. Her short meads and beers get fermented in the same area with the same gear. Whether this cavalier approach is due to foolhardy bravery or a NYC-enforced lack of the storage necessary for maintaining a whole separate line of gear, it still plays out that she's able to reuse her stuff without cross-contaminating her beverages. Just pay attention to your sanitation, and you'll be fine.

From Inspiration to Execution with Mary

I find inspiration everywhere. I'm super-crazy about cocktail menus right now. Although I often imagine strolling into a speakeasy-style bar after work, slipping onto a bar stool, and elegantly sipping a stylish cocktail, it never happens.

The craft beer bar bars have a stronger siren song (and usually someone I know in front of or behind the bar). So while I don't drink that many cocktails, I drool over cocktail menus. New York City has some primo cocktail artists and the creativity, passion, and thoughtfulness that goes into their cocktails are nothing short of incredible—and oh-so inspirational. Inventive cocktail menus are basically a cheat-sheet for flavor combinations.

> **DENNY:** In other words, it's not cheating if you find your flavors by looking around you. One of Drew's favorite recipes—Jasmine Dragon—occurred to him because his wife had discovered jasmine-infused Dragon Pearl Tea from a local teashop. The aroma is intriguing, with the interplay of the jasmine flowers and the earthy spiciness of the tea. Naturally, the next thing to do was capture it in a tincture and add it to a soft saison base that would emphasize both of those aspects.

I'm also inspired by foods—the Elvis Sandwich short mead (page 164) is an example of this, obviously. I was invited to brew some beverages for a public festival at one of the hippest BBQ joints in NYC. I wanted to make something that would grab people's attention, and I've always been fascinated by the Elvis Sandwich, so the Elvis Sandwich short mead was born.

Seasonal produce is a big one. I love to play what I call "The Greenmarket Speed Brewing Beverage Challenge." I stop by a greenmarket (usually at Union Square, which is one of the largest in NYC) on the way home from work and pick up everything I need to make a beverage (well, almost—complementary spices are allowed).

I've had a ton of fun with rhubarb, gooseberry, peaches, beets, and so much more. My Heart Skips a Beet Short Mead (beets and star anise) is one of my favorite drinks to come out of this.

There's a wonderful book called *The Flavor Thesaurus: A Compendium of Pairings, Recipes and Ideas for the Creative Cook* by Niki Segnet that's a great place to start when you have a flavor in mind that you want to build around.

Food is always a challenge to deal with since we're never certain how fermentation will change the flavor of things until we actually try them out. The classic example we can think of is oranges. They taste great raw and fresh, brimming with acid and sugar in their juice. It never fails that when you ferment the juice, what you end up with is earthly, funky, and deeply unsettling in a vomitus sort of way.

Now, the tricky part is how to go from inspiration to execution. In short, it's a combination of research, intuition, and experience.

I find that developing short mead, cider, and sugar-based spirited soda recipes are quite liberating in comparison to beer recipes. Not only is it often easier to extract flavors from fruit, spices, herbs, and so on, but almost anything goes. And most of it works.

I have a lot of ingredients that I'm a hard-core believer in—freeze-dried fruit, for example. They work every time, especially beautiful but hard-to-capture fruit like strawberries and blueberries.

After I have a flavor combination in mind, I'll research online how others have used it, combine that with any experience I have, and go from there. For the first batch of the Elvis Sandwich Short Mead, I actually made four different 1-gallon batches: a banana, two peanut butter batches with differing amounts of PB2, and a plain batch, and blended at kegging.

I wanted to make sure that all the flavors were in

balance since I was making it for an event. This is a bit extreme, but these are trickier flavors. For the bacon element, I contemplated using smoked malt or infusing with bacon, but Liquid Smoke won out: it's 100-percent natural and super easy to add at kegging. Win-win all around.

I'm a huge believer in ½-gallon batches. I have quite the inventory of ½-gallon Mason jars, reCAP lids, and No. 5.5 stoppers after writing my book. They're a great combo for experimenting without much commitment.

The use of "alternative" sugar sources is also quite liberating when developing recipes.

Once I have a flavor combination, I figure out which substrate will compliment it best. Will barley be the balance, or do I want the clean backdrop of sugar? Will a slight apple tartness benefit, or honey? So many delicious choices.

It's been a liberating and delightful experience to explore the full world of fermented alcoholic beverages. And I am now committed, not only to barley and wheat but apples, honey, straight-up sugar, and any other fermentable sweetness I can get my grubby paws on. I hope you have as much fun as I do with this alternative universe of fermented booziness.

DENNY: So there you have it: in Mary's world, the small batch is the key because it allows for play and exploration. Maybe it's time that we all stop and think how we've been trained to always make 5 gallons.

Mary's Recipe

★

MEMORIES OF MEKONG

Falling into the realm of what Mary calls a "spirited soda," consider this drink a first step on your way to kombucha, if you'd like or just sit back and enjoy a fantastic porch-sipping beverage. It's radically different than your usual sweet tea. (For more information on boozy kombucha and spirited sodas, check out Mary's book, Speed Brewing.*)*

FOR 3.0 GALLONS AT 1.034 OG, 0 SRM, 0 IBUs, ABOUT 5% ABV

INGREDIENTS

40 grams	Trader Joe's Coconut Lemongrass Ginger Green Tea (or other flavored green tea)
2.25 lb.	table sugar
0.25 tsp.	yeast nutrient

WATER
3 gallons   dechlorinated water

YEAST
1 packet dry Champagne yeast

INSTRUCTIONS

1. Bring 8 cups of water to a boil and let cool slightly. Stir in tea and yeast nutrient, and steep for 10 minutes.

2. In a carboy, add 8 cups of chilled water, the sugar, and strained tea/nutrient mixture. Stir/swirl to combine.

3. Top up with enough chilled water to reach 3 gallons, swirl to combine thoroughly, and pitch the yeast.

4. Ferment between 65 and 80°F for 5 to 14 days until you reach your target sweetness. Mary prefers the final gravity to land around 1.008–1.010.

5. Crash and package.

Mary's Recipe

★

ELVIS SANDWICH SHORT MEAD

Mary has made quite a specialty of short meads. Think of all the ease of making mead with the sessionability of beer that allows the brewer to play with a crazy spectrum of flavors. For this one, she reaches out to The King for inspiration with her banana-peanut butter-bacon-sandwich-inspired short mead. Make sure to crash this out a little early to preserve some sweetness.

FOR 3.0 GALLONS AT 1.032 OG, 0 IBUs, 3 SRM, 4.5% ABV

INGREDIENTS

4.00 lb.	honey
0.70 grams	Trader Joe's freeze-dried banana slices, crushed
75.00 grams	defatted peanut butter powder (PB2)
0.25 tsp.	yeast nutrient

WATER

3.5 gallons dechlorinated water

YEAST

1 packet dry Champagne yeast

ADDITION

8 to 10 drops liquid smoke

INSTRUCTIONS

1. Bring 3 cups of water to a boil. Let cool slightly and pour over the bananas, peanut butter powder, and yeast nutrient. Stir to dissolve and rehydrate.

2. Add your honey and 1 gallon of water to your sanitized fermenter. Seal the fermenter and shake/stir to dissolve the honey.

3. Add the peanut butter/banana slurry to the honey must and top with additional water to reach 3.5 gallons of must. Shake/stir/swirl to combine.

4. Pitch the yeast and attach the airlock. Ferment in the 70°F range for 1 to 2 weeks. (Mary prefers 1.008 to 1.012 as her target final gravity.)

5. Cold crash the mead at 34°F to clear up the mead.

6. Add liquid smoke and bottle or keg.

VARIANTS: PBJ SHORT MEAD

Substitute 1.2 to 1.8 oz. of freeze-dried berries for the bananas and skip the liquid smoke.

The Recipe (and Ingredient) Innovators

★ ★ ★

*C*raft beer has a reputation for pushing the envelope. The best of beers can even create incredible new experiences. Whether it's a beer inspired by crazy new hops, the humble pumpkin, or a desire to tell outlandish tales, the recipe at the heart of the magic is what excites the Recipe Innovator.

In a short list of malts, hops, water adjustments, yeasts, and other additions, these brewers see an infinite universe. Yes, the recipe is their brush with which they paint a beery landscape—whether it be profoundly subtle or absurdly strange. In fact, there's a real split in this archetype with some of the brewers looking at their recipes with an eye toward style and tradition and others who want to put the innovation pedal through the floorboards in an attempt to blow everyone's minds. No matter, all Recipe Innovators are driven by their creative impulses.

- **The Cloner:** These "innovators" are obsessed and will stop at nothing until they figure out the trick to making a flavor duplicate of their target beer. No matter if it's the rare bitter they fell in love with in the UK or something commonly available, they won't stop.
- **The Ingredient Hound:** These brewers never met a homebrew store, grocery store, farmer's market, or convenience store that didn't serve as a possible source of inspiration for the next beer. Sometimes it's as simple as a stack of leftover tortillas. Other times it's that new weird hop or syrup folks have just noticed.

  Denny: Permit me to rant a bit here . . . and I'm gonna do it whether you permit it or not! First, let me say that I admire people who can take an unusual ingredient and actually make it work in a beer. I really do. But, for the love of all that's foamy, just because you spot an ingredient in the natural foods grocery aisle doesn't mean it necessarily belongs in a beer! Think about the final beer and what the ingredient, or combo of ingredients, will do to it. Think about the flavors, not the weirdness. Think of the children!

- **The Recipe Hoarder:** For these brewers, the brewing is almost an afterthought. They while away the hours (usually at work) playing with their favorite brewing software, formulating a massive stockpile of recipes that will probably never exist except in their fevered imagination.
- **The Shocker:** These demented people get a charge from watching people recoil at a beer concept. A few years back, that was pretty simple (looking at you, Bacon Beer). Nowadays, they've got to try harder and find the next gross-out factor.
- **The Stealth Innovator:** We tend to get hung up on the flashy brewers, but the stealth brewers are the ones that bring a measure of sanity to the whole game with tweaks and twists to classics that become "a thing." (Later in this chapter, read about Vinnie Cilurzo and his invention of double IPA.)
- **The Storyteller:** These are the folks who see the world as one great big book waiting to be shared, and their preferred medium is the pint glass. It's also one of Drew's biggest passions, as can be seen in recipes like his Cookie Celebration Ale (page 176). Everything has a story to tell, and the recipe reflects that.

The Positives

Whereas the Scientist is driven by a thirst for knowledge, the Innovator wants to make magic. Ultimately, he or she thinks a bit like a chef—a dash of this, a pinch of that—to create an experience. Sometimes it's flashy and sometimes it's not, but we'll look at both sides.

For a classic example of the Innovator writ large, you only need to look at Sam Calagione and the continuing collection of crazy beers that he and his crew at Dogfish Head produce on a daily basis. Looking at the homebrew level, you have the folks in this chapter, of course. Both are known for attracting a ton of attention by creating far-out beers and concepts.

However, a number of Innovators take a quieter inspiration. Almost all of the "American" styles got their start this way, in fact. Looking through the survey responses for this type, we repeatedly saw reference to serious research efforts applied to recipes, which demonstrates the care that these brewers take before embarking on a brew day.

For example, what's an American pale ale or American IPA but an increase of hops and another tweak or two to separate them from their classic British predecessors? Or think of sour beer: how many "American sours" exist as inventive spinoffs of the wild ales of the Belgians? So, even though it's fun to talk about the wild and crazy brewers

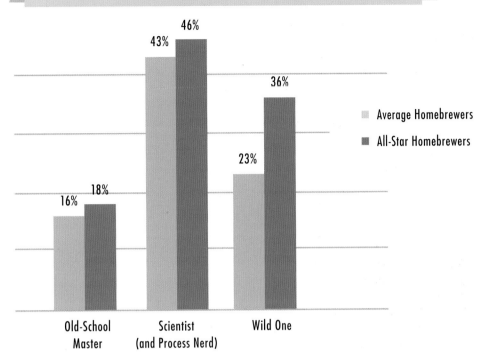

SUBTYPES FOR RECIPE (AND INGREDIENT) INNOVATORS

- Average Homebrewers
- All-Star Homebrewers

Old-School Master: 16%, 18%
Scientist (and Process Nerd): 43%, 46%
Wild One: 23%, 36%

of the Innovator, we would be remiss not to give a heaping helping of praise to those quiet explorers who extend our beery world by taking smaller steps in a new direction.

The Negatives

You know how homebrew and craft beer has a bad reputation amongst some folks? The awful beers that make people say, "What was wrong with beer-flavored beer?" Well, it's all the fault of the Recipe Innovators.

Wait, how is it their fault? It starts with an affliction common to many brewers: the kid-in-the-candy-store syndrome. You know, the impulse that hits when you walk into the homebrew shop and can't resist the lure of all the choices you have. Unfortunately, what a lot of "innovative" recipes end up looking like is a kitchen sink brew with a little bit of everything

in the mix. For example, Drew once was offered something along the lines of a rose-infused, smoked, strong American brown ale aged on tequila-soaked oak. That's about three too many things added to a recipe! It's this eager puppy-like level of enthusiasm that many seasoned brewers find tiring and leads the laments about "when beer was beer."

A final complaint lobbed at the Recipe Innovator: they're accused of being attention seekers. It's true that in a world of IPAs, brown ales, and stouts, the wacky and wild will stand out and catch a lot of attention. Sometimes it's not even something that complicated—but witness the hype train built around barrel-aged stouts or the bitterness war of the single/double/triple IPA. Lots of grumbling gets directed at high-concept beers or beers with catchy names.

DENNY: Since this is Drew's chapter (see page 172), I'll just say my piece. Of all the sub-archetypes, I think Stealth Innovator is closest to how I approach recipe design. Yet I also look at a recipe as a target, something to strive for as I learn how it all goes together. I tend to imagine flavors in my head before I start on a recipe, then put together whatever ingredients I need to get that flavor into the beer. I don't use ingredients just to use them, even when I use off-the-wall stuff like mushrooms. I think about what I want the finished beer to taste like, then use the brewing process to learn how to get those flavors and make them work together. To that end, I brew most new recipes multiple times in order to fine-tune the flavors and learn how the ingredients and processes work together. I often start with a style or recipe that's "normal," then add specialty ingredients—traditional or untraditional—to create new flavors.

Computers were invented so we could use them to write and edit beer recipes, right?

Innovators by the Numbers

Here's an interesting fact that we found digging through the results: while almost all homebrewers are ale-centric, the Recipe Innovators are even more so—for the average homebrewer in this type, just 4 percent brew lagers more often! We could speculate that's because ales lend themselves to rapid experimentation and a broad base for playing with flavors, but then something interesting happens when you look at the All-Star's answer to the same question: the percentage jumps to 18 percent.

The All-Stars are much, much more likely to be playing in the lager space. It's not surprising, since the All-Stars on a whole tend to tackle lagers more frequently, but the difference really stood out with the degree of ale-ness to the average brewers. These brewers have a lot of opinions about beer styles and what they like to brew (with over one hundred different styles mentioned in their responses). However, the most popular styles should come as no surprise since they read like a super-trendy beer list!

Innovators' Most Popular Styles to Brew

1. American India pale ale
2. American pale ale
3. Saison
4. Stout
5. Porter
6. Sour
7. Brown ales
8. Belgians
9. Double IPA
10. Pilsner

All-Star Innovators' Most Popular Styles to Brew

1. American pale ale
2. Belgians (tie)
3. IPA (tie)
4. Sour (tie)
5. Experimental
6. Czech pilsner (tie)
7. German lagers (tie)
8. Porter (tie)
9. Saison (tie)
10. American wheat (tie)

- "Secondary fermenters are for chumps."
- "Yellow beer can be fantastic."
- "Conventional wisdom would have people believe that the more of a good thing the better. However, in recipe formulation I've found that using specific ingredients in moderation is not only 'better' but more palatable."
- "I'm always told weird flavors/flavor combinations in recipes don't work as well as traditional recipes, but I've made some amazing, award-winning beers with my weird flavor combinations."
- "Brew through the problems. Don't quit."
- "Creating is almost as fun as the finished product."
- "Brewing in my eyes is a wonderful collision of art and science, and if you can see both sides with equality, then you can make beautiful art."
- "Recommended ingredients: alfalfa hay with a saison, kaffir lime leaves in a kölsch, roasted figs in a Belgian winter ale, and coffee in an IPA."
- "Ingredients to avoid: honey and wormwood in a wheat beer (don't ask), oak in a west coast IPA, gefilte fish, and ghost pepper."

Choice Quotes from Innovators

We asked all of our survey respondents to provide us with some thoughts about homebrewing. Collected below are some of the best responses we received from the regular brewers. For the All-Stars, read on for their profiles! (Yes, we know some of the quotes throughout the book are contradictory, but that's what you get when it comes to homebrewers.)

Drew Beechum

Drew has been an active member of the homebrewing world for more than fifteen years. Beyond the writing bit (books and just about every homebrewing magazine, plus plenty more online), he's served as his homebrew club's president and chief cheerleader, as well as on the AHA Governing Committee. He continues to teach and spread the gospel of homebrewing. Plus, he has some really wacky weird ideas on how to brew.

BREWING SINCE: 1999

BREWING MOTTO: It sounded like a good idea at the time!

BREWING PHILOSOPHY: Keep it simple, keep it interesting.

FAVORITE BREW STYLES: Double IPA, mild, saison

FAVORITE BREWING COUNTRY: Belgium

BREWING METHODOLOGY: All-grain batch sparge

BREWING LOCATION: A stand-alone, 300-square-foot garage/workshop with a sink and hot water heater, stereo, TV, and two chest freezers and a mini-fridge on override thermostats. There might be a beer sign or two and a beer glass collection that's larger than his wife knows about.

BREWING SYSTEM: Three kettles on a homemade Unistrut stand (see 74 for more), dual-stage wort chilling, two 10-gallon corny kegs as primary fermenters with twenty-six 5-gallon kegs for secondary and draft.

HOW HE GOT STARTED: Way back in the early days of the Internet, when Drew was in college, he sat down and brewed with a few college buddies, mostly from the sidelines. Turns out "cheap" beer was hard work.

When he was twenty-five, he worked on one of those projects that you're told "makes or breaks" your career—one-hundred-hour work weeks for nine months. There were no weekends, no holidays, no nothing. His only break time was a weekly run off to his local brewpub for a couple of pints.

On his first Saturday off in ages, he sat on the couch and enjoyed a nap and a book. On Sunday, he started to do the same thing only to realize that the long work cycle had wiped out all memory of what he used to do that was fun. In fishing around for what to do, he remembered that college batch and the pressure-relief pub visits and decided to explore the hobby again.

He drove fifteen miles to his nearest homebrew shop and was immediately greeted and treated like family. That was that—from there it was a short fall to the second batch. By his sixth batch, he was doing all-grain, kegging, yeast starters—the whole nine yards.

FANCIEST PIECE OF EQUIPMENT: "Take your pick: either a digital refractometer or my pair of 10-gallon corny kegs I use as fermenters."

BREWING INSPIRATION: "I'm a sucker for a good story. Sometimes it's a story like memorializing the Gonzo spirit of Hunter S. Thompson with a barleywine that incorporates tequila, Coke, mushrooms, hemp, and poppyseeds. Other times it's trying to tell a tale of my 'farmhouse' like the Saison Guacamole, flavored with ingredients from my backyard."

FAVORITE INGREDIENTS:

- Blend of Maris Otter and American 2-row for almost every American ale. He likes this blend because it gives some of the toasty oomph of the Maris Otter while still retaining the crisp neutral edge of the 2-row for the clean presentation of hops.

- Oat malt: It's rich and self-converting. Drew says to combine it with toasted oats for a power punch of goodness.

- Magnum, Target, or Warrior hops for clean, neutral bittering. Warrior goes into the hoppy Americans whereas Target goes into anything British or Irish, and Magnum is used for everything else. This simplifies some of the hop additions and allows him to buy in bulk.

FAVORITE YEASTS:

- ECY08 Saison Brasserie: "Great complex yeast character."

- WLP585 Saison III: "Unique flavor profile and a surprise winner in a taste-off of saison yeasts."

- WLP022 Essex Ale: "Not too dry, not too sweet with enough esters to be interesting without smelling like a fruitcake."

- WY3711 French Saison: "The go-to for those hoppy Belgians. It's reliable and a monster fermentation strain. It also somehow provides extra mouthfeel while drying out. A relatively boring character for a saison yeast provides the perfect base for crazy experimentation."

- WY1275 Thames Valley: "Use this for anything English. Like the Essex, it's clean, dry, and minerally, but still distinctly English."

- WY1056 American Ale / WLP001 California Ale: "The ultimate neutral hard workers that provide a perfect base for hops and other flavors."

- Yeast Bay Vermont Ale: "Interesting cross of American ale cleanliness with a bit of that fruity English character to round out the experience."

MOST UNUSUAL INGREDIENTS:

- Just about anything in the magical buckets of flavors: homemade tinctures galore in mason jars or the jars full of oak cubes that have been soaking for about ten years.

  DENNY: I had a chance to visit Drew's brewery/ garage recently, and these tinctures were some of the coolest things around. Drew seems to make them when he gets an idea for a flavor, and then they sit until he's inspired to brew something with the flavors he's created. Very cool, very creative, and they're always ready to go.

- Avocado honey for molasses-like weirdness.

- Fenugreek makes things taste more maple-like than maple syrup.

- Clams (see 178).

Drew on Transforming Recipes

When I'm working on a new recipe, I want a reasonable shot of producing a decent beer right out of the gate. Sure, I do my research on the style and look at a few recipes not written by me, but ultimately, the one source I know I can trust is my own recipe archive. I have a few hundred recipes in the recipe bank and *something* in there is bound to be close to what I want to make. Plus, I know—or at least have notes on—how well they work for my palate and my system. How do I go from one recipe to another? It's all a matter of transformation.

Think about it this way: beer is made up of water, malt, hops, and yeast. While we find massive variations derived from these four simple ingredients, there are close similarities between different styles—close enough that a few simple tweaks can make one recipe into another.

Changing one beer recipe to another isn't a mystery when you think about it as a transformation.

DREW'S FIVE RULES FOR TRANSFORMATION

- Pay attention to location: ingredients
- Pay attention to location: water
- Practicality
- Embrace and extend (or contract)
- Pay attention to history

PAY ATTENTION TO LOCATION: INGREDIENTS

Location informs our ingredients. After all, not everything grows everywhere, and until recently you could only brew with the ingredients found locally. This explains why you see so many styles that look roughly the same, but vary by specific ingredients.

Want to change your brown ale recipe to the basis of a Munich dunkel? Start by changing all your ingredients to German. Change those malts! Switch out those distinctive earthy English hops for spicy German noble varieties. So long, Fuggles! Hello, Hallertauer! Use a German lager strain instead of an English ale strain. Voila!

PAY ATTENTION TO LOCATION: WATER

Water is insanely important. It's 90 to 95 percent of our beer, and it influences the beer's characteristics. The primary difference between a classic Bohemian pilsner and a North German pils is all about that mineral-laden German water that accentuates the hop bite. Or take the IPA: would it be nearly as assertive without the sulfate?

Pay attention to the overall quality of the water of your area. Is the water mineral laden? Is it higher in sulfate than chloride? What you want to aim for is a water profile that mimics the overall ratio of the water, not the exact numbers found in a moldering table somewhere. Need another reason to gently adjust your water? Water changes. By nudging my water, instead of trying to fit it procrustean-like to those tables, I'm not making changes so drastic they kill a beer. This means for hoppy beers, I adjust with 1 to 2 teaspoon of gypsum. For the malty beers, I use 1 to 2 teaspoons of calcium chloride instead. That's about all I do.

PRACTICALITY

One rule I live by is that if it wouldn't be practical for a commercial brewer to do it, don't do it at home. The brewers who were creating the style weren't going out of their way to do anything that wasn't absolutely necessary. For the most part, beer styles are the invention of well-fed bearded folks (a.k.a. obsessive brewers).

A simple example can be found in sacks of grain, which come in standard sizes, 50 pounds for US domestic malts and 25 kilograms (55 pounds) for imported malts. A commercial brewer is rarely going to deal with quantities lower than a half-sack because who wants to try and stash forty different partially filled bags of stuff? So most commercial recipes won't call for a million specialty malts. They're carefully selected and often move across a brewer's recipes.

EMBRACE AND EXTEND (OR CONTRACT)

American craft brewers have a reputation for amping up their beers, constantly increasing the booze and hopping levels. Look at the difference between a bitter, a pale ale, an IPA, and a double IPA. Each step of the way, what we see is a bit more malt and hop to eventually reach the heights of "wow." My suggestion for these increases, though, is not to simply multiply everything by the same factor. When you want to make a beer bigger, try increasing the base only at first and see where that gets you. Increasing the specialty malts or late addition hops tends to lead to muddier flavors. Conversely, if you want to follow the British trend of beer development, start big and go small as they did from the time of the Industrial Revolution until just a few years ago.

As an example, look at my Pliny the Toddler recipe on page 179. You can make the "Unwanted" version simply by increasing the amount of base malt and the first bittering addition.

PAY ATTENTION TO HISTORY

Just like the example of British beer strength, sometimes it pays to know your history when you want to change recipes around. There's a caveat here: the history that we know and love and have read over and over again is mostly romantic folderol. Often we're just drinking stories told by brewers to beer drinkers that contain as many plausible facts as the urban legends about albino alligators in New York City's sewer system.

For an example, look no further than Belgian golden strong. This style is the combination of two pieces of history colliding. The first is the worldwide prohibition movement. Just like the United States, at the dawn of the 1900s, much of the world was caught in alcohol prohibition fever. Belgium, reeling from the devastating onslaught of the Great War, banned the sale of spirits at bars and introduced minimum sale quantities at stores. This prohibition lasted from 1919 all the way until 1983! The second factor was the rise of the pilsner (exercise for the reader: search for the story of the creation of Westmalle's classic tripel).

With spirits banned, Belgian brewers pounced and began reversing the trend of lighter and lighter alcohol levels. They intended to replace strong booze with strong beer. Brouwerij Moortgat jumped into the fray with its "Victory Ale," brewed to celebrate the end of World War I. Later the beer earned the nickname "Devil" (or "Duvel," if you're Flemish) because of the strength. But until recent times, it was a strong Scottish-inspired beer: big, dark, and brown. With pilsner changing everyone's eye toward golden-color beers, Duvel was transformed into the new stylish devil we know today. Is it a true story? It seems to be backed up, but then again, beer drinkers and stories.

How does knowing your history help? If you combine what you know about one style and what the history was at the time of other styles, you can pretty quickly surmise that Duvel, being strong and in response to pilsners, would be pilsner-like, only bigger. Like our previous example, you'd take a pilsner recipe (100-percent pils malt, noble hops) and add some sugar (20-percent sugar) to boost the gravity and swap in appropriate yeast.

COOKIE CELEBRATION ALE

"There's only one thing I love more than homebrewing, and that's my animals. I have a small army, but my girl is the now 7-year-old Chihuahua/Corgi pup that we adopted from our local humane society. Unfortunately, in addition to her goofy little legs and spirit, she inherited a genetic disorder that paralyzed her a few months after she joined us. Thankfully, spinal surgery corrected the issue, and she's running around like a champ. In celebration of her recovery, I brewed this oatmeal brown ale infused with rum-soaked raisins."

FOR 5.5 GALLONS AT 1.077 OG, 14.8 SRM, 23 IBUs, 8.1% ABV

GRAIN BILL

12.50 lb.	Maris Otter malt
1.00 lb.	flaked oats, toasted at 350°F for 20 minutes
0.50 lb.	British crystal 55°L malt
0.50 lb.	oat malt
0.33 lb.	Dingemans Special B malt
0.12 lb.	Weyermann Carafa III Special malt

MASH

Rest   150°F   60 minutes

HOPS

0.5 oz.   Magnum   13.1% AA 60 minutes

YEAST

WY1469 Yorkshire Ale or WLP090 San Diego Super

ADDITION

0.25 lb.	raisins, soaked in spiced rum for 1 week (add at 60 minutes)
2 tsp.	powdered ginger (add at knockout)

Drew's Recipe

CLAM CHOWDAH SAISON
(pictured on page 166)

"This one started as a dare. While writing this book, Denny sent an email to our All-Stars reminding them to get their information to us. In the course of the email he threatened, 'If you don't get your answers back, Drew has threatened to brew a Manhattan Clam Chowder Saison.' Naturally, with my family heritage rooted deeply in New England, I took grave offense as tomatoes in a clam chowder is a sin against humanity. So instead I threatened to make a New England Clam Chowder Saison, but I decided to push it further by forcing Denny to brew with me. The day before we flew to a Brazilian homebrew convention, Denny, John Palmer, and I brewed a potato- and herb-infused saison with clams. Just to keep things normal, the second portion was chilled without clams and had Earl Grey tincture added to the keg." (**DENNY:** *Only Drew would call that normal!*)

FOR 5.5 GALLONS AT 1.058 OG, 4.4 SRM, 33 IBUs, 6.8% ABV

GRAIN BILL
5.0 lb.	2-row pale malt
3.5 lb.	Maris Otter malt
1.5 lb.	oat malt
1.0 lb.	wheat malt
1.0 lb.	flaked potatoes (straight potato, no butter or milk solids)

MASH
Rest   149–151°F   60 minutes

HOPS
0.60 oz.	Magnum	12.9% AA	60 minutes
0.50 oz.	US Fuggles	4.5% AA	10 minutes

YEAST
WY3711 French Saison

ADDITIONS (added after knockout during the whirlpool)
1	bay leaf
1.0 tsp.	black peppercorns (whole)
4 sprigs	thyme
8.0 oz.	clam juice (with clams)
1.0 tsp.	salt
0.5 lb.	lactose

EARL GREY ADDITION (in lieu of Chowdah Spices)
4 Earl Grey teabags (remove tea from bags)

4 oz.   vodka

1. Soak tea in vodka for one week, filter through a coffee filter. (Or use Drew's speed tincture technique found in *Experimental Homebrewing*). Add to keg to taste.

2. Chill to 63 to 65°F. Pitch, cap fermenter with foil—no airlock—and keep below 70°F for 2 to 3 days. Allow the fermenter to warm up to the high 70 to low 80°F range.

Drew's Recipe

★

PLINY THE TODDLER / PLINY THE UNWANTED

"Years before the whole 'session IPA' became a thing, I designed a beer to be called Pliny the Toddler. It was an attempt to make a lighter-weight beer in the hoppy vein of Russian River's masterful Pliny the Elder. Since Vinnie Cilurzo, owner and brewmaster of Russian River, already made Pliny the Younger, I just figured we needed to get really young. The first brew day got messed up when I added way too much pale malt to the mix, making an accidental triple IPA called Pliny the Unwanted. That beer was great, but eventually we went back and made the proper Pliny the Toddler so we could have a few without falling over sideways. In a way, this mirrors Vinnie's creation of the original Double IPA at Blind Pig in Temecula, California, where he took his IPA recipe and made it bigger because he was worried about his new brew system's efficiency. He ended up making a style that revolutionized the craft beer world!"

FOR 5.5 GALLONS AT 1.048 OG, 3.7 SRM, 56 IBUs, 4.7% ABV

GRAIN BILL

3.5 lbs	2-row pale malt
3.5 lb.	Maris Otter malt
1.0 lb.	cara-pils dextrine malt
0.5 lb.	table sugar

MASH

Rest   152°F   60 minutes

HOPS

0.75 oz.	Warrior	15.5% AA	60 minutes
0.75 oz.	Columbus	11.4% AA	10 minutes
0.75 oz.	Centennial	8.5% AA	10 minutes
0.75 oz.	Cascade	8.5%AA	0 minutes

ADDITIONS

5 grams gypsum to boil kettle

YEAST

WY1056 American Ale, WLP001 California Ale, or Fermentis Safale US-05

VARIANT

Pliny the Unwanted Triple IPA: increase both Maris Otter and 2-row pale malt to 7.25 lbs. each. Increase the first Warrior addition to 1.5 oz.

Jeff Gladish

Plenty of homebrewers win awards, but not many brewers can do so both for clean, classic lagers and for spiced or smoked ales. Jeff came in second in the Pilsner Urquell "clone" competition sponsored by the brewery, and his recipe for Poblano Wit, brewed as a collaboration with Cigar City Brewing in Tampa, Florida, took first place in the 2013 GABF ProAm competition. He also took a gold medal at the National Homebrew Competition for a smoked porter and a bronze for smoked braggot. Jeff is also great about sharing his knowledge and experience online, in the AHA discussion forum and elsewhere.

BREWING SINCE: 1990

BREWING MOTTO: Stay calm. It's only beer.

BREWING PHILOSOPHY: Pay attention to the whole picture and don't sweat the small stuff.

FAVORITE BREW STYLES: Rye IPA, smoked beer, pepper beer, German pils, classic American pilsner

FAVORITE BREWING COUNTRY: Germany

BREWING METHODOLOGY AND SYSTEM: Jeff brews all-grain, single-infusion batches. He brews on an "antique" Sabco rig that he's modified a bit. After selecting a style to brew, he researches the recipe. "I research by buying commercial examples of the beer, read winning recipes in *Brewing Classic Styles* or the link to gold medal-winners at NHC or ask the brewer. Then I modify that to the ingredients I feel would be best and plug it all into Beer Smith for percentages." He selects his ingredients and preps his water the night before brew day. On the day of the brew, he mills his malt as the water heats to mash temperature. He usually does a 60-minute mash, recirculating with a pump for most of that time. After a mash out, he sparges for an hour onto his first wort hops. He boils for at least an hour, then uses recirculated chilling to cool the wort before oxygenating with an O_2 system.

BREWING LOCATION: Outdoors on the patio

HOW HE GOT STARTED: "I've always loved beer, especially local stuff wherever I've been. A friend from England gave me a kit [Dogbolter Bitter] in 1990, and soon I was trying to make all-grain beer."

FANCIEST PIECE OF EQUIPMENT: His antique Sabco system

FAVORITE INGREDIENTS: Jeff likes to use Weyermann pilsner malt because he feels it adds a tart flavor to his beers that he can't get with other malts. He even uses it in his American IPA recipes. He also uses Weyermann Munich II malt, saying "any beer is better with a little Munich malt." He's a big fan of Amarillo hops and says he loves the aroma he gets from them.

FAVORITE YEASTS: For lagers, Jeff prefers WY2206 Bavarian Lager or WY2308 Munich Lager. He says he's had great luck with them because they make the beer turn out so well. Fermentis Safale US-05 is "easy and very clean." He uses WY3944 Belgian Witbier for witbier because "it's nicer than the other brands, in my humble opinion—less fruity, less saison-y, more witbier-y."

MOST UNUSUAL INGREDIENTS: Jeff's most unusual ingredient is the smoked malt he makes in his smoker. His home-smoked malt was used in Swamp Head Brewing's (Gainesville, Florida) Smoke Signal, which took gold medal for smoked beers at the 2014 World Beer Cup.

Cold Smoking Malt

Jeff has made some tasty and award-winning smoked beers, and one of the best things about them (other than they're delicious!) is that he makes them with malt created with his own two hands on his homemade smoking system. It makes Denny's "Cheap 'n' Easy" sensibilities dance like Drew when he's had too many barleywines.

DREW: Actually, I prefer to get silly on saison.

Jeff uses a cold-smoke system; he notes that he's even used it to smoke cheese. Here's his description of the system and how it works.

"My system uses cold smoke because I don't want to change the character of the grains by smoking them over a heat source. Hot smoke may be fine for a porter or another dark or roasty style, but for lighter or more delicate styles, cold is the way to go. When using cold smoke, there is no need to rest the malt for a week to off-gas any chemicals that may come by using hot smoke. In fact, I recommend using the malt right away.

"The box you see at right contains several 1.5-inch-deep sliding shelves with bottoms made from aluminum window screening. Once the shelves are filled with grain, the front is closed and duct taped shut to prevent the smoke from escaping out the sides. The object is to have

the smoke flow from the bottom, up through the grain in all the shelves, and out the top. Each tray holds about 7 pounds of malt, so when full, it can smoke a whole sack. Obviously, you could create the same thing on a smaller scale, though."

Check out Jeff's homemade malt smoker in action. *Photos courtesy of Jeff Gladish*

Where there's smoke, there's smoked malt. *Photo courtesy of Jeff Gladish*

"For smoke, I use a kettle-style grill with a lid modified to accept a section of 4-inch-diameter, flexible aluminum dryer ducting. I place the grill about 16 feet from the smoker box and keep the section closest to the grill slightly elevated to keep the flow of smoke constant. The temperature inside the box is never much more than 5 or 10 degrees above ambient.

"I smoke the malt both dry and whole before crushing —although the malt may pick up slightly more smoke flavor if each tray is spritzed with some distilled water. If I go that route, I make sure to use the malt as soon as possible to avoid mold growth.

"I use citrus wood often because I have a ready supply in my backyard. It lends a smoke flavor similar to beechwood with a slight citrus note. Other woods that make great smoke are oak, birch, apple, pecan, valder, and peach. I avoid strong-flavored smoke such as mesquite.

"One package of chips purchased at the barbeque or hardware store is about 200 cubic inches or 3 quarts. This is enough to produce smoke for about an hour, adding wet chips onto the coals a handful at a time.

I have made beers using 100-percent smoked malt, but most people find this a bit overly aggressive, to put it politely. Twenty percent may be sufficient to make a smoky beer without overpowering the base style. Although any grain can be smoked this way, I tend to use either base malts like 2-row or pilsner or Munich malt. My latest smoked beer was a lager made with 100-percent pecan- and citrus-smoked Munich malt. It was delicious."

POBLANO WIT

This beer has won multiple awards and state competitions, but the most impressive was when Jeff teamed up with Tampa Bay's Cigar City Brewing Company and won the Great American Beer Festival's Pro-Am Competition with this beer. It brings enough heat to let you know something's up, but it's the poblano that shines through. If you hate chile beers, you really need to give this a try before writing them off completely.

FOR 5 GALLONS AT 1.074 OG, 2.8 SRM, 22 IBUs, 8.2% ABV

GRAIN BILL
6.0 lb.   Rahr white wheat malt
6.0 lb.   Weyermann Pilsner malt
1.5 lb.   rolled oats

MASH
Cereal mash: wheat, oats, 1.5 lbs. of pils with 13.5 quarts of water at 150°F for 20 minutes.

Main mash: Strike 4.5 lbs. pils with 6.75 quarts of water to rest at 148°F.

Cereal boil: Bring the cereal mash to a boil for 20 minutes, stirring constantly.

Main mash: Add the boiled cereal portion to the main mash to rest about 156°F for 60 minutes.

Mash out: Raise to 168°F for 10 minutes and sparge.

HOPS
2.7 oz. Cascade   5.5% AA   60 minutes

YEAST
WY3944 Belgian Witbier

ADDITION
1.00 oz. Indian coriander seed: flame-out

0.75 oz. fresh orange peel: flame-out

0.50 oz. chamomile: flame-out

3 poblano peppers, roasted, seeded, and peeled: added to secondary or keg

0.50 habanero pepper, roasted, seeded, and peeled: added to secondary or keg

NOTES
Pasteurize the peppers in the oven for 20 minutes at 200°F.

Chill to 64°F and pitch yeast.

Ferment at 64 to 68°F until complete.

Either rack the beer to a secondary and add the peppers for 3 days, or keg the beer and add them to the keg.

NOT CRAIG'S SMOKED PORTER

Home-smoked malt is a heck of a thing, but you don't need to jury rig a cold smoker like Jeff's to take advantage of his recipe. Look around, and you'll find a couple of varieties of smoked malt that are available, but seriously, if you're taking the time to brew a beer, find a way to smoke your malt! If you can only hot smoke it, make sure to give it a few weeks to off-gas first, and use less in the recipe.

FOR 5 GALLONS AT 1.070 OG, 30 SRM, 44 IBUs, 7.1% ABV

GRAIN BILL
10.00 lb. Rahr 2-row pale malt, home cold-smoked (see page 181 for process)
1.25 lb. Weyermann Munich II malt
0.75 lb. chocolate malt
0.66 lb. crystal 60°L malt
0.25 lb. black patent malt

MASH
Rest   153°F   60 minutes
Mash out 168°F
Note: Collect 5.5 gallons of wort.

HOPS
0.25 oz.	Magnum	14.0% AA	First wort hop
1 oz.	Willamette	5.0% AA	120 minutes
1 oz.	Styrian Goldings	3.2% AA	30 minutes
0.5 oz.	Amarillo	8.5% AA	10 minutes

YEAST
WY1968 London ESB

NOTES
Chill to 64°F and pitch yeast. Ferment at 64 to 68°F.

BREWER'S PROFILE

Mike "Tasty" McDole

Tasty is known as the creator of some incredible homebrew recipes. Not only have his beers been brewed by thousands of homebrewers, but they've also been made by some of the finest craft breweries in America. The version of his Janet's Brown Ale recipe brewed by Russian River has become legendary. In addition, he's possibly the grumpiest of the hosts on The Brewing Network podcast, where he regularly dispenses wisdom while enduring jokes about his impending death.

Denny: Hey, Mike, that was Drew's comment!

Drew: Can't argue with the truth!

BREWING SINCE: 1993

BREWING MOTTO: It's not tasty until Tasty says it is.

BREWING PHILOSOPHY: Keep your process as similar to commercial processes as reasonably possible.

FAVORITE BREW STYLES: Tasty is a fan of American styles like APA, IPA, and brown ale. He's also developed a love of American-style session beers.

FAVORITE BREWING COUNTRY: America

BREWING METHODOLOGY AND SYSTEM: Tasty brews all-grain fly sparge and uses a multi-step mash. He brews 10-gallon batches using a system with a 26-gallon kettle and hot liquor tank. He has three separate burners to power his brew day. He fills the hot liquor tank with reverse osmosis (RO) water and adds water treatments appropriate to the style he's brewing.

During the mash, he strikes with 9 gallons for every brew, regardless of grist, and uses a direct-fired RIMS to maintain mash temperatures. He sparges for forty-five minutes, measures his preboil gravity, and adjusts either by diluting or adding dry malt extract if necessary.

He boils for ninety minutes and takes a gravity reading fifteen minutes before his anticipated flame out. At that point, before adding finishing hops, he'll make adjustments by either diluting or extending his boil. At flameout, he whirlpools for ten minutes, then lets the wort rest for twenty minutes to form a "trub cone" in the center of his kettle.

He chills to 2 degrees below his intended fermentation temperature, then pitches the yeast and aerates for ninety seconds with an O_2 system. Mike lets the temperature free-rise after five days. He dry hops for three days, then racks to a keg, fines with gelatin, and carbonates the keg.

BREWING LOCATION: Outside on the deck

HOW HE GOT STARTED: Tasty started enjoying craft beers. Being a DIY kind of guy, he decided to DIH (Do It Himself).

FANCIEST PIECE OF EQUIPMENT: His custom-made mash tun.

FAVORITE INGREDIENTS: Tasty prefers Rahr 2-row pale malt over other domestic malts like Great Western. He feels like Rahr makes more of a "statement" in his beer flavor, which he says is important as he makes smaller beers. In his lighter session beers, he uses a significant portion of Maris Otter along with the Rahr pale malt to bump up the malt flavor.

He's also a big fan of English crystal malts, particularly those from Crisp. Again, he says it's a case of how much flavor they add to his smaller beers. He also uses Weyermann Carapils and other cara malts and likes Castle Pils malt.

Mike says that he's so focused on malt flavors that he really doesn't fuss with hops too much. He says that he buys fairly large amounts of Cascade, Centennial, and Warrior hops at the beginning of his brewing season and pretty much builds his recipes using them. He's familiar with what they add to his beers, so he can concentrate on the other flavors in the beer.

DENNY: I admire Mike's swimming upstream on this point. I feel the same way, but it's remarkable how many homebrewers follow a silly "rule" about the percentage of crystal malt you're "allowed" to use. The most recent example of that is a "session" triple IPA. He uses 18-percent cara malts and shoots for 100 IBU.

DREW: I tend to like rules as guidelines and not strictures, and the rule about crystal is a good example of saying, "You know, until you know what the heck you're doing, how about not going overboard?"

MOST INTERESTING DISCOVERY ABOUT HOMEBREWING: A low finishing gravity isn't always desired. Also, just how much fun he has hanging out with other homebrewers.

FAVORITE YEASTS: WY1056 American Ale or any neutral yeast that lets the malt and hops shine through.

HIS ADVICE TO NEW BREWERS: More than anything else, get a handle on your fermentation temperature control.

Fast Lagers

One piece of valuable knowledge that's not widely disseminated is Tasty's fast lager schedule. Tradition dictates that when we talk of lagers, we talk of long, slow, cold ferments and aging that brings about smooth, crisp, refreshing characters. Drew used to brew an Oktoberfest beer each year in March and lager it all through the summer before tapping for an annual O'Fest party. After all, that's what they used to do back in the day!

A quicker fermentation schedule for lagers has been kicking around for a long time, most notably in the book *Abriss der Bierbrauerei* by Ludwig Narziss. It's the holy grail of the global pilsner industry. Mike has played with and refined what he considers the perfect fast lager schedule for us homebrewers. It may seem radical or even impossible when you first read about it, but the technique has produced delicious and award-winning lagers for many homebrewers.

Here's how Mike describes it: "I pitch and oxygenate at 55°F and hold until the gravity drops 50 percent of the way to terminal gravity. For example, if my OG is 1.052, and I expect to finish at about 1.010, then a drop of 21 gravity points would be 50 percent."

The math works like this:
Original Gravity (OG) = 1.052 or 52 points
Final Gravity (FG) = 1.010 or 10 points
Total Gravity Drop (TGD) = OG – FG = 52 - 10 = 42

Mike is watching for a 50 percent gravity drop or 21 points (42 divided by 2) for this hypothetical lager. In other words, when the beer reaches 1.031 (52 minus 21), it's time to move onto the next step.

Mike continues: "I then raise the fermentation temperature by 3 degrees to 58°F and hold until the gravity drops 75 percent of the way to terminal gravity."

For our example beer, the ferment at 58°F would continue until it reaches 1.020 to 1.021. We arrive at that figure by calculating our total gravity drop × 0.75 and subtracting that from the original gravity or:

Target gravity = OG – (TGD × 0.75)
Target gravity = 52 – (42 × 0.75)
Target gravity = 52 – 31.5
Target gravity = 20.5

Onto the next step with Mike: "I then raise the fermentation temperature by 4 degrees to 62°F and hold until the gravity drops 90 percent of the way to terminal gravity."

Target gravity = 52 – (42 × 0.9)
Target gravity = 52 – 37.8
Target gravity = 14.2
So, hold at 62°F until about 1.014.

Finally to the finish line: "I then raise the fermentation temperature by 4 degrees to 66°F and hold until I reach terminal gravity.

"With this method, 75 percent of the fermentation takes place at 58°F or below, 90 percent at 62°F or below.

"In my experience, the first part (50 percent gravity drop) can be as short as four to five days. The important thing is to check the gravity—no guessing! A high gravity lager will take longer to reach this point than an 'average' 1.045 to 1.055 OG lager.

"But the most amazing part of this technique is that a lager can be in your glass in as little as two weeks after brewing it. No guarantees, of course, since it depends on your beer, but it's proof that you don't need months to make a great lager."

THE TASTY FAST LAGER SCHEDULE IN LIST FORMAT
Calculate your total gravity drop based on original gravity and yeast strain choice (75 to 80 percent is usual).
1. Chill the wort to 55°F and pitch the yeast
2. When the ferment is 50 percent complete, raise temperature to 58°F.
3. When the ferment is 75 percent complete, raise to 62°F.
4. When the ferment is 90 percent, complete, raise to 66°F and hold until at terminal gravity.

If you look around, you'll see some alternative fast lager ideas floating around there. Another of our All-Stars (and star of many of our photos), Marshall Schott (page 94) has a hybrid method that incorporates a traditional lager cold crash. Instead of Mike's gravity-based checkpoints, Marshall waits for the beer to hit 50 percent attenuation and then ramps the temperature a steady five degrees every twelve hours until he reaches 65 to 68°F. Once the beer is stable and without diacetyl (butter) or acetaldehyde (green apple), Marshall chills the beer 5 to 8 degrees every twelve hours until it reaches 32°F. Once there, he lets it hang for two to three days to clarify.

Water Profiles

In the face of so many lessons about the importance of nailing your water profiles precisely, Mike has a very simplified approach with two primary water treatment approaches. His classic that he uses for almost every beer (easy to do when most of your beers are hoppy) is as follows:

HOPPY BEER WATER TARGET PROFILE

CALCIUM (CA)	MAGNESIUM (MG)	SODIUM (NA)	SULFATE (SO$_4$)	CHLORIDE (CL)
110 PPM	18 PPM	17 PPM	350 PPM	50 PPM

Tasty gets there by calculated additions of gypsum ($CaSO_4$), Epsom salt ($MgSO_4$), salt (NaCl) and calcium chloride ($CaCl_2$). We're not giving you addition amounts because the amounts would depend on your base water profile. You'll notice with this water that it's really geared toward hoppy beers. Why? Look at those last two columns: sulfate and chloride. The accepted general belief states that sulfate boosts hop character (dryness) and chloride boosts malt character. By boosting the overall sulfate in relation to the chloride (7:1, in this case), you drive a brisker hop character.

"OTHER" BEER WATER TARGET PROFILE

CALCIUM (CA)	MAGNESIUM (MG)	SODIUM (NA)	SULFATE (SO$_4$)	CHLORIDE (CL)
75 PPM	12 PPM	35 PPM	120 PPM	100 PPM

Now compare that to his "other" beer water profile that he developed while brewing for the challenges on "Can You Brew It." You'll notice that this water profile is far more balanced in terms of the sulfate and chloride, providing for a happy medium between malt and hop characters.

Gypsum, Epsom salt, calcium chloride, and salt are all you need for this simplified approach to water adjustment.

Tasty's Recipes

★

TASTY'S DORTMUNDER

(pictured at right)

This is Tasty's standard lager recipe—clean, simple, and ready to go in short order. He's won plenty of accolades for it. He'll win even more when he doctors it with a little fruit extract which makes it the perfect "I Don't Like Beer" beer. Try this with his fast lager fermentation schedule and see how little work it takes to always have a lager on hand

FOR 6 GALLONS AT 1.050 OG, 5 SRM, 23 IBUs, 5% ABV, 90-MINUTE BOIL

GRAIN BILL

6.00 lb.	pilsner malt
2.00 lb.	2-row pale malt
2.00 lb.	Munich 10°L malt
2.00 lb.	flaked wheat
1.00 lb.	cara-pils dextrine malt

MASH

Rest	143°F	10 minutes
Saccharification rest	151°F	30 minutes
Mash out	170°F	15 minutes
Sparge	170°F	45 minutes

HOPS

0.75 oz.	Santiam	6% AA	60 minutes
2.00 oz.	Hallertauer	4% AA	Hop back

YEAST

WLP833 German Bock Lager

NOTES

See page 187 for Tasty's recommended fast lager schedule.

JANET'S BROWN

The American brown ale seems to be heading for a renaissance, and Janet's Brown is a good example of why it's deserved. There's a ton of sweet, crackery, toasty notes that can fully support the bombastic American hop character. Note that Tasty is using nothing but old-school American hops—none of these new-fangled tropical hops for him. Want the commercial version? Head to Russian River in the fall and who knows: you'll probably run into Tasty himself.

FOR 6 GALLONS AT 1.066 OG, 19.3 SRM, 63 IBUs, 7.35% ABV, 90-MINUTE BOIL

GRAIN BILL

12.00 lb.	2-row pale malt
1.25 lb.	cara-pils dextrine malt
1.25 lb.	American crystal 40°L malt
1.00 lb.	American wheat malt
0.50 lb.	American chocolate malt

MASH

Saccharification rest	154°F	30 minutes
Mash out	165°F	15 minutes
Sparge	170°F	45 minutes

HOPS

1.00 oz.	Northern Brewer	6.5% AA	Mash hops
1.25 oz.	Northern Brewer	6.5% AA	60 minutes
1.00 oz.	Northern Brewer	6.5% AA	15 minutes
1.50 oz.	Cascade	6.0% AA	10 minutes
1.50 oz.	Cascade	6.0% AA	0 minutes
2.00 oz.	Centennial	9.0% AA	Dry hop

YEAST

WLP001 California Ale

WATER

See page 188 for Tasty's hoppy water profile.

BREWER'S PROFILE

Roxanne Westendorf

Roxanne is extremely active in her homebrew club, the Bloatarian Brewing League of Cincinnati, Ohio. She is also chair of the AHA's Governing Committee where one of her primary efforts has been increasing the diversity of brewers in the homebrewing world. She works at Rivertown Brewery in Cincinnati as ExBEERience Architect and Beer Evangelist—she says that means she works in the taproom, on tours, and on the educational programming. Together with her husband, Rob, she also brews small batches for the brewery.

BREWING SINCE: 1994

BREWING MOTTO: Ja-eeep (it's a Bloatarian thing!)

BREWING PHILOSOPHY: Because I can.

FAVORITE BREW STYLES: Belgian styles (almost any); culinary-inspired beers

FAVORITE BREWING COUNTRY: Belgium

BREWING METHODOLOGY AND SYSTEM: Roxanne brews primarily 5-gallon, all-grain, fly-sparged batches in a basement walkout, although she has brewed some of her beers in commercial breweries. She uses a natural gas double burner, converted kegs as kettles, and a Blichmann mash tun. She chills using a Chillzilla counterflow chiller.

HOW SHE GOT STARTED: Roxanne's husband, Rob, is also a homebrewer. She says, "My brother got us a homebrew kit for Christmas in 1994. New Year's weekend we brewed our first batch and haven't looked back."

> **DENNY:** It's interesting how many times the phrase "never looked back" shows up when you talk to homebrewers about how they got started.

> **DREW:** It's almost like we're all on the run from something!

FANCIEST PIECE OF EQUIPMENT: Blichmann mash tun

FAVORITE YEASTS: Roxanne's favorite yeast is the Westmalle strain (WY3787 Trappist High Gravity or WLP530 Abbey Ale). She likes it because it was the yeast in her "gateway beer," Westmalle Dubbel. When she and her husband were just starting to explore beer, they went to a bar where Roxanne ordered it because she thought the name was interesting. Her beer journey had begun! Other favorites include:

- Ardennes yeast (WY3522 Belgian Ardennes or WLP550 Belgian Ale): "During our first trip to Belgium, Rob asked one of the brewers, 'If you were starting from scratch, how would you pick your yeast?' I think the brewer was Karol Goddeau from Schlagmulder/Witkap, and DeCam. He said he'd look at his brewery's water profile and pick a yeast from a brewery with similar water. We happen to have water very similar to the Ardennes region. And we happen to love Belgian beers."

- WLP090 San Diego Super: Roxanne says you can ferment this yeast cool for clean lagers and warmer for ales. "It's also a great workhorse yeast. Yeast flavor is set somewhere in the first seventy-two hours—that's less than one week of fermentation. Many Belgian yeasts don't like to have their temperature drop, but it happens in the basement sometimes despite our best efforts, and the fermentation stops. This yeast works great to finish off a fermentation while leaving the base yeast flavor profile intact."

Roxanne: A Culinary Approach to Beer

I generally brew thinking about complementary flavors and aromas since it fits with my culinary style. I have an Italian background, and our family has a style of cooking called "schway schway." It essentially translates into finding what I have around that can be combined into a meal.

> DREW: Roxanne refers to "complementary" flavors. In the world of food and beverage there are the "Cs". While there are many variants, the common Cs are "cut," "complement," and "contrast." When you choose a flavor pairing (like beer and a course, or beer and a spice), you can think of the impact by whether it "cuts" through a richness or fattiness; "complements" and emphasizes common flavors; or "contrasts" by presenting the opposite tone and note (e.g., sweet and sour).

When it comes to using non-traditional ingredients in beer, my approach varies based on the inspiration. Generally I'll start with a Belgian style, but it could be a brown pale ale or bock depending on the inspiration. For example, if a yeast produces peppery or spicy phenolics, then build on them. The same goes for citrus flavors.

As far as drawing inspiration, Rob and I go to a lot of beer dinners and see a ton of pairings. Of course, there are also books—both brewing books (specifically Randy and Stan's books) and my collection of over 500 cookbooks. Inspiration also can strike in the real world, when I'm out and not necessarily thinking of beer. For example, Rob and I are headed to Spain soon. My goal there is to come back with a good sangria recipe, a good gazpacho recipe, and cool ideas for beer. But, hmm—what about sangria beer or a beer with a gazpacho influence? (Oh my, Rob will think I'm nuts if I try a tomato beer, but I just might.)

Here are a few notes I've made over the years on various ingredients:

SEASONAL SPICES: Beers can be more refreshing—and more appropriate year-round—when using savory spices. Some of these spices don't always taste or smell like we think they do. Mustard seed is very different than prepared mustard, for example. Some spices will add citrus and/or spicy notes. I usually eliminate aroma hops when using spices (unless I'm complementing hop aroma) and sometimes will eliminate flavor hops if I want the spice/herb flavor to be more noticeable.

MAPLE SYRUP: I played around with maple syrup one day after I won a gallon in a raffle. I fermented it like I would honey with nothing else added. It was clean and slightly sweet to start but bland. Six months later, it went kind of soy-like, and three years out, it was like Amaretto! I blended it into some meads and found some extraordinary flavor blends (especially with buckwheat mead).

> DREW: Technically, fermented maple syrup or sap (with or without added water) is a maple wine. Add in honey, and you've created an Acergyln (or maple mead).

Roxanne uses a variety of sugars and syrups for interesting flavors.

SUGARS: Maple was the start of an exploration of other sugars. A bunch of us in the Bloatarian Brewing League have done a lot with agave nectar and have a 100-percent "mead" made from that. We came into several drums of agave nectar recently, so everyone in the region is playing with it. Having the 100-percent fermentation helped people understand the flavors that agave would bring to a mead or beer.

The other notable sugars I've used are molasses and date palm sugar. The date palm sugar had a horrible aroma but it vented off within a few minutes of opening the bottle. The flavor was sublime. I think we sometimes take sugar for granted (or think of it poorly as just a way to increase alcohol and dryness versus thinking about the flavors it has on its own).

SMOKE: Most people just buy smoked malts. At a friend's recommendation, I smoked my malt for my Rauchbier. I was amazed at how much fresher and cleaner my malt smelled compared to commercial malts. (I've found that Bamberg malts can be very inconsistent.) Plus, nearly all commercially smoked malts are pale malt–based. I smoked Munich malt over cherry wood. And, of course, I smoke my homemade cheese too (mmm . . . Gouda smoked over orange wood).

DREW: Roxanne brings her cheeses to the governing committee meeting every year. They're another fine example of the fermentation arts.

ODD FRUIT: We have two native paw paw trees in our yard. We got them as sticks from the county extension service after we built our house. One day I finally noticed fruit on them hidden under the leaves. So began the paw paw saison.

Unfortunately, paw paws have *no* shelf life. You can't pick them early; they have to start ripening on the tree, are ripe in less than a week, and rotten within a week after that. So the key is to pick, peel, pulp, seed, and freeze until all are harvested. They also have a ton of papain enzyme, which means the skin on your hands will be a disaster unless you wear gloves. Anyway, I have added the pulp to the secondary for wondrous flavors. If you know what paw paw tastes like, you know it's there, but it's not a sweet, limited fruit beer. The paw paws are complex.

DREW: If you don't know the paw paw, it's the largest edible fruit indigenous to the United States. The custardy fruit is sometimes called a prairie banana and tastes like a cross of banana and melons. Papain is a protease enzyme which attacks and helps digest meat. It's commonly found in a number of fruits, especially its namesake papaya. Powdered papain is sold as meat tenderizer, which is why it can do a number on hands.

Roxanne's Recipe

CAPTAIN MAVERICK'S FLYER

This is Roxanne's beery take on the flavor trend of blending good dark chocolate with caramel and sea salt. She says, "The cocoa husks and nibs came from Maverick Chocolates, located in Findley Market in Cincinnati. An earlier test batch had used Maverick's husks but generic nibs. Use the good stuff; it makes a big difference. If you have a local craft chocolate maker, you can probably get the husks from them as they are essentially a waste product for someone who starts with the cocoa beans."

FOR 6 GALLONS AT 1.068 OG, 25 IBUs, 7% ABV

GRAIN BILL

8.5 lb.	2-row pale malt
1.8 lb.	crystal 80°L malt
1.5 lb.	flaked oats
1.5 lb.	cocoa husks
0.5 lb.	roasted barley
0.6 lb.	chocolate malt

MASH

Rest 150°F 60 minutes (do not mash the roasted barley and chocolate; add them before a 170°F sparge).

HOPS

0.9 oz. Perle 8% AA 60 minutes

YEAST

WLP090 San Diego Super

WATER

Filter and adjust pH as needed. (Roxanne doesn't adjust the water further, but she has fairly hard water; if your water is low on calcium and carbonates, adjust with calcium carbonate salt.)

ADDITION

0.5 lb.	caramelized sugar (see below) for 60-minute boil
3.0 oz.	cocoa nibs for 5-minute boil
12.0 grams	pink Himalayan sea salt for 5-minute boil

NOTES

Add sugar in boil to dissolve.

Add cocoa nibs and salt in the last 5 minutes of boil.

CARAMELIZED SUGAR:

1 lb. cane sugar

¼ cup water

¼ tsp. lemon juice

Boil without stirring until caramelized. Don't leave it: Once it starts caramelizing, it can go from caramel to burnt very quickly. Pour onto a parchment-lined tray (with sides) to cool. Break up before adding to the boil.

SNAKE IN THE GRASS
BASIL LEMONGRASS BELGIAN BLONDE

More thinking like a foodie: Here's Roxanne's travel-inspired beer that combines the minty, licorice, herbal hit of basil with the bright, zesty, lemon pop of lemongrass. Both combine with the spicy phenolics of the Belgian yeast to give a complex mix of palate sensations. Use it as an inspiration for your own combinations.

FOR 5 GALLONS AT 1.062 OG, 1.008 FG, 24 IBUs, 7.1% ABV

GRAIN BILL

9.75 lb.   pilsner malt

0.50 lb.   Munich 10°L malt

0.25 lb.   abbey/aromatic malt

1.00 lb.   table sugar (15 minutes before end of boil)

MASH

Rest   147°F   90 minutes

HOPS

0.8 oz.   Perle   8% AA   60 minutes

YEAST

WLP550 Belgian Ale

WATER

Filter and adjust pH as needed (Roxanne doesn't adjust the water further, but she has fairly hard water.)

ADDITION

6.00 oz. fresh lemongrass after trimming (trimmed, outer layers removed and chopped)
10 minutes before end of boil

1.25 oz. fresh basil (leaves only, no stems) at knockout/whirlpool

NOTES

Ferment at ambient temperature and allow to free rise.

Gordon Strong

Gordon is a three-time (in a row!) winner of the Ninkasi Award, given for scoring the most points in the first round of the National Homebrew Competition. He is also the recipient of the American Homebrewers Association Governing Committee Recognition Award, given for exceptional service to homebrewers. (It's kinda like a lifetime achievement award.) He is the author of the books *Brewing Better Beer* and *Modern Homebrew Recipes*, which outline his brewing philosophy and recipes. Gordon is also the president of the BJCP (Beer Judge Certification Program) and the principal author of the BJCP Style Guidelines.

★

BREWING SINCE: 1996

BREWING MOTTO: Brew better beer.

BREWING PHILOSOPHY: Brew like a Jedi Master. These are not the water salts you're looking for.

FAVORITE BREW STYLES: Almost anything that doesn't involve sour, smoke, or wood.

FAVORITE BREWING COUNTRY: Belgium

BREWING METHODOLOGY: Gordon brews all-grain and fly sparges. He normally employs a multi-step mash. He uses reverse osmosis (RO) water and adjusts the pH to 5.5. He mashes his base malts with some $CaCl_2$ (calcium chloride) added to the mash and uses a thin mash. Crystal and dark grains get added during the vorlauf and/or mash out.

He does a twenty-minute whirlpool stand after boiling and may or may not add hops then, depending on the recipe. He's discovered that bitterness from whirlpool additions don't work for him the way conventional wisdom says it does. Instead of 0 IBUs, he calculates an effect similar the addition being boiled for twenty minutes.

After the whirlpool, he uses a counterflow chiller, and then allows the sediment to settle out of the wort before racking to a fermenter. He oxygenates the wort before pitching yeast.

Gordon has developed a process that he enjoys and that produces great results, but he realizes that it may not be for everyone. "There are more ways to brew than you can imagine, so don't believe anyone who tells you there is only one way you can do things. Never stop learning and improving. There's always more you can learn. It's up to you to decide what you include in your own process. Life's too short to brew like someone else—make your own decisions."

BREWING LOCATION: "The shed in the backyard where I store my equipment (and yard stuff) is built on a concrete slab that has a little 'patio' out front. I set up there."

BREWING SYSTEM: "I use a three-vessel, half-barrel system from Pico Brewing in Ypsilanti, Michigan, from the late

'90s, modified a bit. I also use a Phil Mill with a 5-gallon hopper and a Blichmann Therminator chiller that I won—and, of course, various other crap that does the right thing at the right time."

HOW HE GOT STARTED: Gordon didn't discover craft beer until he was out of college. He wasn't even really a beer fan at that point. But two friends introduced him to various beer styles and how to appreciate the flavors. A few years later, he tried some of their homebrew and loved it. He decided to give it a go himself. It's safe to say it worked out for him.

FANCIEST PIECE OF EQUIPMENT: Walk-in cooler

FAVORITE INGREDIENTS: Gordon likes to use German dark Munich malt because he gets a deep malt flavor from it without any roast or biscuit notes. He says that if you use all light Munich malt and still don't get enough malt presence in your beer, using dark Munich or aromatic malt will boost the malt flavor. It's a good accent malt to give more depth and complexity, "especially when trying to simulate the lightly oxidized Maillard flavors found in darker, malty German import beers. My Belgian dubbel recipe just isn't the same without it, but I also use it in most non-pale German styles."

Gordon says that English brown malt gives him "kind of a deep nutty-toasty flavor that's much richer and less dry-dusty than biscuit malt. It's an unmistakable flavor in London-type porters. It has a darker flavor, almost hinting at chocolate but with a much stronger nutty flavor. It's strange; if I use it in English styles like mild or brown ale in almost any quantity, my head keeps telling me it tastes like a porter."

Amarillo was the first non-citrusy or resiny hop that Gordon used. He says that getting the clean, bright, stone-fruit flavor (apricots, mostly) without the citrusy-resiny and dank qualities is the reason. It's still one of his favorites, particularly paired with Simcoe. (That's also one of Denny's favorite pairings.)

Gordon lists RO water as one of his most important ingredients. He says that he hates harsh beers and much

of that harshness comes from water. By using RO water, he's able to avoid that harshness that comes from using his heavily carbonated tap water. He likes the clean flavors he gets with only minimal water salt additions. It has simplified his brewing process and improved the flavor of his finished beers. In other words, don't go crazy with the water salts.

Gordon likes to use honey in his beers in place of sugar. "It's a signature ingredient of mine in pale hoppy beers. When using good quality varietal honeys, it also allows for added flavor complexity, such as when I use orange blossom honey to boost floral aromatics. Pairing honey variety with the flavor and aroma components of hops, malt, and yeast is an interesting exercise, and it often leads to a more complex and interesting beer."

FAVORITE YEASTS: Gordon has several favorite yeasts, depending on the beer style he's brewing. We'll let him tell you about them.

- **WY1968 London ESB Ale:** "My favorite cask yeast, this one flocs very well. It's fruity and clean, and can be successfully used in English and American styles. Fermented cool, it behaves more like an American yeast with a clean profile. Fermented warmer, more fruit emerges. Either way, it tends to favor malty beers. It can leave some residual sweetness, so be careful using it in styles where they must be highly attenuated."

- **WY1272 American Ale II:** "My favorite American yeast strain and it's my go-to IPA choice. I think it has a little more character than the more common Chico yeast, especially as it adds a little fruitiness. I like how it works in malty styles, and it's more attenuative than WY1968 London ESB Ale, but I use it in much the same way."

- **WY1335 British Ale II:** "This yeast has become my new favorite all-around English strain, as it seems very balanced. Many English yeasts tend to favor one specific flavor (malty, dry, minerally, fruity, etc.), but this one has aspects of all of them. So it adds complexity but in a relatively unobtrusive way."

- **WY2124 Bohemian Lager:** "One of my favorite lager strains; this one is very clean and malty. It has a more neutral fermentation profile than WLP833 German Bock Lager. It attenuates well, but doesn't go overboard, allowing malt flavors to remain. It's stable during lagering."

- **WY3787 Trappist High Gravity:** "My first choice for Belgian yeasts, particularly when I want a classic Trappist-type fermentation profile. It's spicy, peppery, phenolic, with balanced fruit and quite complex. It attenuates very well. The fruit character changes with fermentation temperature. It can be a little picky about fermentation, as it likes a rising temperature to completely finish. It works equally well in pale and dark beers, malty and hoppy, and of varying alcohol levels. It's capable of fermenting big beers. Just give it time to fully attenuate and clean up after itself."

- **WLP833 German Bock Lager:** "My other favorite lager strain, this one has a characteristic richness that just says 'Ayinger' to me. It enhances the malty finish of a beer, but also seems to add some flavor richness. While a no-brainer in bock beer styles, I also like using it in non-traditional styles like American lagers; I find that it increases the flavor dimension and makes the beers more interesting. I have used it in classic American pilsners and dark American lagers equally well, but it really shines in malty German lagers."

MOST UNUSUAL INGREDIENTS: "I'm not about unusual for unusual's sake. I like building my own spice blends to use in different seasonal beers, such as a chai spice blend for a summer beer, pumpkin pie spice blend for a fall beer, and a Christmas spice blend for a winter beer. Working with different individual spices to create the blend is more fun for me than using a prepackaged mix, and it lets me tune the beer to my palate. Some of those spice blends will use a half-dozen or more spices."

Gordon on How to Keep Water Easy

Minimal water fiddling can be quite rewarding. I've seen many homebrewers drive themselves into the ditch by over-adjusting their water. Using minimal water additions and low mineral water greatly simplifies the mash process and allows character ingredients to be used in a way that best preserves their character. I get more consistent, reliable, and tasty results since adopting this approach.

> **DENNY:** In thinking about Gordon's water advice, keep in mind that he has pretty poor water for brewing, so starting with RO water and building it up is a logical, practical alternative for him. It might be for you too. Or you might have great water like I do. In either case, though, Gordon's advice to keep mineral additions to a minimum is good advice. I've learned through sometimes sad experience that you want to do the least treatment that will get you the results you want. Don't think you need to add every mineral listed in your water program! I've found that small mineral additions along with acid to get my pH in line will make a far better beer than going crazy throwing minerals into the water. Even when I make an IPA and target sulfate in the 300 ppm range, I try to split that sulfate addition between gypsum ($CaSO_4$) and Epsom salt ($MgSO_4$) so that neither will overpower the beer.

Gordon on Blending

Don't be afraid to blend to get the flavor profile you want. Not as a crutch, but you can sometimes get fewer side-effects or have better control of the balance of a complex beer by blending individual components. It can let you optimize the flavor of key components without making as many compromises. Mixing old and young versions of the same beer is often a way to get more complexity in a finished beer that you couldn't easily get otherwise, and it's a long-established tradition in many brewing cultures. Plus it's a great way to train your palate and improve your judging.

DENNY: Blending beers is something that too few homebrewers try, and that includes Drew and me! We've both done some blending, but not to the extent that Gordon has. Here are some tips about how to do it:

- Think carefully about the finished beer flavor. Sure, you can just toss some stuff together and see what happens, but you'll likely get better results if you approach the blending with a goal in mind.

- Think outside the box. Blend a wee heavy with an American pale ale? Why not try it on a small scale and see what happens? Blend in your glass and see if you can create a new beer flavor that's never been done before. How about a wit and a hefeweizen? Porter and bock?

- Measure! Pour a measured amount (I use 4 oz. just to make calculations easy) of whatever you want the base beer to be into three or four glasses. Then measure out different amounts of the beers you're blending in and add them to the base. Taste carefully, take notes, and decide which blend you like best. You can then scale those amounts up to the size of your batch.

  It's difficult to give recommendations for exact amounts to use; that will depend on the beers you're using and what you want to end up with. But for the testing outlined above, I'd start with the base to blender mix of 4:1, 3:1, 2:1, and 1:1. Decide which version suits your tastes the best and scale those amounts up to the size of your batch. If none of the blends tastes right to you, pick the closest one and do another round of testing. That's right, you've got to drink more beer—thank me later!

DREW: The world of homebrewing is filled with an odd sense of what's right and proper, and the art of blending doesn't appear to fit in that code of conduct. It's a crying shame because so many beer styles are best executed by blending. It becomes even more important when you're dealing with sour beers where blending is realistically the only way to generate a perfect beer. In other words, get over it!

Blending beer isn't top of mind for most homebrewers, but it's a useful technique with a variety of applications.

Gordon's Recipes

LONDON PORTER

This is about as classic a London porter as you're ever going to see. Gordon builds his "Londonesque" water profile from scratch with clean RO water. Notice that he doesn't strain to replicate everything about the city's water profile you see in brewing water tables and instead focuses on enough calcium for the mash to work and enough chloride to round out the malt profile.

FOR 5 GALLONS AT 1.054 OG, 31 SRM,
20 IBUs, 5% ABV

GRAIN BILL
6.50 lb.   Maris Otter malt
0.75 lb.   Munich 10°L malt
1.00 lb.   brown malt
1.25 lb.   British crystal 65°L malt
0.50 lb.   British chocolate malt

MASH
Rest   153°F   60 minutes
Batch sparge

HOPS
1.18 oz. Fuggles   4% AA   60 minutes
0.60 oz. Fuggles   4% AA   10 minutes

YEAST
WY1968 London ESB

WATER
Reverse osmosis water with ¼ tsp. 10% phosphoric acid per 5 gallons

1 tsp. calcium chloride ($CaCl_2$) in mash

ADDITION
Add ½ tsp. calcium chloride ($CaCl_2$) to boil.

NOTES
Collect 8 gallons.
20-minute whirlpool
Ferment at 66°F.

TOM FITZPATRICK MEMORIAL SAISON
(pictured at right)

Gordon's take on a saison include a healthy blend of different continental malts and a small kick in the teeth of the very dank, new American hop, Apollo. The long boil will strip most of the distinguishing characters, leaving just a faint hint of something different. Gordon also uses an unusual technique of forcing the mash to cool back to a lower temperature in an effort to encourage a drier final mash character by favoring the activity of Beta Amalyse.

FOR 5 GALLONS AT 1.055 OG, 1.002 FG, 4 SRM,
23 IBUs, 7% ABV, 75-MINUTE BOIL

GRAIN BILL
8.50 lb.   Belgian pils malt
1.00 lb.   wheat malt
0.50 lb.   golden promise malt
0.33 lb.   German rye malt
0.25 lb.   Munich 10°L malt

MASH
Rest   153°F Recirculate, and allow to cool to 140°F
Mash out   Ramp slowly to 170°F while recirculating

HOPS
0.42 oz. Apollo (pellets)   16.5% AA   60 minutes

YEAST
WY3711 French Saison

WATER
½ tsp. calcium chloride ($CaCl_2$) in mash

¼ tsp. calcium sulfate ($CaSO_4$) in mash

¼ tsp. 10% phosphoric per 5 gallons (19L) in sparge

NOTES
Ferment at 73°F.

SPRING IPA (MAIBOCK-STYLE IPA)

You know how sometimes you feel like a nut and sometimes you don't? Well, sometimes you feel like an IPA, but you don't as well. Gordon tackles the problem by combining the clean, sweet malt of a German maibock/hellesbock with an IPA's hop kick. He mitigates the harsher bitter character of many IPAs with a hop selection that favors softer, more "noble" hops with some interesting edges added by Centennial and the winey, grapey Nelson Sauvin.

FOR 5 GALLONS AT 1.064 OG, 1.014 FG, 60 IBUs, 6.6% ABV

GRAIN BILL

7.25 lb.	German pils malt
1.50 lb.	Vienna malt
1.50 lb.	Munich 10°L malt
0.50 lb.	dark Munich malt
0.50 lb.	Weyermann Carahell malt
0.50 lb.	table sugar

MASH

Rest	131°F	15 minutes
Sacchraification rest	144°F	30 minutes
High alpha rest	158°F	15 minutes

Collect 8.5 gallons.

HOPS

0.79 oz.	Liberty	3.7% AA	First wort hop
0.79 oz.	Hallertauer Tradition	6.8% AA	First wort hop
0.79 oz.	Spalt (whole)	2.2% AA	20 minutes
0.79 oz.	Centennial (whole)	10.3% AA	15 minutes
0.39 oz.	Nelson Sauvin	12.5% AA	15 minutes
0.39 oz.	Nelson Sauvin	12.5% AA	5 minutes
0.79 oz.	Centennial (whole)	10.3% AA	0 minutes

YEAST

WY1272 American Ale II

WATER

Reverse osmosis water with ⅛ tsp. 10% phosphoric per 5 gallons.

Mash water used ⅛ tsp. 10% phosphoric, 1 tsp. calcium chloride (CaCl$_2$)

Sparge water used ¼ tsp. 10% phosphoric for 5 gallons

NOTES

Ferment at 68°F.

Keith Yager

Keith has twenty years of brewing experience that he shares freely on the Internet in various discussion forums. He has since parlayed that experience into owning a commercial brewery, but he still homebrews, experiments, and posts about his brewing. He's always willing to answer questions from homebrewers and discuss ideas for recipes and ingredients.

★

BREWING SINCE: 1995

BREWING MOTTO: Yeast is the key!

BREWING PHILOSOPHY: Brewing is a craft, and all crafts are life-long fine-tuning experiences.

FAVORITE BREW STYLES: German and Belgian

FAVORITE BREWING COUNTRY: America

BREWING METHODOLOGY: Keith has his homebrew rig set up at his commercial brewery, Yellowhammer Brewing in Huntsville, Alabama. It's now his pilot rig. He says, "I mainly brew German- and Belgian-style brews with an American twist. I do a single infusion with a target of 150 to 152 mash for most beers. I do a forty-five-minute mash and fifteen-minute vorlauf. For smaller batches—12 gallons or less—I batch-sparge. I boil most beers for ninety minutes. I cool, aerate, and pitch most ales at 64°F and most lagers at 48 to 52°F depending on the yeast strain. After two to three days, I start raising the temperature 2 degrees per day—never higher than 70 to 72°F for ales and 58 to 62°F for lagers. I let all beers sit for two to three days after fermentation appears to be complete, then crash cool and cold-condition it for at least a week, sometimes longer. All beers go into a bright tank (either commercial-style BBT or stainless keg), and in some instances they're fined for clarity. Then everything is carbonated and packaged. I am very careful to remove as much oxygen as possible once beer has been fermented."

BREWING LOCATION: At the brewery

BREWING SYSTEM: Keith's system has a converted keg (legally obtained) for the mash tun and a 14-gallon brew pot. It also utilizes a Chillzilla counter flow chiller and a March pump and a stainless steel burner.

HOW HE GOT STARTED: Keith's mom gave him a homebrewing kit as a Christmas gift. There were beers he'd heard about and wanted to try that he couldn't get a hold of, so he learned how to brew them. One of the first beers he brewed was an IIPA.

FANCIEST PIECE OF EQUIPMENT: His temperature-controlled fermenters. He says he "couldn't live without them."

FAVORITE INGREDIENTS: Keith says he really likes German malts and mainly uses Best Malz. He finds beers made with it to have a more complex malt "backbone" and a richness that he doesn't find in American malts. When he uses American malts, he goes for Rahr 2-row pale malt. He also likes Briess Midnight Wheat and pale ale malts. He says pale ale malt has a cookie-like sweetness that he enjoys.

For English/Scottish/Irish-style beers, Keith relies on Thomas Fawcett Maris Otter and Golden Promise, as well as the company's rye malt, 45°L crystal, chocolate malt, and roasted barley. When he wants to use crystal malt, he uses Caramunich and Caravienne in both German and American styles.

Keith is a big fan of American-grown crystal hops. He describes them as kind of an American noble hop, like a slightly citrusy/fruity Hallertauer Mittelfruh. For IPA he likes to build off of a base of CTZ (Columbus/Tomahawk/Zeus) hops along with Centennial, Cascade, and Amarillo. English styles get East Kent Goldings, often with Challenger as a bittering hop. He says that blending some Willamette in with those two makes an interesting combination. For German styles, Keith goes to Hallertauer Mittelfruh and loves using Tettnanger for aroma. He also likes the tangerine-like qualities of Mandarina Bavaria hops.

FAVORITE YEASTS: Keith brews mainly German- and Belgian-style beers, so it's no surprise that the Weihenstephan lager strain (WY2124 Bohemian Lager or WLP830 German Lager) is his favorite yeast for lagers. For German styles, he uses WY1007 German Ale fermented around 54°F. (Denny is also a big fan of this yeast at low temperatures.) Kölsch gets WLP029 German Ale/Kölsch for its "unique apple/chardonnay" character.

For his Belgian styles, he's become a fan of WY1214 Belgian Abbey, the Chimay yeast. He says that you have to use it carefully to mitigate the banana (isoamyl acetate) esters it can throw. He uses control of pitching and fermentation temperature to minimize that as much as possible.

For his English-style beers, Keith uses WLP007 Dry English Ale for its "complex English ale yeast" flavors, high attenuation, and clarity, even though he's found that it sometimes needs rousing to finish on higher gravity beers.

Keith: Know Your Yeast

You know, I have always taken exception to the notion that "malt is the soul of beer." To me, malt is the body of beer. Yeast is the soul of beer. Yeast can be responsible for up to 80 percent of the flavor characteristics of beer. Yeast is literally the personality of beer. Take any recipe

Have you smelled and tasted your yeast slurry? Keith recommends it.

and change the yeast and you can completely change the beer. The way you handle yeast has a profound effect of the flavor of beer. Yeast can affect everything from head retention to shelf stability and longevity. Many brewers spend most of their time thinking about recipe development and flavorings and aging while often taking yeast and fermentation for granted. But the truth is, without yeast and fermentation, you won't have beer. And without properly controlled fermentation, you won't have great beer!

Commercial brewers need to have a detailed understanding of their yeast to maintain consistency and stabilize shelf life. But homebrewers can have a much more organic approach to understanding yeast. Obviously, the hobby brewer can take the craft as deep as he or she wants, and go so far as to count cells using a hemocytometer and high-powered microscope. But experience can be an even better teacher. Observing the vigor of fermentation; tasting the beer throughout the stages of fermentation; and noting the color, consistency, flavor, and smell of a yeast slurry will be invaluable indicators to any brewer. As any thoughtful brewer gains experience, understanding yeast becomes more intuitive. Getting a feel for how much yeast to pitch, noting how healthy a slurry or yeast starter is, will become an invaluable part of honing the craft.

DENNY: Keith makes an interesting statement about discovering that most yeasts will work well below the temperature range that the manufacturer lists for them. I've discovered the same thing and always advise people to begin fermentation at or below the low temperature that's suggested. There seems to be a persistent myth in the homebrewing community that if you're trying to ferment a beer in warm weather that you should use a Belgian yeast because they like high temperatures. I haven't found that to be good

advice. In his excellent book, *Brew Like a Monk*, Stan Heironymus points out that most Belgian breweries start most fermentations at temperatures lower than American homebrewers have been led to believe were used. Now, it's also true that after fermentation is well underway, they let the temperature rise to create the esters that Belgian beers are noted for, as well as to make the yeast more active. That ensures that these beers finish with the low gravity and dry "digestibility" that Belgian styles are noted for. But they don't start the fermentation at high temperature. Based both on reading and my own experience, I find that most esters and fusels are created in the first seventy-two to ninety-six hours of fermentation. After that, you can safely let temperatures rise in order to complete the fermentation.

DREW: And for me, the same thing applies to my favorite yeasts—the saisons (WLP565 Belgian Saison I, WLP566 Belgian Saison II, WY3724 Belgian Saison, and WY3711 French Saison). A lot of folks view a saison strain as an excuse to just pitch hot and ferment hot. "That's how you get the saison strains to ferment!" I've said it many, many times—but don't do it. It's a recipe for a mess. If you're running hot and goosing the yeast, you'll end with fusels and phenols and some rather unpleasant flavors. Instead, I run a very similar profile to what Denny and Keith recommend. I chill the wort into the low 60s (°F), pitch with a healthy colony of yeast and then hold it in the low 60s (°F) for seventy-two hours. Then I let it do the saison ramp into the 90s (°F). That, combined with open fermentation, makes short work of any ferment I've done. In fact, I've grown so fond of the technique that now all of my Belgian ferments are run this way.

YELLOWHAMMER BELGIAN WHITE

What started as a homebrew recipe inspired by a lime tree has now become one of Keith's flagship beers at his Yellowhammer Brewing Company in Alabama. Here's his word about spices, which many people are tempted to overuse in a wit: "Go easy on the spices. Resist the urge to make this a ginger and lime beer. The spices are there to add accents to the yeast. The yeast characteristics are the main driver here; spices play a minor supporting role."

FOR 5.5 GALLONS AT 1.050 OG, 1.010 FG, 18 IBUs, 5.2% ABV, 90-MINUTE BOIL

GRAIN BILL
5.50 lb.   German pils malt
4.33 lb.   German wheat malt
1.00 lb.   flaked rye

MASH
Rest   152°F   45 to 60 minutes

HOPS
0.4 oz.   Magnum pellets   14% AA   60 minutes

YEAST
WY1214 Belgian Abbey

ADDITION
0.80 grams   lime leaves (do not overdo the lime leaves—a little goes a long way)
0.75 oz.   fresh ginger
0.40 oz   chamomile

NOTES
Chop ginger and lime leaves and soak for 10 minutes in 185°F water.
Puree in blender until finely ground. Add puree and chamomile at flame-out during whirlpool.

Cool to 64°F. Aerate well and pitch yeast. Ferment 7 to 10 days;
crash cool to 32 to 34°F for 3 days.

This beer can be ready to drink 10 to 13 days from brew day.

VARIANTS
I used to add a small amount of Amarillo with the hops at flame-out because it added a small amount of orange/tangerine character (about .25 ounces per 5 gallons). It can make an interesting addition. A small amount of black pepper at flame-out can be interesting. Lime zest can be substituted for lime leaves.

- CHAPTER 7 -

Bringing It All Together

*Y*ou've now spent the last four chapters with a whole crazy collection of All-Star Homebrewers. We hope that you've found them inspiring, but we also hope that you do two other things.

First, find your local all-stars! There are so many out there that we couldn't hope to cover them all unless we somehow managed to con our publisher into producing a twenty-volume set bound in rich brown leather suitable for any office or brewery.

Secondly, and arguably more important, you need to become an All-Star. We hope you've realized by now that the most important character traits for an All-Star are a blend of curiosity, enthusiasm, and a willingness to be open to new ideas. Granted, we might be biased toward education with our backgrounds, but we really do feel it's an important aspect of the whole hobby. The only reason we know half the things we know is because people have dropped the "secret and proprietary" routine when it comes to the brewing process. Sure, you might be able to be a homebrewing rock-star, but we've seen that paycheck, and it's much more rewarding to be an awesome member of the community.

DENNY: We've found that being a "famous" homebrewer and $3 will get you a good cup of coffee.

Keep Learning and Find Your Own All-Stars

The very first thing we recommend is to read. Of course, you have our book in hand, so we're hoping this isn't a shocking suggestion. However, it's not just books we're talking about. Read everything that interests you. Read every magazine, every blog post, Facebook group, forum, and, yes, all the books you can find as well. Compared to when we started out, there's so much useful information out there about beer and homebrew that it's unbelievable and overwhelming, but trust us—you've got to grab ahold of the material.

DREW: When I first began brewing, I'm pretty certain I bought one of every homebrewing book that existed and then kept going. These days that would exhaust anyone, but it was a great way to jam my head full of stuff.

DENNY: Keep this in mind: the more information you collect, the more contradictory information you'll find. So as you go about your knowledge quest, learn to consider the sources. Look for consensus between various sources. And most important of all, once you find consensus on a process, ingredient, recipe, or whatever, try it for yourself and see if it works for you. In the end, that's all that really matters.

A very lively segment of the homebrew informational market is the podcast space. Every year it feels like more and more folks are turning on the microphones and opening their mouths to spill forth what they know. In fact, you'll be able to find a lot of wit and wisdom from folks featured in this book spilling out on the audio Internet every day. Tasty McDole and Nathan Smith are found on various Brewing Network shows. Mary Izett has her Fuhmendaboutit program out of New York City. Self-promotion alert: we're also on the airwaves, so check out

---

★ HOW TO BECOME A FULL-FLEDGED ★ MEMBER OF THE CLUB

- **Pay your dues.** Besides the legal reasons behind dues collection in many areas, the club needs your dues to make things happen.
- **Bring beer.** Everyone in a club is into beer, so your gift will never be refused. "But I don't think my beer is good . . . " Everyone has also gone through that phase. Just bring the beer and listen to the critique. Only the worst of jerks would belittle you for your efforts. If someone does critique your beer, listen honestly, ask questions, and don't assume they're one of the jerks.
- **Volunteer.** No club is run by professionals. We're all volunteers in the effort, and you know what every club needs? More help! Ask what you can do and cheerfully pitch in. That will make you better loved than the 95 percent of schlubs who bolt whenever work is mentioned.
- **Make things happen.** In our experience, everyone has ideas about how things should be done. Unfortunately, most think someone else should implement his or her ideas. Instead, make great things happen. Work with the club to make a new event and watch how people respond. It doesn't have to be fancy. It can just be, "Hey, let's go visit this new brewery on Friday. I'll call them and see if they'll offer us a special deal."

DREW: To give you an idea, when I joined the Maltose Falcons I noticed a group of passionate folks with no real website. I had the skills to fix that, so I created www.maltosefalcons.com and began setting up a bunch of online resources for the club to use. Next thing you know, I was part of the club's board. From there I just absorbed as many lessons as I could.

our Experimental Brewing podcast! Virtually everyone else has appeared on programs in the past. So go out there and listen!

JOIN THE CLUB

Far and away the easiest way to learn is to find your local homebrew clubs. They are a source of brewing experience and knowledge that is unparalleled. Look around your local brewing scene; find your local homebrew club via the American Homebrewers Association (www.homebrewersassociation.org/community/clubs/find-a-homebrew-club/); and do anything to get involved with other brewers. Why? Because we still feel the best way to learn the ins and outs of this craft is by brewing with others.

Sure, sometimes it's hard to really "join" a club. We don't mean paying your dues—that part typically comes fairly easy. We mean it can be difficult getting integrated into the fabric of the club. Like other human gatherings, clubs tend to have cliques and power structures that for any newbie can be daunting to penetrate. So what's a brewer to do? Hang out? Drink a few beers? It's a thing you can do, but the club experience is much deeper if you can become more involved than the casual beer drinker.

If it turns out a particular club isn't right for you, no harm, no foul. Most major cities offer more than one club. If not, maybe the time is right to found your own. Each club has a different personality. Some are uber-organized and competitive. Some are more chaotic and loose. Some are a bunch of drinking buddies, and some are brewing fiends. So keep searching to find the one that matches your interest. The truly crazy people with a sickness join multiple clubs and are active in them all.

If you don't have a local club, look to the AHA. The organization fights for your rights as a homebrewer, but it also provides an amazing amount of content for members. For instance, you can currently look through all the issues of their magazine, *Zymurgy*, since 2000, or download conference panels and lectures to learn a bunch of amazing stuff. Also, we can readily suggest online forums and virtual clubs for those situated far away from any physical club.

CLUB BREW DAY IDEAS

In addition to meetings, brewery visits, and competitions, club members should always consider getting together on brew days. While that can be as simple as one or two members visiting a third, it can also be even bigger. Here are a few ideas.

CLUB BREW LESSONS

Arguably the easiest idea of the bunch, encourage your club to hold regular brewing sessions that teach newcomers how to make beer. Drew's club actually has two monthly brew sessions, one focused on brewing extract (Brew 101) and another on brewing all-grain. Even better, the sponsoring shop offers a discount on ingredients so participants can take home 5 gallons of wort for a lower cost. This encourages all sorts of fun and experimentation. A day like this not only provides a load of great beer, but also a chance for new members to get involved with your club.

GROUP BREW DAY

Most everyone can get their system (or a hastily assembled system) on the road. So get the group together at a common location, set up the systems, and brew away! Some affairs are completely free-form—it's all about the brewing. Others have structure around them, like the AHA's "Big Brew Day" in early May with a few national choices of recipes. So fire up the grill, make some sandwiches, and enjoy some beers while wandering between different setups to see how people do their magic.

Club brew days are a great way to learn from experienced homebrewers in your town.

BREW WITH A BREWER DAY

The problem with the big group brew day is that people change how they brew just by leaving their house. Maybe all the fancy gear couldn't make the trip or maybe someone is just missing his lucky colander. Instead of making everyone leave their comfortable home setups, bring the guests to the brewers.

When Drew's club does it, four or five veteran members of the club volunteer to open their homesteads to guests. Each location only takes as many signups as they can handle. It helps to have each location decide on an educational angle as well. Drew, for instance, has taught his theories on recipe design, batch sparging, making pressure canned starter wort, and so on. Other members have done lessons on decoction mashing or building a massive brew rig.

How You Can Be an All-Star

With the group exploration concluded, there are other steps to take to become an All-Star. Start kicking butt and help push the hobby forward.

BREW

It all starts with beer. You can theoretically know everything about brewing just by reading, but none of it means a thing until you get behind a kettle and coax the alchemical magic out of water, barley, yeast, and hops. It's not just about the raw number of batches under your belt. We're both a few hundred in (okay, Denny's is maybe seven-thousand-plus in), but we feel that the more important metric is frequency of brew. Like the old line about Carnegie Hall, it's all about practice, practice, practice.

DREW: I've met amazing brewers who were blowing my palate after brewing for less than a year. The trick: they brewed every week for their first nine months and had their process down cold. They had an opportunity to try every crazy thing they read about while building up their brewing muscle memory.

Brew every chance you can and vary your brew days. Either follow Drew's approach and visit other people's breweries or bring others' experiences to you. Also, try to have a specific goal in mind for each brew beyond, "I want to make a beer." Your goal could be to explore a new hop, dry hopping technique, fermentation control, flavoring, etc. Try to learn with every batch.

Consider hosting a brewing party like AHA's Big Brew Day. Bring new brewers into the brewery to glean what lessons people need. And always, always be gracious about teaching and people's attitudes about beer. Don't be "that guy" who embodies the bad side of passion and truly deserves the less flattering version of the sobriquet "Beer Snob."

COMPETE

This is the easiest one to execute, but one of the trickiest to successfully make happen. Brew a bunch of great beer, enter it into a bunch of competitions, get a little lucky, and win medals. Win enough of those shiny disks and ribbons, and people will know you know how to make a mean batch of beer.

Do you want to take on the heights achieved by Jamil Zainasheff, Gordon Strong, or Mark Schoppe by winning the AHA's coveted Ninkasi Award? You'll need lots of luck and some absolutely stellar beer when you enter the AHA National Homebrew Competition.

Other great opportunities to win big on a national stage include the Great American Beer Festival's Annual Pro-Am Competition, where a BJCP competition-winning homebrewer collaborates with a craft brewer to create a beer for judging during the GABF competition. It's the best of both brewing worlds competing on the same stage. In a similar vein, Boston Beer Company (a.k.a. Sam Adams) runs its annual Long Shot competition to choose three homebrews (one employee and two regular homebrewers) for a six-pack release across the nation.

WRITE AND TAKE PHOTOS

Okay, sure, we're both semi-professional curmudgeonly writing types, but with the rise of the Internet and multiple publishing platforms, there's nothing stopping you from writing up your misadventures and sharing them with the universe. Look to Marshall Schott, Lars Marius Garshol, Chris Colby, and Mike Tonsmeire for inspiration. They have fantastic blogs that can inspire you.

Worried you don't have something interesting to say? If you focus on the learning piece we described, then every brew will yield something to share. Even if it's a less than stellar effort, there's something to be remembered. And by writing it down, you'll have a journal of lessons that's handy for when you want to revisit an idea.

Dont rite 2 gud? Take advantage of the mobile studios we carry in our pockets and document your brew with a few well-chosen photos, videos, and audio clips.

PARTY

Last but not least, whatever you do, do not lose the sense of fun. Homebrewing, after all, is really just a great excuse to have fun. We've yet to meet anyone we'd consider an amazing brewer who didn't still have a sense of giddiness about the whole practice. So keep the spark alive and have a party or two or three or however many you need to remind your brain that this is a great and goofy way to waste time. Maintain that and your enthusiasm and passion will carry through to your other pursuits! We don't presume we need to teach you how to throw a beer party, do we?

Amanda Burkemper (page 66)
Club: Kansas City Bier Meisters
(www.kcbiermeisters.org)

Annie Johnson (page 49)
Club: North Seattle Homebrewers
(www.wahomebrewers.org/
community/110?task=view)
Website: www.picobrew.com

Brandon Jones (page 154)
Brewery: Yazoo Brewing Company
(www.yazoobrew.com)
Website: www.embracethefunk.com

Chris Colby (page 106)
Website: www.beerandwinejournal.com

Curt Stock (page 54)
Club: Saint Paul Homebrewers Club
(www.sphbc.org)

Denny Conn (page 84)
Club: Cascade Brewers Society
(www.cascade-brewers.com)
Media: Experimental Brewing Podcast
Websites: www.experimentalbrew.com,
www.dennybrew.com
Other Writings: *Craft Beer for the Homebrewer*,
Experimental Homebrewing, *Brew Your Own*,
Zymurgy

Drew Beechum (page 172)
Club: Maltose Falcons (www.maltosefalcons.com)
Media: Experimental Brewing podcast
Website: www.experimentalbrew.com/
Other Writings: *The Everything Homebrewing
Book*, *The Everything Hard Cider Book*, *Experimental*

Homebrewing, *Beer Advocate* magazine, and
Zymurgy

Fred Bonjour (page 42)
Clubs: Ann Arbor Brewers Guild
(www.aabg.org), Clinton River Association of
Fermentable Trendsetters (CRAFT)
(www.crafthomebrewclub.org), Kuhnhenn Guild
of Brewers (KGB) (www.kgb-club.org),
Society of North Oakland Brewers Society
(SNOBS)

Gary Glass (page 130)
Club: Hop Barley and the Alers
(www.hopbarley.org)
Website: www.homebrewersassociation.org
Other Writing: *Zymurgy*

Gordon Strong (page 198)
Club: Saint Paul Homebrewers Club
(www.sphbc.org)
Website: www.bjcp.org
Other Writings: Brewers Publications (*Brewing
Better Beer*, *Modern Homebrew Recipes*), *Zymurgy*

Janis Gross (page 118)
Club: Hop Barley and the Alers
(www.hopbarley.org)
Website: www.homebrewersassociation.org

Jeff Gladish (page 180)
Club: Tampa Bay B.E.E.R.S
(www.tampabaybeers.org)
Other Organizations: Best Florida Beers
(www.bestfloridabeer.org)

Joe Formanek (page 60)
Club: Urban Knaves of Grain
(www.knaves.org)

John Palmer (page 112)
Club: Crown of the Valley
(www.crownofthevalley.org)
Websites: www.howtobrew.com,
www.palmerbrewingsolutionsinc.com/
Media: The Brewing Network *Brew Strong*
(www.thebrewingnetwork.com/category/shows/
brewstrong)
Other Writings: *How to Brew, Brewing Classic
Styles, Water*

Keith Yager (page 206)
Brewery: Yellowhammer Brewing
(www.yellowhammerbrewery.com)

Kent Fletcher (page 72)
Club: Maltose Falcons (www.maltosefalcons.com)
Other Writing: *Zymurgy*

Lars Marius Garshol (page 36)
Website: www.garshol.priv.no

Marshall Schott (page 94)
Club: BT6 / San Joaquin Worthogs
(www.sjworthogs.org)
Website: www.brulosophy.com
Other Writing: *Brew Your Own*

Martin Brungard (page 100)
Club: Foam Blowers of Indiana (FBI)
(www.foamblowers.com)
Website: www.sites.google.com/site/brunwater
Other Writing: *Water, Zymurgy*

Mary Izett (page 160)
Brewery: Cuzett Libations (www.cuzett.com)
Club: New York City Homebrewers Guild
(www.nychomebrew.com)
Media: Fuhmendaboutit! (www.
heritageradionetwork.org/series/
fuhmentaboudit)
Website: www.mylifeoncraft.com
Other Writing: *Speed Brewing, Zymurgy*

Mike Karnowski (page 148)
Brewery: Zebulon Artisan Ales
Other Writing: *Homebrew Beyond the Basics*

Mike McDole (page 186)
Club: Diablo Order of Zymiracle Enthusiasts
(http://clubdoze.com)
Media: The Brewing Network *Brewing with Style,
The Sunday Session*

Mike Tonsmeire (page 142)
Club: DC Homebrewers
(www.dchomebrewers.com)
Website: www.themadfermentationist.com
Other Writing: *American Sour Beers*

Nathan Smith (page 122)
Media: The Brewing Network *The Sunday Session*

Roxanne Westendorf (page 192)
Club: Bloatarian Brewing League
(www.bloatarian.com)
Brewery (where Roxanne gets to play with her
ideas): www.rivertownbrewery.com
Favorite sources of ingredients:
www.maverickchocolate.com,
www.junglejims.com
Other Writing: *Zymurgy*

Drew Beechum

Drew has been brewing and writing about brewing since he first picked up a kettle in 1999. He is the author of *The Everything Homebrewing Book*, *The Everything Hard Cider Book*, and *The Homebrewer's Journal*, and coauthor of *Experimental Homebrewing*. Beechum has also written for *Zymurgy*, the journal of the American Homebrewers Association, writes a regular column for *Beer Advocate*, and is the cohost of the Experimental Brewing podcast. He lives in Pasadena, California, with his lovely wife, a dedicated brewery, and his loyal army of dogs and cats.

Denny Conn

Denny brewed his first batch of homebrew in 1998 and since then has brewed over 500 more. He is a BJCP national-ranked beer judge and has been a member of the governing committee of the American Homebrewers Association for nine years. His recipes have been brewed by several commercial breweries in both the United States and Europe. He was a contributing author to *Craft Beer for the Homebrewer* and coauthor of *Experimental Homebrewing*. He currently consults for several breweries, is a field educator for Oakshire Brewing in Eugene, Oregon, and cohosts the Experimental Brewing podcast. He lives in the foothills of the Coast Range in Oregon with his wife, five cats, and two dogs.

★ ACKNOWLEDGMENTS ★

Drew: There's no way a book like this happens without the incredible patience of my lovely wife, Amy. Not only are there the long hours spent staring at a computer screen, but then there's the grump that appears around deadline time. Thank you, honey, for once again understanding that my brain runs in its own track!

Thanks to Denny, the man with two red shoes (Converse, natch). He's been the Ben to my Jerry, the Statler to my Waldorf, the Laverne to my Shirley. He's always maintained a sense of fun and play, and that's just what this book needed, man!

Lastly, thanks to all of our All-Stars, both here on the page as well as the ones in our beery lives. Remember to keep on rocking, teaching, and generally just being awesome. Good people drink good beer. Great people brew beer!

Denny: You can't write a book without thanking a lot of people, so here goes . . .

Many thanks to my incredible wife for her support while we wrote this book. Without knowing she was behind me all the way, it never would have happened.

I can't imagine how you could find a better coauthor than Drew. The back and forth banter in the book is a mirror of our real-life friendship and is what makes doing these books fun and interesting. Thanks for taking up the slack and keeping me going. And a big thanks to our editor, Thom O'Hearn. At no point during the writing of this book did I want to fly to North Carolina and strangle him. That's a breakthrough for me!

And of course, mega thanks to all the homebrewers who contributed their time and effort to this book. Over five hundred homebrewers took time to fill out our initial survey. And to the twenty-three amazing homebrewers who are featured in the profiles, thanks for your information and your patience as I badgered you about getting us material. In spite of the threat to send you all Clam Chowdah Saison, you really came through and made this an incredible book!

INDEX

Recipe titles appear in bold face.